E

The Lady of the Place

Mary in the history and in the life of Carmel

EDIZIONI
CARMELITANE

- Portuguese (Brazil): *A Senhora do Lugar*, co-edition by the Istituto de Espiritualidade Tito Brandsma Goiana PE – Livraria e Editora do Carmo Curitiba, Paranavaì, 1994.
- Italian edition revised and enlarged: *La Signora del Luogo. Maria nella storia e nella vita del Carmelo*. Edizioni Carmelitane, Roma, 2001
- Spanish translation: *La Señora del Lugar. María en la vida y en la historia del Carmelo*. Edizioni Carmelitane, Roma, 2001
- English translation: Edizioni Carmelitane, Roma, 2001

The illustrations at the beginning of every chapter are taken from the book, *Beauté du Carmel* (Brussels, 1660) and are by the painter Abraham Van Diepenbeke. (1596-1675).

Other photographs and etchings are from the General Archive of the Carmelite Order in Rome.

English translation by Joseph Chalmers, O.Carm. and Míceál O'Neill, O.Carm.
Layout and editing by Antonio Ruiz, O.Carm.

© Edizioni Carmelitane

Collana: *Carmelitana, 2*

First Printing: 2001
Second Printing: 2015

Edizioni Carmelitane
Via Sforza Pallavicini, 10
00193 ROMA, Italia
E-mail: edizioni@ocarm.org
Web: http://ocarm.org/edizioni

ISBN 978-88-7288-068-5
ISSN 2421-5775

Finito di stampare nel mese di ottobre 2015
dalla tipografia Città Nuova della P.A.M.O.M. - Via Pieve Torina, 55 - 00156 Roma

Preface

Dear Brothers and Sisters,

> "May the Most Holy Virgin confirm you
> in your CARMELITE VOCATION.
> May she conserve within you the desire
> for spiritual things.
> May she obtain for you the gifts
> which the saints had
> and the attainment of the knowledge
> of divine things....
> That SHE may make you models of fraternity
> in the CHURCH OF GOD."

This is what I desire for all of us, repeating the words of Paul VI in his discourse to the Carmelites in 1967. I repeat those words because they are appropriate to explain the underlying reason for this work, "THE LADY OF THE PLACE", which I have the joy of sharing with my sisters and brothers of the Carmelite Family.

The fundamental motive which led me to undertake the study, meditation and research was, without doubt, love for her who is our Flower of Carmel, our Mother and Sister, the first to whom I dedicate with tenderness, the time, the commitment, and the result of all this work.

The publication in 1994 of this work, which enlarged upon a text previously available in photocopied sheets in 1993 and then in the magazine "Carmelo Lusitano", (no. 2, 1994), develops further some points on the marian aspects of Carmel contained in the book, "Come Pietre Vive". The essential objective of this work is to share the marian heritage of Carmel with whoever desires to know it and to deepen his or her knowledge. With gratitude, I recognise the stimulus received from the Carmelite Sisters in Italy and the Carmelite Sisters of Divine Providence in Brazil, with their request to have a text on the marian aspects of Carmelite spirituality for use in the work of formation, in order that they might have a broad vision, from the historical and spiritual point of view, of the "marieform" Carmelite life. This present edition, reviewed and enlarged, is offered for the Marian Year, which the whole Order celebrates in 2001.

The title of this book, "THE LADY OF THE PLACE" was chosen to underline the foundational relationship that Carmelites have with Mary, the Mother of the Lord of the place, according to the medieval expression. As Lady, Patroness and Mother, she is present with her maternal protection, on our journey towards the fullness of life in Jesus Christ.

The way which will help us to reach a systematic understanding of the whole marian dimension of Carmel, is the historical method, or rather, the verification of how our "marian" memory was formed over the course of time. For this reason our attention was focused on all that appeared spiritually significant for the marian aspect of our Order. This led to the decision not simply to make a collection and presentation of facts. We have tried to go beyond individual facts in order to seek out their real and deepest meaning so that we can in turn understand the interior dynamic that moved generations of Carmelites to love the Virgin Mother of God and to express this in various ways. We have attempted to verify the values that have been transmitted to us and to which we must be faithful.

In order to assist the discovery and interiorisation of these values, the work is organised in a didactic form. We therefore have the following elements:

A basic text in which there is the presentation of the essential content of each topic. The content of the text shows the development in the understanding of various historical events, from the origins to our own days, thus revealing the evolution of the Carmelite marian experience and the reflection within the Order. The style is simple but not simplistic and summarises that which the historical and spiritual research has thus far produced on a particular topic. In some parts of the book we have included the result of original research based on archival sources and serious works of reference.

Inserts that provide interesting information on particular issues. These texts are intended to help the reader understand the particular values and interiorise them. They may also offer a stimulus for further reflection.

Original texts offered at the end of each chapter, taken from Carmelite spiritual authors and from official Church and Order documents. The point is to enable a direct contact with these sources. These pages assist in the understanding of the basic text and also can stimulate further reflection.

Suggestions for deepening our relationship with Mary. There are questions for further study and suggestions for our prayer and for our way of life.

Iconography – there are some illustrations presented to show how over time "Our Lady of the Carmelites" was depicted and what marian values were expressed in each work of art.

Bibliography – an essential bibliography is offered at the end of each Chapter. This can be of help in setting up and developing a community library and in any future research into our marian spirituality. The bibliography is not restricted to one language and it takes account of the value of the studies that are mentioned. If such works appear in a language different from the original, that is expressly pointed out.

I have tried to respond in some way to those sisters and brothers who seek help for their initial and ongoing Carmelite formation.

I want to thank the community and the residents of the home "S. Antonio di S. João del Rei and "Lar Comunitario" of Guarani. I also want to thank those other communities and individuals I have met and with whom I have shared the contents of this book.

If I may ask something of you, the reader, it is that you will use this book to grow in the commitment which leads us to

"DO EVERYTHING HE TELLS YOU"

In this way I shall be happy and more than compensated.

Emanuele Boaga, O.Carm.

HYMN TO MARY

HYMN TO MARY

LOVING PRESENCE, bringer of good,
Lady always loved
And always desired!
From the very beginning of your and our Order
You are the one and only, "Lady of the Place".

HEAVENLY LADY, your children always give you praise
Yesterday and today.
You look lovingly upon us, are always generous with us.
You cover us with the mantle of your special protection;
You are our Patroness, always with us!

Oh Mary, you are our MOST BEAUTIFUL SISTER,
A precious pearl and the masterpiece of the Creator,
You are without equal!
In you resounds the divine melody.
You are a treasure for your brothers!

We desire A LIFE HIDDEN WITH YOU, in communion with you.
    God is in you and you are in God.
    You savour of eternal life!
For each one of us you are an invitation, a bridge and a gate.
    You are the promise of OUR GREATEST GOOD.

MOTHER OF THE SCAPULAR, you are always gracious.
    You are a certain help in this life.
    You are the presence of God in sorrow!
You free us from sin, oh gate of heaven
    And flower of Carmel!

You GATHER US TOGETHER as one Family.
    Your sons and daughters, brothers and sisters, imitate you,
    Honour you and praise you!
Guided by your hand, they will securely arrive
    At their homeland in the HEART of our GOD.

FEAST OF LOVE, the whole of Carmel exults with immense gratitude
    And celebrates your presence faithfully in every age.
    Your protection is so well known throughout our history
Oh Lady of Mount Carmel!

TOGETHER WE WALK, united with the whole Church,
    Having you, our Sister, at our side;
    Take us by the hand and lead us, oh Mother!
Guide us, Star of the sea,
    To live with pure heart in allegiance to your Jesus.

SKILLED ARTISTS so often desired to paint your features
    So many sweet images came from their brushes
    But no-one could ever fully express your beauty
VIRGIN-MOTHER, AND SPLENDOUR OF CARMEL.

YOUR PRESENCE TODAY is as gracious as ever,
    Heavenly Lady, most beautiful Sister,
    In union with you, Flower of Carmel,
In the feast of love, united in fraternity,
    We walk together with the Church,
    In the light of your sweet image

    My mother,
        my Sister,
            MARY.

(A Carmelite Sister of Divine Providence)

Bibliography

There are several books which can be consulted for information on some specific aspects of marian spirituality or for general themes. For our study, at each stage, the following works are fundamental.

a) For Carmelite marian spirituality in general:

- N. Geagea, O.C.D., *Maria Madre e Decoro del Carmelo. La pietà mariana dei Carmelitani durante i primi tre secoli della loro storia.* Roma, Teresianum, 1988 (There is a Spanish translation of this book by Editorial Monte Carmelo, Burgos, 1989).
- V. Hoppenbrouwers, O.Carm., *Devotio mariana in Ordine Fratrum B. Mariae Virginis de Monte Carmelo a medio saeculi XVI usque ad finem saeculi XIX.* Roma, Institutum Carmelitanum, 1960 (There is a Spanish translation of this book by Cesca, Onda).

b) For an historical-doctrinal synthesis of the marian dimension of the Order see:

- V. Hoppenbrouwers, O.Carm., *A Virgem Maria e a Ordem do Monte Carmelo*, in *Citoc*, 1 (Fatima, 1960), pp. 15-22.
- Id. *Come l'Ordine Carmelitano ha veduto e vede la Madonna*, in *Carmelus*, 15 (1968), pp. 255-277.
- Id. *Carmelitani: Vita mariana*, in *Dizionario degli Istituti di Perfezione*, II, Roma, 1975, col. 502-507.
- L. Saggi, O.Carm., *Santa Maria del Monte Carmelo*, Roma, ed. Centro Stampa Prov. Romana dei Carmelitani, 1986 (reworking and enlargement of the article in Saints of Carmel).
- E. Boaga, *Carmelite Devotion toward Our Lady*, in *Carmel in the World*, 28 (1989), I, pp. 29-36
- Id. *La presenza di Maria nella storia del Carmelo*, in AA.VV., *Maria Icona della Tererezza del Padre. La spiritualità mariana nell'esperienza del Carmelo*, Palermo, Ed. Augustinus, 1992, pp. 49-61.
- N. Geagea, O.C.D., *La spiritualità mariana dl Carmelo nel suo organico sviluppo*, Roma, Edizioni OCD, 1997.
- R.M. López-Melús, O.Carm, *El Carmelo y Maria*, Onda, Amacar, 1995.

c) On particular aspects of marian spirituality and on authors and notable figures within the Order see:

- *Mary, Model of the Christian Life*, Carmelite Marian Commission, Rome, 1985.
- AA.VV. *La dimensione mariana del Carmelo*, 2 vols, Rome (Centro Stampa della Prov. Romana), 1989. This contains studies by various authors in preparation for the National Marian Congress held in Italy in 1989.
- AA.VV. *Maria icona della tenerezza del Padre. La spiritualità mariana nell'esperienza del Carmelo*, Palermo, ed. Augustinus, 1992. Acts of the above mentioned Italian Congress of 1989.
- Ildefonso de la Inmaculada, O.C.D., *La Virgen de la contemplación*, Madrid, Editorial de Espiritualidad, 1973.
- R. Valabek, *Mary, Mother of Carmel. Our Lady and the Saints of Carmel.* 2 vols. Rome, Institutum Carmelitanum, 1988 (Carmel in the World Paperbacks, 3 & 4).
- P. Garrido, *La Virgen de la Fe. Doctrina y piedad mariana entre los Carmelitas españoles de los siglos XVI y XVII*, Roma, Edizioni Carmelitane, 1999.
- Other studies will be mentioned under the appropriate chapters.

d) For the historical sources, the following editions have been used:

- *Medieval Carmelite Heritage. Early Reflections on the Nature of the Order, critical edition of texts with introduction* by A. Staring, Rome, Institutum Carmelitanum, 1989.
- Daniel of the Virgin Mary, Speculum Carmelitanum, 2 vols, Antwerp, 1680.
- V. Hoppenbrouwers, *Devotio mariana*, pp. 335-445.
- *Acta capitulorum generalium ordinis fratrum B.V. Mariae de Monte Carmelo*, ed. G. Wessels, 2 v., Rome, 1912-1934.
- *Bullarium carmelitanum*, ed. E. Monsignani – J. Ximénez, 4 v., Rome, 1715-1768.

e) For a bibliography on marian themes, see:

E. Boaga – E. Caruana, *Bibliografia sulla Marianità Carmelitana*, Rome, 1986.
M. Caprioli, O.C.D., *Bibliografia mariana carmelitana*, in Quaderni Carmelitani n. 4-5 (1988), pp. 257-275.
Further studies are to be found in the *Annual Carmelite Bibliography* which appears each year in *Carmelus*.

1

A LOVING PRESENCE

Dum fluet unda Maris, curretque per aethera Phoebus
Vivet Carmelus candidus Ordo mihi

As long as the waves of the sea roll, And Phoebus goes on his course through the heavens,
The pure Order of Carmel Will live forever for my honour.

(Attributed by some to Bl. Baptist of Mantua)

A LOVING PRESENCE

The Presence of Mary at the Origins of the Carmelite Order

1. The Marian characteristic of the Order

A distinctive element of the spirituality of Carmel is the profound influence exercised by the presence of the Mother of God. For this reason it is said that, "Carmel belongs totally to Mary" which means that Carmel is eminently Marian. However it surprises some that Our Lady is not mentioned in the "formula vitae" written by St. Albert of Jerusalem to the Latin hermits on Mount Carmel, from whom the Order of Carmelites takes its origins.

One scholar explains that the absence of any mention of Mary is due to the particular character of the albertine document, which was rather a practical laying out of the fundamental ideal of the Latin hermits rather than a theoretical exposition with details of their life. The same author tries to confirm this argument by means of a brief parallel with the rules of other institutes of monks or canons, notable for their Marian dimension. Finally he concludes, "devotion towards the Blessed Virgin, even though it is not prescribed by legal norms - not excluding the Rule - flourished in spirits kindled by faith; in the soul which was naturally Christian and inseparably Marian." (N. Geagea).

Is there really a Marian characteristic present at the origins of the Carmelite Order?

Scholars in this area generally look for the presence, in the experience of the first generations of Carmelites, of elements that, according to the medieval mentality, illustrate the Marian character proper to a religious order or association. They affirm that the Marian characteristic is present from the beginning by means of the dedication to Mary of the first oratory on Mt. Carmel, at the Wadi 'ain-es-Siah, and from this flows the understanding of Mary as Patroness of the Order.

This choice of Mary as Patroness, understood in the feudal context, marked the spiritual orientation of the original group of Carmelites and their attitude towards her because they saw in her the "Lady of the place" in the land of the Lord Jesus, whom they were pledged to follow. In this way, the patronage, applied to the relationship of the faithful with Mary, implied two aspects or dimensions of life: on the part of the faithful, it implied the "traditio personae", the "*servitium*" and the "*mancipatio*", that is that they be dedicated to Mary in order to honour her; and on Mary's side, her "*protectio*" or "*patrocinium*", with the mediation of graces and blessings. In this way, every good thing came from God through Mary.

This understanding of the bond between Carmel and Our Lady, according to the feudal notion, was developed and was several times reaffirmed in the course of the 13th century. The sense of the special dedication of the Order to Mary appears in the documents of the time and Pope Urban IV makes it explicit in 1263 Later, a greater understanding grew of the nature and characteristics of the Marian patronage of the Order until we arrive at that union of principles and practices which nowadays we call the Marian spirituality of the Order.

There still remain some questions about the Marian origins of the Order:-
- What was the preceding experience of the men who formed the first group of Latin hermits on Mount Carmel
- What was the dynamic that led the hermits to dedicate their first oratory to the

Blessed Virgin Mary?
- Is the only reason they chose Our Lady their desire to be recognised as a group, even if only by the local bishop?
- Is it enough to consider in the dedication of the first oratory only the medieval relationship, of servants and patroness, with the spiritual orientation which that implies?

For an adequate response it is necessary to understand why the Latin hermits dedicated their first oratory to Our Lady. This was done not only in the context of the feudal "mancipatio" but also in the more general context of Marian piety in the West, and more specifically in the Holy Land at the time the Order had its beginnings.

2. Marian spirituality in the 9th-13th centuries

Here I want to present a panorama of Marian spirituality in the West from which the first hermits on Mount Carmel emerged.

In Europe, from the 9th century and more especially in the 11th and 12th centuries, the theological elaboration of mariology took place within Christology. It was based on the relationship between Mary and Christ, the God-man, and her role in the work of salvation. The Marian aspects which are commonly treated, are the Assumption and the Immaculate Conception. Furthermore, reflection on the divine maternity led people to see her also as Mother of the faithful. This theological reflection brought out the mercy and the mediation of graces obtained through Mary. Various other Marian themes were treated like the New Eve, Our Lady the type of the Church, and the woman of the Apocalypse.

Marian spirituality at this time united the liturgy with popular piety. The preferred theme was the relationship between the joy of Mary in being the Mother of God and the joy that comes to the one who celebrates this fact. In this way the individual participates in her joy. The theme of participation in the joy of Mary was more pronounced than sharing in her sorrows, even though the theme of compassion was not unknown. Among the most venerated Marian mysteries from the 10th and 11th centuries is the Annunciation.

In the feudal context of the following of Christ, Mary's divine maternity established a relationship with descending and ascending aspects:
- Descending aspect: The maternal mediation of Mary or her protection;
- Ascending aspect: The virtues of the one who is devoted to Mary: praise, trust, supplication, "mancipatio" or "servitium".

This type of relationship finds its fullest expression in the form of patronage described above.

St. Bernard (+1153) took up and propagated the medieval Marian devotion in three ways, using the themes of "obsequium" and service:
1. *To honour Mary*, the Mother of God. Never can enough be done to honour Mary. Jesus is the model because he placed in her all power for good.
2. *To pray to Mary* with great confidence. This attitude is founded upon the doctrine of mediation and patronage that St. Bernard described amply. Everyone must look to Mary, invoke her name and obtain her help. Mary is the advocate at the side of Jesus. Her goodness assists us in trusting her in her role as dispenser of graces, a doctrine espoused by St. Cyril of Alexandria and John Damascene and which St. Bernard enlarged upon, made more precise and propagated.
3. *To imitate the virtues of Mary*. This, united with prayer, is the best way of obtaining her protection.

In the writings of St. Bernard, we see all the tenderness of feelings and attitudes of the medieval person in relationship to Mary. These elements, presented by St. Bernard, characterised medieval Marian spirituality and piety.

The teaching of Guerrico d'Igny (+1157) was

very well known among devotees of Our Lady, especially in France and in Religious Orders. According to this teaching, Mary is seen as the spiritual model for everyone because, through a mystical conception of Christ, in her pure and virginal heart, she progressed in love.

In the 12th and 13th centuries in Europe, more than in previous centuries, spirituality took as its starting point the humanity of Christ. This christocentric tendency led to the contemplation of the Lord in his infancy, and of the Saviour on the cross, and by that fact to a contemplation of Our Lady's role in the life of the Lord, in Bethlehem and the other mysteries of the infancy through the public life to the passion. Prayer was directed to Mary as the Mother of mercy, Queen of the universe, taken up to heaven and seated at the right hand of her Son.

In the context of "service to Mary", there was a plethora of liturgical texts, salutations, collections of "miracles or prodigies" (a symbolic literary production of the era). A privileged place was reserved for the Mother of God in art. In her name were dedicated in increasing numbers, monasteries, hospitals, churches, cathedrals and many religious orders that were being founded at that time. Many expressions of Marian piety spread within the monastic orders and the new religious institutes, both within the liturgy and in private devotions. Also within monastic and mendicant Orders there was a widespread Marian interpretation of their religious habit. From the 11th century within the monastic reform movements, there was a strong relationship between Marian devotion and the "reform of the Church" (also taken up later by the Mendicants). An expression of this is the inclusion of the name of Mary in the formula of religious profession. So the Mother of the Lord appears as the means, the guarantee and prototype of the renewed life of the Church.

Finally we must not forget the phenomenon of the medieval knights which spread from around the middle of the 12th century and dominated much of the culture of the various groups of society: lower class, middle class and the courtly class, with a strong influence on religious literature. It is significant that St. Francis compared his companions "to Charles, the Emperor, to Orlando and Olivero, and to all the knights and strong champions who distinguished themselves in combat", or to the knights of King Arthur: "these are my brothers, the Knights of the Round Table, who are hidden in distant and solitary places so that they can dedicate themselves more attentively to meditation and prayer". In this context an "order of Marian knights" also came into being, in which men (friars, devotees etc) understood themselves to be ministers and servants of Mary, wearing her colours.

In the East, Marian spirituality, flourished in the 12th and 13th centuries and was expressed above all in the liturgy, in relation to the mysteries of Christ. Frequent mariological themes were: "Theotokos" (Mother of God), Virgin, "All Holy". In relation to the intercession of Mary, they speak of her gifts rather than her mediation. There are a great many expressions of Marian devotion in the liturgy, in prayers and in the veneration of icons.

3. Marian spirituality during the Crusades

With relation to the Crusades and to the Holy Land, the most important sources for Marian spirituality are those literary sources known as "*itinera ad loca sancta*" (written memoirs of journeys to the Holy Land undertaken by pilgrims during the Middle Ages). They are notes that were used as guides for other pilgrims to the Holy Land and which reveal to us the piety of the author.

The principal points of these memoirs regarding Mary are:
- Mary was born in Magdala and lived for three years in Jerusalem where the Church of St. Anne was built;
- The house of Mary in Nazareth, during the Crusades, was transformed into a basilica. The seat upon which Mary sat at the

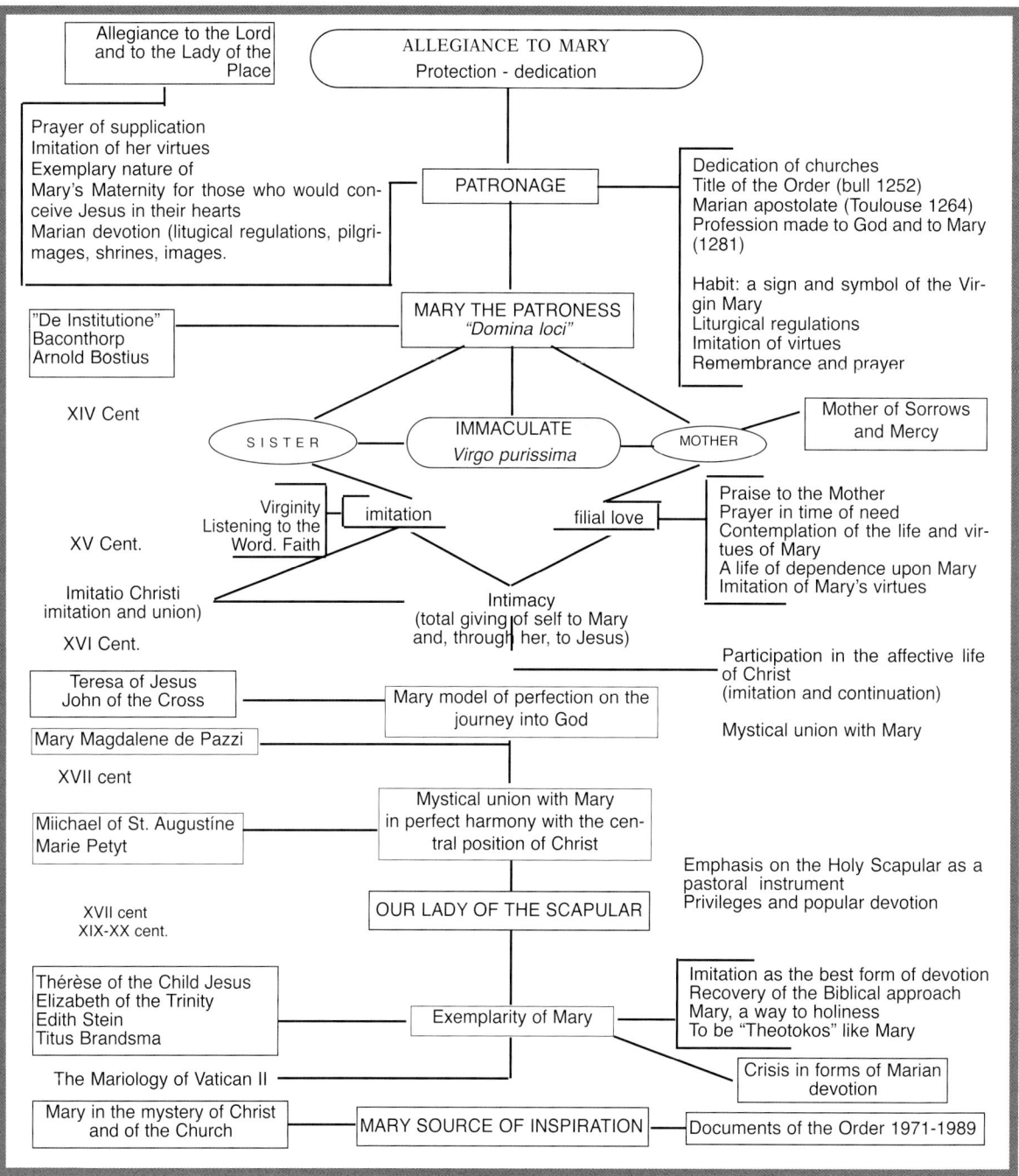

1 A LOVING PRESENCE

Annunciation was preserved in the little town of Diocesarea, where the "amula" (little vase), and the "canestellum" (little basket) which had been used by Our Lady, were also preserved;

- In Nazareth there was a well where Our Lady drew water; in the same little town of Galilee two churches were built dedicated to the Mother of God;
- There was a stone on which Mary rested during her journey to Bethlehem, when she got down from the donkey; the stone was blessed by Mary's presence.
- In Bethlehem there was the table at which Mary received the Three Kings;
- During the flight to Egypt, in the place where Mary rested, a spring of clear water flowed; while in Egypt she lived in Memphis;
- In Nazareth, in the synagogue, there was a beam on which the child Jesus played while Mary joined with the people in prayer;
- In Cana, a visitor could see the jars used in the miracle which Jesus performed at Mary's request;
- In Jerusalem one could see the "ligamentum" (a type of binding) and the ribbon with which Mary tied her hair;
- As well as all this, the pious pilgrim was told that Mary had embroidered a piece of linen with the words of the Creed recited by the apostles and with a representation of the Lord.

Medieval pilgrims felt the necessity to have very concrete connections with the holy places which they could touch, feel and see. This kind of contact with places and things spoke to the pilgrim of the values that Mary had lived, and nourished in the pilgrim a profound love and tenderness towards Our Lady, even though many of the things shown the pilgrim were based on legends. Certainly the historical sense of the time was very different from what it is today and the desire to live the faith was greater than trying to define it.

The written itineraries also mentioned churches and altars built in honour of Our Lady. These churches and Marian altars were erected above all in places associated with an event in the Gospels connected with Our Lady, for example the construction of the altar dedicated to Our Lady of Sorrows on Calvary and others in Nazareth, Bethlehem, and in the vicinity of the Holy Sepulchre. There also existed other churches connected to events related in the Gospel (the Annunciation in Nazareth, in Accon and on Sinai; the Visitation in Ain-Karim; the "Nutrition" and the Holy Family in Nazareth; Our Lady of Tears on the Via Dolorosa; St. Mary of the pinnacle near the Temple). Moreover some traditional events were remembered, for example the "*Dormitio Virginis*" in Sion; Our Lady of the milk in Bethlehem, and the small chapel at the Sepulchre of Our Lady in the valley of Josafat.

As well as these churches, many others were dedicated to Our Lady in Jerusalem, in the city of Acre and in various other places in the Holy Land (Tyre, Sidon, Antarados etc) with various legendary references to the life of Mary.

In all these places worship of the Lord was associated with the veneration of Mary. Devotion to Mary had a European imprint above all in the emergence of new forms of devotions and prayers. The "Hail Mary", the "Hail Holy Queen" (in an embryonic form), the "Angelus" and the "Praises of Mary" recited in the Holy Land acquired a spiritual value, in connection with the holy place which recorded an event in the life of Our Lady and a corresponding value in the daily life of the pilgrim.

One can see very clearly from reading these itineraries, that pilgrims had great interest in those places of the Holy Land connected with Our Lady. In visiting the places sanctified by Jesus, Mary was seen always in intimate union with her Son. She was above all venerated as the Mother of God. We can find confirmation of this in the Arabic histories of the 12th and 13th centuries which make reference to the devotion of Christians to Mary, explicitly called the Mother of "the

Spirit and Word of God, the Mother of Light".

Among other testimonies to Marian devotion during the Crusades are the celebration of liturgical feasts, some of which were not at the time officially recognised by the Universal Church. There also exists a substantial series of things which bear witness to the Marian piety of the times. These include stones, epigraphs, graffiti, and many representations of Our Lady in mosaics, pictures and seals. This type of testimony illustrates abundantly and at times rather tenderly, confident prayer to the Mother of God and the awareness of her mediation. There are several elements that point to Mary as an example of prayer. The emerging mariological themes which one can see represented in pictures are: the Annunciation, the Mediation, the "*Dormitio*" and the Assumption.

Based on what we know about Marian spirituality at the time of the Crusades and in the Holy Land throughout the 12th and 13th centuries, we can draw some conclusions:

a. Marian spirituality at the time of the Crusades was very intense. The content of this spirituality and its theological references are the same as that which was spread throughout Europe during the medieval period, maintaining all its western and Latin characteristics. It is possible to discern influences, or perhaps better, stimuli, coming from contact with the Byzantine East, where the veneration of Our Lady was very strong as in Europe, and which had very ancient traditions especially in places which had some connection to her life.

b. At the time of the Crusades, Mary was always seen in intimate union with her Son Jesus. A reference to Mary leads always to Christ.

c. The most well known Marian mysteries at the time of the Crusades, were the Annunciation, the Mediation, the "Dormitio", and the Assumption. In particular, very often the Annunciation, the "Dormitio" and the Assumption, were put together as various ways of being in connection with Christ. This can be seen above all in epigraphs and in paintings. This understanding might derive from a desire to explain the totality of the plan of God in all that referred to Mary and her spiritual journey from the beginning (the Annunciation) to the end (the Assumption), her journey of complete transformation.

d. The sources and testimonies at the time of the Crusades refer to the presence of Mary in three ways:
- The experience of a contact with a place or with a memory connected with Mary, supported by a Gospel story or by a local tradition; this type of experience led people to recognise the spiritual value of the presence of Mary in each place.
- The prayer of intercession and the awareness of Mary's mediation because of her presence as Lady and Patroness of the place; the consequence of this is the imitation of her virtues as a way of giving honour to the "Lady of the place".
- The inspiration that people found in Mary for their own lives.

4. The Dedication of The Oratory on Mount Carmel

In order to understand the profound meaning of the dedication of the oratory on Mount Carmel to Our Lady by the Latin hermits, it is necessary to situate this fact in the context of all that has already been said in relation to Marian devotion: the facts, the dynamic and the orientation.

As has already been affirmed, the historical fact of the dedication to Mary of the oratory is beyond doubt, because it is confirmed by the concordance of sources and of the writings of the 13th century. However, all sorts of arbitrary and legendary accretions also surrounded it. For example it was said that the oratory was constructed in the year 83 CE and that it was therefore the first Christian church dedicated to Mary.

This dedication of the oratory exercised a fundamental influence on the later developments of Marian spirituality within the Order. When this dedication is examined within the context of the Crusades in the Holy Land, it can be seen that it is not the cause of the Marian devotion but is in fact an effect. We must seek the cause in the hearts of the hermits, according to the customs of the times and in particular, those of the Holy Land during the Crusades. Without a doubt, this devotion, in Europe firstly and then in the Holy Land, induced the hermits to choose Mary as their Patroness. The Latin hermits were men of the 12th and 13th centuries and lived and reacted in accord with their times. It is important not to forget this.

As we have seen, the fact of dedicating a church to Mary in the Holy Land, always had something to do with the belief of Mary's connection to the place dedicated to her. This is true whether the affirmation is valid or not according to our scientific point of view. It was certainly valid for those times. Was this also the case for the Carmelites?

The whole of Mount Carmel, and the Wadi 'ain-es-Siah where the first Carmelite monastery rose up, was surrounded by a host of sacred traditions referring to Elijah and Mary. As understood by various Fathers and early Church writers, the Bible contains references to the relationship between Mary and Carmel, even before the arrival of the Crusaders in the Holy Land. The affirmations of these Fathers and writers were well known at the time by pilgrims to the Holy Land and Christians who already lived there.

The writers applied two biblical references to Mary: "your head is adorned like Carmel" (Sg. 7,6) and the vision of the little cloud by Elijah on Carmel (1 Kings, 18,42-45). To offer some examples, for the first passage we have the beautiful paraphrase of Honorius de Autun: "O Blessed head (of Mary), beautiful and virtuous like Carmel, which inclined so often to kiss the Son of God" and the text of Philip of Harveng from the 12th century, who offered a Marian interpretation of Sg 7,6, basing what he said on the etymology of the word "Carmel", interpreted by many Fathers and writers of the Church as "scientia circumcisionis". This theme reached a greater profundity in the monastic spirituality of the Middle Ages. We can see in these examples the relationship between Mary and the desire to be free from sin and to grow gradually in virtue, all of which is suggested by the word "Carmel". So Mary is the model of the spiritual journey and by the way she lived she became the most beautiful flower of Carmel. The devout and hopeful pilgrim, who visited the holy sites, was led to reflect on this point.

The application to Mary of the text of Is.35,2 ("The glory of Lebanon was given to her, the beauty of Carmel and Sharon") does not appear to have been present at the time of the Crusades in the Holy Land, even though it may have been known in Europe.

As for the second biblical passage regarding the little cloud (1Kings 18, 42-45), it should be remembered that one of the examiners of the "Formula vitae" written by St. Albert, Cardinal Hugh of St. Caro, reaffirmed the interpretation of this passage. Before him, there were several Fathers and ecclesiastical writers who repeated the same thought, like Crisipus of Jerusalem, in the 5th century, and John Damascene later. The symbolism of the little cloud, based especially on the texts of Isaiah (19, 1 and 45, 8), was applied to Mary, the Mother of God, the Virgin and channel of graces. This was frequent in Christian antiquity, used for example by Pseudo-Methodius, St. Cyril of Alexandria, Psuedo-Epiphanius, Germanus of Constantinople, Theodorus the Studite, and Leo VI. We can also find references to a Marian interpretation of the little cloud of Elijah in texts by St. Jerome, Procopius and St. Ambrose.

Witness of Pilgrims to the Church on Mount Carmel

From the journeys of pilgrims to the Holy Land between the 13th and 15th centuries we have various descriptions of the little church (oratory) that the Carmelites built and dedicated to Our Lady, in their place of origin on Mount Carmel. Bringing together elements of these descriptions, we have the following picture: on Mount Carmel there exists a place, near the fount of the Prophet Elijah in the Wadi 'ain-es-Siah, which is most pleasant and picturesque, with abundant water. It is quite distinct and distant from the Abbey of St. Margaret where the Greek monks live, and from the Abbey of St. John of Tyre. In this place, where Latin hermits live, later called Carmelites, there is a little church or oratory, beside which there is a monastery dedicated also to St. Mary, the Virgin Mother of God.

After the fall of Accon (1291), the place became uninhabited and the monastery was destroyed. The little church was used for a certain time afterwards but was then abandoned and consequently fell into disrepair sometime between 1333 and 1458.

Below are some statements:

• "Behind the Abbey of St. Margaret, on the slope of the same mountain, one comes across a picturesque place where Latin hermits, called Carmelites, live. In that place there is a little church of the Holy Virgin. There is also a great abundance of good water that gushes down the cliffs. The Abbey of the Greeks is about a league and a half away from the Latin hermits." (Anonymous, La Citez de Hierusalém, written between 1220 and 1231).

• "After the Abbey of St. Margaret, on the slope of the same mountain, one sees a lovely and pleasant place where Latin hermits called Carmelites lived. They have a lovely little church of Our Lady. In this place there are large gardens irrigated with good water which flows down the rocks of the mountain." (Les chemins et les peregrinages de La Terre Sainte, redaction A, before the year 1265).

• "On the mountain, to the left, there is a beautiful and holy place where can be found the monastery of the Latin hermits who are called Carmelite brothers. In this place there is a church of Our Lady and nearby flowing water, abundant and good, with abundant vegetation." (Les chemins, redaction B, 1268).

• "Two miles after the monastery of St. John of Tyre, there is the monastery of Saint Mary of Carmel. It is a marvellous place, with a mild climate, situated in a valley between the mountains where some Latin hermits lead a penitential life." (Br. Philip Busserio, between 1285-1291).

• "Those who wish to go from the city of Acre to Egypt and Babylon, as we did to seek from the Sultan a letter of safe conduct and his protection which are necessary for the journey, may, if desired, pass by Mount Carmel which is about eight miles distant from Acre. There is to be found a chapel, quite favourable for prayer, built in honour of the Blessed Virgin Mary. From this mountain and from this chapel, as they themselves affirm, the name of the Carmelites has its origins. These are called brothers of Blessed Mary of Carmel." (Umberto of Dijon, 1332).

• "About ten miles from Acre, along the seafront, there is Mount Carmel. The blessed Prophet Elijah was there many times. On this mountain there is a church of Blessed Mary, beside which lived the Brothers of the Order of Carmelites, at the time when Christians governed Acre. Now no-one lives in this place." (Giacomo of Verona, 1335).

• In this place a little church was built in honour of Our Lady, the most glorious Virgin Mary, called Saint Mary of Mount Carmel. The Carmelite Brothers take their origin and their name from here, which they conserve to this day. Now this church is in ruins and only a few Saracen peasants live there." (Roberto of S. Severino, 1458)

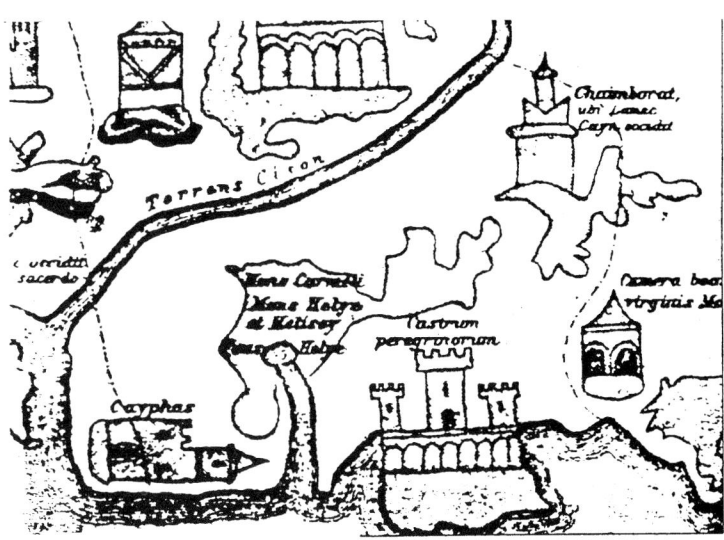

Map of Mount Carmel, drawn c. 1235.

Moreover, those who visited Mt. Carmel, or lived there, felt the presence of Mary and then became aware of biblical references to her.

It is very interesting to note that these biblical passages (Sg & Kings), with their Marian interpretations, are also taken up by Carmelite writers of the 14th century and later, in particular by Baconthorpe and Ribot. From that time onwards, these texts have become obligatory points of reference in the Order's self-understanding.

Similarly, Carmelites took up traditions from the Middle Ages which connected the figure of Elijah to the spring at the Wadi 'ain es-Siah.

We can find other legends in Carmelite authors between the 13th and 15th centuries. These legends connect Mary with Mount Carmel and they are rich with symbolic meaning. For example, it was said that the angel of the Lord transported Mary, still a child, from the Temple to Mount Carmel where she dedicated her perpetual virginity to God. Other legends had it that Mary visited Mount Carmel and was welcomed by the hermits and that Mary and her virgin companions from Nazareth, went to Mount Carmel.

It is interesting to note that these Carmelite legends are not completely original. In fact they are the result of the development and adaptation of pre-existing elements and legends from outside the Carmelite world. The legend about Mary visiting Mount Carmel and the idea that she had dedicated her virginity to the Lord in imitation of the prophet Elijah during one of these visits is based on the apocryphal writings especially pseudo-Matthew. Also the legend, which tells of the meeting of Our Lady and her virgin companions on Mount Carmel, has a precedent, at least indirectly, in a legend in the travelogue of pseudo-Antonino of Piacenza (6th century). He wrote that the Jewish women of Nazareth are the most beautiful of the whole region and that this was a gift of Our Lady who considered them as her relatives.

It is easy to understand how various legendary elements established a personal contact between Mary and Mount Carmel. These legends were particularly significant to people who were open to symbols, as medieval people tended to be.

As well as the biblical references and the interpretations of them, there also exists an historical reference which connects the figure of Mary with the Wadi 'ain-es-Siah. Nowadays, we are sure, that before the Latin hermits arrived, there was a Byzantine "laura" (a type of hermitage) on Mt. Carmel. We also know that the place used by the Carmelites as a stable was the chapel of this "laura". It is thought that this chapel was dedicated to Our Lady as it was very common for Byzantine hermits to dedicate their chapel to her. If the Marian dedication of the Byzantine chapel at the Wadi is true, the action of the Latin hermits who dedicated their oratory to Our Lady, connects them to this previous Marian devotion.

What has been mentioned up to now, makes clear the significance of the dedication of the oratory on Mount Carmel. The basis of the choice made by the Latin hermits by dedicating their oratory to Our Lady, thus taking her as the feudal Patroness of the place, is her "presence", i.e. the connection of Mary to the place.

This Marian dedication shows us that the first hermits were men of their time with a profound devotion to Mary, according to the medieval mind-set: they contemplated Mary as the Mother of God, had an awareness of her role as Mediatrix, sought in her the model for their own lives as they endeavoured to climb the mount of perfection. It seems to me that this is the underlying dynamism that emerges from the origins and constitutes the basis of the later developments that grew up alongside the concept of the Patronage of Mary.

5. Is the Marian Title Generic or Specific?

The dedication of the oratory to Mary poses yet another question. The first documents (from the first part of the 13th century) which speak of the title of the oratory, affirm that it was dedicated to "Our Lady". The title "Sancta Maria de Monte Carmeli", on the contrary, emerges later and appears in papal documents for the first time most probably between 1245-47. The mention of the virginity of Mary appears in documents certainly in 1252 and 1263. Outside of these papal documents, the Marian title of the Order seems to be present in 1246 or 1247 in England and certainly in 1249 and 1250 in Pisa and Trapani.

One might ask, to what Marian mystery does the title of the oratory refer? Was the title generic or specific? For lack of documentation, it is only possible to present here an hypothesis. We can safely reject some suggestions which were put forward by Carmelite authors of the 14th century onwards, for example its association with the Assumption. These are clearly based on later developments resulting from reflection within the Order, especially during the controversy over the Marian title.

In the context of the Crusades the Marian title of "Our Lady" and of "St. Mary" always have a connection to Christ and are understood as referring to the Mother of God. Having said that, there also appears in the title "Our Lady" the idea of "Domina Loci" (the Lady of the place), the Patroness.

"St. Mary" also has another sense. According to St. Thomas Aquinas, the terms "blessed" and "saint" when applied to Mary, have the same meaning and both refer to her sanctification. Following St. Bernard the "via pulchritudinis" (the way of beauty) is also present in the title "St. Mary". The beauty and the delicacy that flow from Mary, chosen by God, help us to understand how the spiritual journey becomes a way of awe and intense love in contemplating the works of God. This is a nuance that was perhaps present in the choice of the title made by the hermits.

A confirmation that the titles "Our Lady" and "Saint Mary" must be understood as a specific expression of "Mother of God", comes from the most ancient Marian iconography in the Order. The oldest Carmelite images of Our Lady, from the 13th and 14th centuries, which are conserved in the churches of the Order, present the typical iconography of the Mother of God. These are called "the Eleusa". All these images, according to legend, come from Mt. Carmel. The symbolic language of these legends is clear. In the iconography that came from the East, Marian images have a legendary connection with St. Luke. In the west, there were some images that were reputed to have been produced by angels. In this context, to affirm that something came from Mt. Carmel means to imply closeness, that is to say, an affective relationship with Mary, which unites the person to the origins by contemplating Mary as the Mother of God.

6. Conclusion on the Marian origins

In the origins of the Order, reference to Mary is backed up by biblical references, local traditions and also by the awareness of the role of Mary in the mystery of Christ and the Church. The values inherent in the dedication of the first oratory, have, without doubt, reference to Mary as Mother of God, as well as Patroness, the Lady of the place.

From this initial setting, in line with the feudal climate of the Crusades, and through a process of idealisation of the Marian origins, a very affectionate, tender and intimate relationship with Mary arose which went on to include new dimensions and new nuances.

The Marian title of the Order

The title of the Order in official documents shows an evolution. Knowledge of this evolution lets us see how in the title certain marian elements appear often at the same time as debates about the bible book place. Below we set out a list of the titles, as they appear in original documents (as preserved in various European archives and especially in the General Archives of the Order) and not in the transcriptions referred to in the *Bullarium Ordinis*, because these are not always faithful to the original. In order to better understand the diversity of the titles, they are presented in the following way:

1. The change introduced in relation to the preceding title is in italics.
2. The date and type of document in which the title is originally mentioned are given.
3. The titles are in chronological order.

- Hermits who ....live on Mt. Carmel (Formula Vitae of St. Albert, 1206-1214).
- Prior (fratres) *heremi* of Mt. Carmel (Bull of 1226).
- *Hermit* brothers of Mt. Carmel (Bulls of 1245 and 1246).
- Brothers *of the order of hermits* of Mt. Carmel (Bulls of 1245 and 1256; then in two bulls of 1289).
- Brothers *of the Blessed Virgin Mary* of Mt. Carmel (letter of Innocent IV, between 1245 and 1247. If this document was not an interpolation from another document from before 1262, this is the first mention of a marian title in a papal document).
- Hermit brothers of the Order *of St. Mary* of Mt. Carmel (Bull of Innocent IV, 13th January 1252; another Bull with the same title from 1256)
- Brothers of the Order of *Blessed Mary* of Mt. Carmel (Bulls of 1259, 1262, 1265, 1291, 1295, 1297; General Chapters of 1369, 1372, 1375, 1385; Constitutions of 1324, 1327, 1342. It is to be noted that "St." and "Blessed" have the same sense and refer to the sanctification-consecration of Mary by means of the Incarnation. Following St. Bernard of Clairvaux, within the term "saint" is to be understood the via pulchritudinis (the way of beauty).
- *Hermit* Brothers of the Order of Blessed Mary of Mt. Carmel (Constitutions of 1281).
- Brothers of the Blessed *Virgin* Mary of Mt. Carmel (Constitutions of 1357 and 1369).
- Brothers *of most Blessed* Mary, *the Mother of God* of Mt. Carmel (Bull of Urban VI, 26th April 1379).
- Brother of the Order of *the Blessed (Holy)* Mother of God, Mary of Mt. Carmel (General Chapters of 1379, 1381, 1405 and 1411).

Brothers of the Order *of the glorious Virgin* Mother of God Mary of Mt. Carmel (Bull of 1380; General Chapters of 1380, 1381, 1387, 1393 and 1396).

- The Order of the Brothers *of the most Blessed* Mother of God, Mary of Mt. Carmel (General Chapters of 1416, 1420, 1425, 1430, 1434 and 1451).
- The Order of the Brothers of *the Blessed (Holy)* Mother of God, Mary of Mt. Carmel (General Chapter of 1447; Constitutions of 1462).
- The Order of the Brothers *of Blessed Mary* of Mt. Carmel (General Chapters of 1456, 1472, 1498, 1503 and 1593)
- The Order of the Brothers of the *Blessed* Mother of God *and ever Virgin* Mary of Mt. Carmel (General Chapter 1478).
- *Brothers and Sisters of Blessed Mary* of Mt. Carmel (Constitutions of 1499 in one of its parts).
- Brothers *of the Order of the Most Blessed Mother of God and Virgin Mary* of Mount Carmel (Constitutions of 1499 in another part. In the following Constitutions and in later Missals we always find this title. However in breviaries there is no uniformity until 1730).
- Brothers *of the Most Venerable Virgin* Mary of Mt. Carmel (General Chapter of 1580).
- In patent letters ... in place of the word Carmelites, they put .. the title: Brothers *of the Order of the Most Blessed Mother of God and ever Virgin Mary* of Mt. Carmel (decree of the General Chapter of 1680).

Pages from the Anthology

1. MARY AND CARMEL

Text from John Baconthorpe, *Speculum de Institutione Ordinis*, cap. 1, in *Medieval Carmelite Heritage*, ed. A. Staring, pp. 184-186.

It is necessary first of all to notice that Mary has always been praised and preached within Carmel. When he prophesied the incarnation of Christ, Isaiah said that only a virgin (cf. Is. 7,14) would be able to conceive and give birth to this child and that this Virgin would possess the beauty of Carmel. He says of her, "The desert will blossom like the lily," and he continues, "the splendour of Carmel was given to her" (cf. Is. 35,1-2). St. Bernard in his homily "Loquamur" affirms, "The beauty of Carmel was given her because she was covered by the virtue of the Most High and made fruitful and free from corruption".

Carmel proclaims Mary. Solomon, comparing the beauty of a woman to Carmel, says, "How beautiful you are, o love, daughter of delights; your head rises like Carmel. (Sg. 7,6-7). In her song of praise, the Church repeats this, applying it to the Blessed Virgin.

Because Mary is honoured and praised on Carmel, it is also right that in Carmel, which is dedicated to her, we will find Carmelites who venerate her in a special way. This was so in the past, as can be shown by the events predicted through prophecy. Saul constructed his triumphal arch as a sign of victory on Carmel, consecrated to Blessed Mary: I K.15,12 (=I Sam 15,12); on Carmel, Elijah offered sacrifice (III K. 18,23 = I K.18,23). Ahab, after this sacrifice, understood who was God. Elisha made his home on Carmel (IV K. 4,25 = II K.4,25). So we see that Carmel had prophets and kings who by their actions venerated the Lady of the place, Blessed Mary.

In order to continue the veneration of Blessed Mary on her Carmel, the Carmelite Order came into existence. Veneration, which can be found in places where saints lived and died, has its origin in the fact that saints whose lives were guided by God, lived in that place. The same thing can be said of dedication: *De consacratione*, d.3.c. "Pronunciandum". According to St. Augustine in his Letter 29 to Deo Gratias, the redeemed, at the time of the prophets, had venerated the Son of the Blessed Virgin who was to come. Nevertheless, the fathers of Carmel, at the time of Elijah and Elisha, in venerating the Messiah, actually began their Order on Carmel which belonged to Blessed Mary. This was recorded in the ancient history of the Order. In this way the Carmelites take their origin from the veneration of Blessed Mary, and we must believe in the ancient fathers of the Order and what they have said regarding the origins of the Order at the time of the Prophets.

2. MARY: THE STRONG AND UNASSAILABLE CASTLE

Text from Michael Aiguani, *Dicionarium biblicum*, ed. In *Analecta O.Carm.*, 8 (1932-37), pp. 78-80.

The most glorious Virgin Mary is like a very strong and unassailable castle in which the Son of God deigned to enter and dwell for nine months when he came down to earth. A reference to this can be found in Luke 10: "Jesus entered into a castle and a woman received him…".

It should be noted that in order that the castle be adequate for its purpose, it had to meet twelve conditions. These were fulfilled in the glorious Virgin as one can see in what follows.

The castle must be situated on a mountain and so be impregnable. The mountain is to be understood as the contemplative dimension of life, through which the human being, detached from created things, rises up ever closer to God. This happens within the castle, which is Mary, who persevered tirelessly in prayer.

The castle must have water in abundance. This signifies an abundance of tears (sign of purification from sin). According to St. Anselm, in his *Meditations*, in the Virgin Mary this gift of God is greater than that received by any other creature (the fullness of grace).

The castle needs to be protected by a large and deep ditch, which is always defended. Humility is this ditch, dug within the person who is truly humble. Who is more humble than she who reigns over all beings by means of her humility? In Lk.1, we read, "Because He has looked upon the humility of His handmaid".

The castle must be built on rock, indicating stability and perseverance. Regarding Mary, Lk. 2 affirms, "she kept all these things in her heart".

There must be at the entrance to the castle a drawbridge to receive guests. This indicates the piety with which one receives pilgrims and the poor. This piety was very strong in the Virgin Mary when she had compassion on the newly weds at the marriage feast at Cana and she said to her Son, "They have no wine" Jn. 2.

The castle needs to have a fortified wall. This wall is the symbol of the patience of Mary in adversity. In Lk. 2, it is said that the shepherds met Mary, Joseph and the baby Jesus in the manger because there was no room for them at the inn.

The castle needs to have strategic defences against enemies. This points to voluntary poverty, rejecting earthly riches as a form of putting enemies to flight, i.e. the demons. Who was poorer than she who placed her newborn son in a manger because there was no other room to be found? Lk. 2.

An important part of the castle is its protective tower. This tower is chastity, which defends every human being. Mary stands out for her chastity and because she was the first to make it a vow, as Lk. 1 affirms: "Because I do not know man".

A castle is always the property of a king. In this case, Christ. Mary was obedient, always ready to entrust herself fully to God, as Lk. 1 says: "Behold the handmaid of the Lord".

There must be a guard on the castle, or rather the vigilance of the senses that guards the house. Mary had this vigilance over her own house when the angel visited her , as Lk.1 says, "the angel went to her".

The castle must have full supplies. This refers to the devoted meditation on the divine word. Mary did this, conserving each word in her heart. (Lk. 2).

Concluding, the castle must possess arms for fighting against the enemy. Hope and divine grace are these arms. Mary received these arms, according to Lk. 1 – she was "full of grace".

Thus the castle of the glorious Virgin Mary is impregnable. In this castle we must seek refuge with all our being so that we will be safe in this life, protected against the attacks of the demons.

3. "ARISE" LIKE THE DAWN TO ILLUMINATE THE FAITHFUL

Text from Michael Aiguani, *Dictionarium biblicum*, ed in *Analecta O.Carm.*, 8 (1932-37), p. 71

We apply the term ascend or go up in its fundamental sense with respect to the Virgin Mother of sinners. Just as the glorious Virgin Mary in her humility descended more than any other human being, so by her glory she ascended to the highest heavens. Amazed at her assumption, the angelic spirits said one to the other: "Who is this who arises from the desert surrounded by delights?" (Sg.8, 5). The desert is this world. It is from this desert that the glorious Virgin arises to the glory of paradise. In so doing, she leaves us with three analogies:

She rose like a cloud to let fall the dew on the parched earth

She rose like incense in order to comfort the sick

She rose like the dawn in order to illumine the faithful.

The Most Holy Virgin arose like the dawn, to illuminate those who are devoted to her. With good reason we can compare the assumption of the Most Holy Virgin with the rising of the sun, because just as the sunrise puts an end to the night, brightens the earth and puts evil to flight, so too does the glorious Virgin. Firstly, the Virgin Mary made possible for us an end to the travails of sin, leaving us an example of all the virtues.

Secondly, the assumption of Mary Most Holy, gained for us the grace of the dew that falls on all humanity, making men and women capable of producing good works and taking the heat out of the vices and the craftiness of the demon. Since the sunrise is purple in colour, so Scripture associates the assumption with purple: "King Solomon made for himself a carriage of wood from Lebanon; with columns of silver, its roof of gold and its seat of purple cloth" (Sg. 3,9-10). The carriage in which King Solomon was carried represents the true Solomon, that is Christ. Saying that the carriage was made of wood from Lebanon, means the purity of the Virgin, which remained after she gave birth, because "Lebanon" signifies "pure, white". Saying that the columns of the carriage were of silver means that the virtues of the glorious Virgin, by reason of the example that she gave, had a great effect on people. Silver is a very valuable metal. Saying that the roof was made of gold, means that the soul of Mary was full of charity, which is symbolised by gold. "The seat of the carriage was made of purple cloth". This refers to Christ who constituted her Queen of heaven and Lady of the place, that is, of the world, because purple is the colour which royalty wears. This is confirmed by psalm 44: "On your right is the Queen". In her assumption, she was taken up higher than the angels, in accordance with psalm 17: "he was taken up above the cherubim and flew".

Another property of sunrise is that it puts evil to flight. With the coming of the dawn, thieves and murderers flee. So the Virgin Mary puts the demons to flight. For this reason, the holy fathers prayed for this assumption so that by means of her, the power of the demons would be destroyed, in accordance with what is written in Joshua 10,6: "Come quickly to save us and help us".

For Further Study

I. Bibliography

- AAVV, *Maria nella storia della vita religiosa*, in *Dizionario degli Istituti di Perfezione*, V, (Roma, 1978), 917-937.
- E. Boaga, *Maria nell'itinerario della vita spirituale dal Medioevo al Rinascimento (Sec. XI-XV)*. In: *La Madre del Signore dal Medioevo al Rinascimento. Itinerari mariani dei due millenni*, vol III, ed. Ermanno Toniolo ODM, Roma, Centro di Cultura Mariana "Madre della Chiesa", 1998, pp. 176-202
- Id, *La devozione mariana delle Crociate*, in *La dimensione mariana del Carmelo*, I, Roma, 1989, pp. 5-10
- Id, *Origini mariane dei Carmelitani*, in "*Marianum, Ephemerides Mariologicae*", 53 (1991), pp. 183-198 (Spanish translation in Congresso Mariano Internacional, 1989, Madrid 1990, pp. 37-50
- N. Geagea, *Maria, Madre e Decoro del Carmelo*, Roma, 1989, p.55-109 (on the origins of the Order).

II. For personal and/or group study

1. Go over the essential points of the chapter, underlining:
    - The fundamental marian values in the Middle Ages
    - The marian values present at the time of the Crusades
    - The marian elements present at the origins of the Order

2. What significance does the title "Flower of Carmel" have in the relationship between Mary and Mount Carmel?

III. Prayer and Life

1. Pray with the Word of God

    - Sg. 7,6
    - Is. 35, 1-10; 61, 1-8
    - 1 Kg 18,42-45

2. How do the Church and our religious family sustain our devotion to Mary?

3. What mystery in the life of Mary is most important in my relationship with her? How does this influence my life?

4. Read the pages from the anthology and think about how you personally have contributed to the spread of the knowledge of the marian heritage of our Order.

5. What seems most significant to you in this chapter and in the inserts?

6. In our own times are there any aspects of marian devotion similar to those that existed at the origins of the Order? Give reasons.

THE HEAVENLY LADY

O Blessed Mother!
Long have we waited for you, perfect in your organisation,
institution and governance of our Order.
Prostrate at your feet,
holiest of Mothers, Mother of the Carmelite Family!
Living on this mountain,
We drink from your fountain and quench our thirst.
Sincerely we recognise that your own hand directs us,
Assisted by you, and enlightened by you.
Transform us in you and our life in yours.
Remain with us, our Lady.
O Mary! We seek refuge in your bosom;
A mother must live with her children,
A teacher with her disciples,
The abbess with her monks,
The Lady with her servants.

(Arnold Bostius,
De Patronatu et Patroncinio, no. 1531)

2 THE HEAVENLY LADY

Mary as Patroness

1. Different forms of the presence of Mary in the history and life of Carmel.

The connection between Mary and the Carmelites is seen at the origins of the Order, in the fact of the dedication of the first church on Mount Carmel to her. This fact comes from a process that led to the choice of Mary as Patroness and also to profound juridical, ascetic and spiritual consequences for Carmel in the middle ages. At the beginnings of Carmel, Our Lady is encountered as "the Lady of the place", or "Patroness" or "Virgin Mother of God".

Various factors, mentioned in the previous chapter, reveal the form of Marian presence among the Carmelites: -
- The strong christocentricism that pervades early Carmelite life and Marian devotion.
- The Carmelites came to understand the role of Mary (the Mother of the Lord, the Lady of the place) in relation to Christ, the "Lord of the place" within the mystery of Christ and the Church. This led to the discovery of the relationship between Mary and Mt. Carmel, which was strengthened by biblical references and local traditions.
- The choice of Mary, Virgin Mother of God, the Lady of the Place, as the Patroness, had very important consequences. Service or spiritual vassilage is a consequence of the choice and dedication to Mary. So also is the protection-mediation relationship, that is, the ascending and descending elements of medieval patronage.
- There is possibly also an inspiration for their own individual spiritual lives in relationship with Mary, above all in the virginity of Mary, looked at from the point of view of the via pulchritudinis (the way of beauty).

These initial concepts will be repeated down through the centuries with different emphasis, stressing always however the same basic content. Throughout the lifespan of Carmel, the presence of Mary took on different forms that influenced its history.
- Mary as Patroness: Mother of the Lord, the Lady of the place, of the Holy Land (13th-14th centuries).
- Mary, the Most Pure Virgin: the Virgin, Mary Immaculate, "*tota pulchra*" (all beautiful), the Woman of the Apocalypse, that was also united to the figure of the Mother of the Redeemer (14th-15th centuries).
- Mary, Our Lady of the Scapular: she who delivers from purgatory and preserves from hell (16th century to our own days).
- Mary, Mother and Sister; she who reflects the tenderness of the Father. She is a prophetic figure and disciple of Christ and welcomes the Word that has been sown by God in the heart of the world.

In the present chapter and in those following, these forms of Marian presence in Carmel will be analysed.

2. The Presence of Mary as Patroness

This is the kind of presence that the first generations of Carmelites experienced and which will remain always within the Order as a strong and essential inspiration.

The reference to "Patroness" has an initial

meaning that was then enriched by successive nuances and new dimensions. In particular, the choice of Our Lady as Patroness along with the dedication of the oratory, takes for granted first of all the relationship which is contained in the feudal "obsequium", an ascending and descending relationship, which acquires a particular colouring in connection to the Holy Land, as "the land of the Lord". In the 1330's John Baconthorpe used the term "Domina loci", in reference to Mary and correspondingly "Dominus loci" with reference to Jesus Christ. He was the first Carmelite to do so.

a) To the honour and praise of Mary

From the consideration of Mary as Patroness, an understanding quickly arose within the Order that it had been founded for the honour and service of Mary. Here is a list of expressions and facts taken from early sources that help us to appreciate this Marian atmosphere:
- To the novice, during his clothing, was given "the habit of our holy Order dedicated to the honour of the BVM of Mount Carmel" (Prayer of clothing, in the Constitutions of 1281, but the formula preceded the Constitutions).
- In a document of the year 1264, the Carmelites of Toulouse affirm that they "are dedicated in a special way to the Virgin Mary".
- The Prior General, Peter de Millaud, in a letter written in 1282 to seek help for the suspension of the "nota vacillationis", writes: "The same Order was instituted in regions beyond the seas in a special way for the praise and honour of the Glorious Virgin".
- In the Acts of the General Chapter of Montpellier (1287), we find at the beginning the following reference: "The glorious Virgin Mary, Mother of Jesus, in allegiance to whom and for whose honour the Order of Mount Carmel was founded".
- The Constitutions of 1294 order that the BVM "our patroness" be invoked frequently. Also these Constitutions counsel those who seek alms to invoke the most sweet name of Mary.
- In 1300, the Prior General, Gerard of Bologna, in welcoming devout women of Venice, and in making them participants in the benefits of the Order affirmed: "The Order of the Blessed Virgin has been blessed with this special title"
- In 1324 in a prayer for clothing in the habit, we find, "Through the intercession of the BVM whom you gave as the special Patroness of this holy Order, may this novice truly be converted from the vanity of the world."
- John of Malines affirmed that the Carmelites "have a special devotion to the Mother of God".
- In approximately 1370, Carmelites petitioned Pope Innocent IV for permission to build houses "in which they might sincerely serve the Lord and his Virgin Mother, as they themselves desired".

This Marian characteristic of the Order is also recognised by witnesses from outside the Order:
- Pope Urban IV in the bull of indulgences for the construction of the new house on Mount Carmel (20th February 1263) said: "This place is the head and origin of this Order which was founded for the honour of God and of the glorious Virgin, their Patroness".
- In 1296, 15 Italian bishops, giving an indulgence to those who visited the churches of the Order in Germany, affirmed that the Carmelites "are dedicated in a special way to the service of Our Lady".
- Edward II, King of England, in 1311, recommended the Carmelites to the Pope saying, "The same Order was founded for the honour of the glorious Virgin, whom these friars, here on earth, are bound to follow. Pope Clement V, in a bull of the 13th March of the same year, repeats the same thing:

My Brothers carry the Cross of my Son!

"A great miracle took place in Montpellier, near Toulouse. On that mountain which is close to the sea, there were frequent storms that wreaked havoc in the area. In order to free themselves from these difficulties, the local people built a tower and placed a number of saints' relics at the top. Among these was a big relic of the cross of Christ. One day there was a ferocious storm that toppled the pinnacle of the tower, scattering the relics over the countryside.

The canons of the principal church went out in a solemn procession, accompanied by the cross, in order to look for the relics. When they discovered the relic of the holy cross, it was emitting rays of light and they sought to lift it up. It flew from the hands of those who tried to lift it. They followed it and it moved further away. This happened several times. Many clerics and religious of other Orders tried to remove it with the same results.

In the same city there was a new community of Carmelites, our brothers, who lived poorly and in great holiness. One of these, who was very devout, said to the brothers, Let us also go to take the wood of the Lord because last night, in a vision, the Blessed Virgin said to me, I want only my brothers to carry the cross of my Son.

The community then went in procession, the brothers dressed humbly, carrying a simple cross. The holy wood no longer jumped away but let itself be lifted. With great joy, the Carmelites carried the wood of the cross to their humble little home where it remained performing miracles until today (or at least until the 15th century)."

(From Baldwin Leers, *Collectaneum exemplorum et miraculorum*, chap. 12)

"The Order was instituted in honour of the Blessed and Glorious Virgin."

- Cardinal Berengarius Fredol in 1312, records that "the Order is committed with particular devotion to the glorious Virgin and bears the title of her own name."
- The Council of the 27 wise men of Pavia (Italy) in 1316, helped the Order not to fall into poverty "because of the reverence due to its name, which is that of the Blessed and Glorious ever Virgin Mary, because of whom many individuals and cities receive graces."
- Pope John XXII, in the bull of exemption in favour of the Carmelites (13/3/1317), recognises that the Order is "honoured in a special way with the title of the glorious Virgin Mary". The same Pope repeats this idea in other bulls (18/5/1318; 4/7/1319; 1/4/1321). This idea is also expressed by Clement VI in the bull of 19 July 1347. The Constitutions of 1357 repeat the same idea. Pope Innocent VI reminded the members of the Chapter at Narbonne of the sublime example "of your Patroness, Blessed Mary of Mount Carmel" (17 April 1354). The same example "of the Glorious Virgin Mary, your head" was emphasised by Gregory XI to the members of the Chapter at Puy.

b) Various ways of expressing the meaning of Mary's Patronage

In order to better understand the way in which the Carmelites interpreted the Patronage of Our Lady and made it part of their lives according to the mentality of the times, it is necessary to be aware of the various ways they expressed it:

1- The Marian title of the Order was used widely from the middle of the 13th century.
2- The dedication to Mary of numerous churches of the Order in Europe.
3- The insertion of the name of Mary in the formula of religious profession.
4- The symbolism of the habit.
5- The liturgical legislation and the Marian feasts, especially the "Commemoratio sollemnis" (Solemn Commemoration) as the feast of Mary's protection of the Order.

1. The Marian title of the Order

According to an ancient tradition related by John of Cheminot (c. 1337), the Marian title came from the people when they distinguished the Carmelites of Mount Carmel from the Greek monks from the nearby monastery dedicated to St. Margaret. This is quite possible although it cannot be proved conclusively. It could also have come from within the group of Carmelite hermits. In the writings of the 14th century there are some suggestions for this. In the official documents concerning the Order from the first half of the 13th century, the Carmelites are called "hermits" without any specific reference. The first mention of the Marian title of the Order is perhaps to be found in a papal document which dates from around 1245-47 and then certainly in official documents from the year 1252 onwards. However, by the people, the Carmelites were generally called brothers of Carmel, "fratres virgulati" (striped friars), and in a document from the year 1250 (foundation of the house in Trapani), they are called "Brothers of St. Mary of Mt. Carmel". In the second half of the 13th century the Carmelite house in Milan was founded. In the document of foundation, we find a reference to the Marian title of the Order. There is a reference to the desire of the friars to be there in order to propagate devotion to Our Lady.

Apart from this, the specific characteristics of the Marian title of the Order (Virgin, Mother of God) clearly come from reflection within the Order itself, especially in the context of the controversy surrounding the title.

The Marian title of the Order, whatever was its origin - popular, official or from the Carmelites themselves - is always related to the dedication to Our Lady of the first chapel on Mt. Carmel. With this title, the Carmelites justified the nature and Marian structure of the Order. In the Middle Ages, a name or title was considered to represent what it said. Therefore the General Chapter of Bordeaux in 1294 decided that the members of the Order should answer those who questioned its name, by saying that they were members of the Order of Mary. The same General Chapter decided that they would seek alms always under this name

The Marian title of the Order was very quickly contested by various other religious orders and the Carmelites defended themselves. They sought reasons as they worked out a defence. This assisted the maturation of their Marian devotion. According to the mentality of the era, they understood that the title was not just a matter of words but really expressed the vitality and identity of the Order.

In particular, the fact that the Carmelites called themselves "Brothers of the Virgin" was contested. It seems that the strongest opposition came from the "Brothers of Blessed Mary Mother of Christ", otherwise known as "White Cloaks" or "fratres picae", a French Order founded approximately in the middle of the 13th century and suppressed by the Council of Lyon in 1274. They were often confused with the Carmelites. Also, some said that the Patroness of the Carmelites was St. Mary of Egypt, a penitent, and not Our Lady.

The reaction of the Carmelites to these attacks came early. Apart from the already mentioned norm of the General Chapter of Bordeaux in 1294, between the years 1287 and 1292, they obtained many indulgences for those who referred to the Carmelites by the name "Brothers of the Virgin Mary".

It is interesting to note what Carmelite authors wrote throughout this controversy:

- In the book, "De inceptione Ordinis" of 1320, the motivation for the title of the Order is given as the construction of the oratory on Mt. Carmel and the choice of Mary as Patroness. Various papal documents ("privilegia") in favour of the Carmelites are mentioned. The construction of the oratory is remembered in the Rubrica Prima of the Constitutions of 1281 and 1294. However the explanation of the title as in the book "De inceptione Ordinis" is present only in the Rubrica Prima of the Constitutions from 1324.
- Baconthorpe in his " Tractatus de institutione" affirms the origin of the title of the Order by the place - Mt. Carmel - dedicated to Mary (cf. Is.35,1-2), by the construction of the oratory, and the approval of several Popes. His arguments are based on Scripture (Isaiah mentioned above) and in the legal motives that arose from the examination of papal bulls. He also dedicates a whole chapter to the title of the Order that will be the basis of many later writings.
- John of Cheminot in 1337 affirmed the popular origin of the title. To justify the title, he argued that the Carmelites possessed "the beauty and the title of virginity" because the Scriptures attributed to Mary the "caput tuum" (your head) and the "glory of Lebanon", that is the "head" of Carmel and the "praise" of Lebanon (cf. Sg.7,6-7; Is.35,1-2).
- John of Veneta in his Chronicles, repeats the preceding affirmations and adds the invitation to rejoice at the Marian title, "And so, devoted brothers in Christ, here is the reason you should rejoice and exult: you have been chosen from among many to possess as a title: (Mary) the flower of beauty and of virginity".
- In the middle of the 14th century, John of Hisdin points out that St. Cyril of Alexandria, the adversary of Nestorius, had been a Carmelite and that the Council of Ephesus, to thank him, had decided that his Order have the Marian title. This invention is the origin of the story that St. Cyril was a Carmelite.

- In 1370, John of Hildesheim, tried to prove that the "St. Mary" of the Carmelites was not the Egyptian St. Mary, the penitent or hermit. To defend the legitimacy of the title, this author offered seven reasons based on the affinity between Elijah and Mary, the Virgin Mother of God, and the life of the Carmelites.
- At the same time, Philip Ribot, repeated the popular origin of the Marian title, based on the construction and dedication of the chapel on Mt. Carmel.

The high point of the controversy occurred in 1374 when the Carmelite John Hornby defended with success the Marian title against the Dominican John Stokes in the University of Cambridge in England. The University judged in favour of the Carmelites. The arguments of Hornby in favour of the title, were that each group took its name from its place of origin or from its holy founder and that the Carmelite Order had both. The proofs which he offered were: the reference to St. Cyril mentioned above; the relationship which connected the forebears of the "founders" of the Order (Elijah and Mary were both descendents of Aaron). This justified passing on the title of Elijah and Mary; finally that the first Carmelite house was founded in Jerusalem (near the Golden Gate) in the place where Mary was conceived. These ideas repeat some of the arguments of John of Hildesheim against the detractors of the Order.

At this time, there was an addition to the title by the insertion of the term "Virgin", which was against those who called the Carmelites, the brothers of St. Mary the Egyptian. In this way the title acquired its full reference to Mary the Mother of God: "Brothers of the Most Holy Mother of God, the Virgin Mary of Mt. Carmel".

In 1376 the Prior General Bernard Oller sent a letter to the Pope. Regarding the title, he offered the following reasons:
- the construction of the oratory in honour of Mary
- the formula of Carmelite religious profession
- the bulls of several popes.

He also explained that the word "Patron" could be understood in an active sense (one who initiates or founds an Order, for example St. Dominic). However the term could also be understood in a passive sense (three cases - 1. the one in whose honour the Order is founded e.g. the Holy Trinity for the Trinitarian Order; 2. the one who is chosen by the religious themselves e.g. St. Benedict as patron of monks; 3. the one in whose honour certain monasteries are founded.)

According to Oller, Our Lady is patroness of the Carmelites in both senses - active and passive. Also, the title of religious can be based on the service to which the Order is destined (e.g. the Order of Preachers); the virtue that they practice (e.g. humility for the Franciscans); the place of origin (the Carthusians); the patron understood either in the active or passive sense (e.g. the Benedictines). The title of the Carmelites is based on the last two categories: place and patroness.

Finally in 1379 Pope Urban VI gave definitive approval to the title and conceded indulgences to those who called the Carmelites by their Marian title, "Brothers of the glorious Mother of God, Mary of Mt. Carmel".

Nevertheless the controversy was renewed several times. Some prayers and some texts record the Carmelite victory in the controversy. For example, at the beginning of the Collect of the Solemn Commemoration of the 16th July, we have, "O God, who honoured the Order of Carmel with the glorious title of the Blessed Virgin Mary, Mother of your Son.....". Also in the celebrated "testament of St. Brocard" we read, "My sons, out of His goodness, God has called us into the number of the hermits .. and through his singular gift, we are called Brothers of the Blessed Virgin Mary".

2. Dedication of other churches of the Order to Mary

Though the modern person can live without

THE MIRACLE OF TOULOUSE

The foundation of the house in Toulouse (France), between the years 1242 and 1264, was connected with a very interesting and miraculous story.

John of Hildesheim relates (cf. A. Staring, *Medieval Carmelite Heritage*, p.385-388) that there lived in Toulouse a very rich Jewish man who was esteemed by everyone. It was his custom to take a walk in the orchard of his well-appointed house. It was during one of these walks that something wonderful happened. At the leafy top of a particular tree there appeared a woman of rare beauty holding a child in her arms. The man contemplated this vision for a while and then he wanted to get closer. He fetched a ladder and began to climb up, but as he approached, the vision disappeared. When he went down, the woman appeared again. He went up the ladder again, and again the woman disappeared. He made several attempts all to no avail. During sleepless nights, the man tried to understand the meaning of this vision, trying to penetrate its mystery but failed. He then sought help from a priest who was considered to be a saint and very devoted to Our Lady.

He told the priest what had happened and the priest immediately gave him the following explanation: "This is a true sign that Our Lady wants to receive permanent homage in this house in which she has so often been blasphemed." The Jewish man enquired what kind of homage should be given and the priest responded, under divine inspiration, "The Brothers of the Blessed Virgin Mary as yet do not have a house in this city. Offer to them some land to construct a house. Be baptised and become a member of her Order." Immediately the man obeyed. He invited the friars, who came and took possession of the place. They baptised the man with his wife and children and secretly blessed the house. They put up the bell tower and when it was finished, they rang the bells in celebration.

When the representative of the King of France came to know what had happened, he ordered the immediate withdrawal of the friars. However they resisted. Because they would not leave, he had them enclosed behind a big wall. In their isolation, they were secretly fed by devout people who were motivated by the words, "I was in prison and you visited me". They were also motivated by the words of the antiphon which the Carmelites pray at Lauds, "Ave Stella Mattutina", in which they invoke Our Lady with these words, "You console us most kindly in this prison", while piously gazing upon Mary's image. All that held them prisoners collapsed, just like the walls of Jericho.

At this moment, the prefect lost his eyes; they jumped right out of their sockets. In his great suffering, he recognised his sin and he asked to be taken immediately into the presence of the friars where he pleaded with them to pray to Our Lady that he be pardoned.

The brothers then began the Salve Regina. When they got to the words, "Turn then, our advocate, your eyes of mercy towards us," the eyes of the prefect returned to their sockets. It is said that this miracle made the prefect so ardently grateful to Our Lady that he offered to the Order all his properties and he himself became a Carmelite. It was not only this miracle that happened; there were many other stories of miraculous interventions for the benefit of the Order which made it possible to build a beautiful and grand house in honour of the most blessed Mother of God, whose name be honoured for ever!

(From John of Hildesheim, *Dialogus inter directorem et detractorem*, cap. XVII).

being connected or concerned with the patron of his or her social group, it would have been practically impossible for the medieval person to participate in a group without honouring its patron. In this way the Carmelites knew that they were consecrated to Our Lady because their first chapel was dedicated to her as Patroness. As a consequence of this, as the Order spread throughout Europe, many of its foundations were named in honour of Our Lady, so many that it could be said to be a general rule.

"Each Carmelite foundation with its respective church was dedicated in honour of the Virgin Mary" said John Hornby in 1374. John of Hildesheim affirmed the same thing. He said that it came from very ancient times. Bernard Oller recorded, "These dedications were made in imitation of the dedication of the first chapel". Alongside those of Hornby, Thomas Bradley made the same points. We also find in the *Ancient Ordinal* of the Order the rubric for the washing of the altars on Holy Thursday, "The cantor begins the antiphon 'Christi Virgo' or of the glorious Virgin because our chapels are dedicated to her name."

This Marian dedication of the churches refers to various mysteries of Mary's life. The most popular dedication was to the Annunciation. It is difficult to discover the number of churches dedicated in the 13th century to this mystery. Certainly the following were:- Trapani, Catania, Marsala, Agrigento, Sciacca, Grottaminarda, Piacenza, Milan, Pavia, Avignon, and perhaps also Orange. Many more received the same dedication later. In the same period there were fewer churches dedicated to the Assumption. The title of Our Lady of Mt. Carmel spread from the 16th century onwards. The Annunciation was the principal feast of some Provinces and confraternities that had started in Carmelite churches.

3. The formula and rite of religious profession

The Carmelite of the 13th century, in perfect accord with the Marian spirit of the Order, made his religious profession with the formula in which the name of Our Lady figured: "I promise obedience ... to God and to the Blessed Virgin Mary of Mt. Carmel." This formula, which can be found in the Constitutions of 1281, is from an earlier age (perhaps from 1256) and is inserted in the rite of religious profession that was intentionally structured as a ceremony of feudal homage.

With this formula, the Carmelite of that time intended to make a pact, not only with God, but also with the Virgin Mary and so promise consecration to her service in order to be sure of her maternal protection. The practice of inserting the name of Mary in the formula of profession was common to other Orders, as an expression of the commitment of the religious to the reform of the Church. Therefore, professing vows to God and the Blessed Virgin Mary inspired the Carmelite to be a living stone in the Church, the Mystical Body of Christ.

4. The symbolism of the habit

Another very important fact for the mentality of the Middle Ages was the symbolism of the habit. It was an exterior sign of belonging to the Lord whose insignia were worn. To affirm the Marian sense of the habit was an expression of dedication to the service of the Mother of God.

After the migration to Europe (1238), the Carmelites, in some places, because of their striped cloak were called disparagingly "fratres virgulati" or "fratres picae". To stop this name calling as well as for other reasons, the General Chapter of 1287, held in Montpellier, decreed that a white cloak replace the striped cloak. At this time a Marian significance was not given to the white cloak; this came later. John Baconthorpe (+ 1348) seems to have been the first to make the connection and he defined the cloak as "the mantle of Mary". Following from that, the white cloak was interpreted as symbolically pointing to the purity and virginity of Mary.

5. Liturgical regulations.

Another element that showed the self-understanding of the Order in relation to Mary in the 13th and 14th centuries is in the liturgical prescriptions. In line with the present state of research, we can say that reflection on the Marian spirituality of the Order becomes explicit in the liturgy, from the end of the 13th and the beginning of the 14th centuries and in this way the Order demonstrated its love for Our Blessed Lady. We find many prescriptions in rubrics as well as references to Mary in antiphons, offices and celebrations. Many of these prescriptions are met for the first time in the Ordinal of 1312 (the book which contains norms for the liturgical celebrations). However, it may well be that some of these are older.

In particular the liturgical regulations of the Order regarding devotion to Our Lady include:
- The introduction of the name of Mary in the Confiteor (Constitutions of 1294).
- The daily office "of Blessed Mary" and the growth of the daily memoria "of Blessed Mary" (an antiphon with its own prayer) at Lauds and Vespers (Ordinal of 1312).
- The Mass "of Blessed Mary" each day (1312, and sung from the year 1324).
- Each Saturday or some other day of the week, the celebration of the "Commemoration of Blessed Mary" with nine readings, and a Mass "of Blessed Mary" with greater solemnity (1312).
- The singing of the *Salve Regina* at the end of Compline (1312) and the recitation of the same antiphon at the end of each canonical hour (1324). As a result of this, the practice began very early of reciting the *Salve* at the end of mass (in 1328 it was prescribed for the Province of Lombardy, and for the whole Order in 1357).
- As well as the universal Marian feasts (Purification, Annunciation, Assumption, Nativity), the Immaculate Conception as the principal feast of the Order was added in 1306. From the end of the 14th century "The Solemn Commemoration" of July 17 (later 16th), became the principal feast as a thanksgiving for the protection of Mary of the Order. Other Marian feasts from 1383 are: Our Lady of the Snows, the Visitation, and the Presentation in the Temple. More Marian feasts were introduced later.
- The office of the Annunciation was celebrated each week of Advent with the exception of the last week (1324).
- The addition of the Gloria in each solemn mass "of Blessed Mary" throughout the year (1324); for the Tuscan Province, the Credo was also added (1405).
- The office "of Blessed Mary" with nine readings during Lent (1375).
- As a sign of reverence to the name of Mary, the rule was introduced that friars should bow their heads at each mention of her name in prayers and in solemn masses (1281), and also during the Divine Office (1324, 1369).
- With reference to Our Lady, the feast of St. Anne was introduced into the calendar of the Order with an office of nine readings in 1281; from 1375 (and again in 1381 and 1411), there was a memoria of St. Anne after the memoria of Our Lady in the divine office.
- As a result of this we find the "duplex" feast of the sisters of St. Anne, Mary of James and Mary of Salome. This was established for the 25th May in 1342 and again in 1357. From 1369 a proper office was added.
- There was a particular manifestation of Marian devotion at the house in Paris with the singing of the hymn "Inviolata" before the image of Our Lady every Saturday and on the eve of Marian feasts after vespers, and in Lent after Compline. An indulgence was attached to this usage by Pope Urban V on 23rd November 1367.

The Shrine of Loreto and the Carmelites

The Carmelites at the service of the shrine

The famous shrine of the "Holy House" of Loreto (Italy), was entrusted to the care of the Carmelites of the Mantuan Congregation. According to tradition, the "Holy House" kept within the shrine was the same as the house in which Mary lived in Nazareth. The tradition tells that the house was transported by angels from Palestine to various places until it ended up in Loreto.

Bl. Baptist Spagnoli (the Mantuan or the Christian Virgil) requested that this shrine be given into the care of the Carmelites and his request was granted in 1489 by Cardinal Girolamo della Rovere, bishop of Recanati. Bl. Baptist stated that this same holy house had been cared for by the Carmelites in the Holy Land. He thanked the Cardinal and declared that the Mantuan Congregation, of which he was Vicar General, would do all in its power to imitate the example of the Carmelites of the past. On 22nd September 1489, he sent the Cardinal a short work, entitled, "Redemptoris mundi Matris Ecclesiae Lauretanae Historia".

In the summer of 1488, thirty Carmelites were sent to Loreto but in a short time, more than a half of them had died due to the unhealthy air and an outbreak of the plague. For this reason they asked for and obtained a house at Recanati, near the church of St. Vito, for where they were able to continue the care for the nearby shrine of Loreto. Very soon, the friars became well known in both cities for their austerity and apostolic zeal, which was very edifying and pleasing to the people. Unfortunately for various reasons (the unhealthy air, the high cost of maintaining the community, and difficulties with the local clergy), it was decided in 1497 to give up the care of the shrine. This actually took place the year later. The Carmelites remained for some years at Recanati but in 1524 they finally left.

Cf.: L. Saggi, *I Carmelitani a Loreto*, in *Il Santuario di Loreto*, Loreto 1957, pp. 306-310; A. Martino, *Il B. Baptista Mantovano e la S. Casa di Loreto*, in *La Madonna del Carmine*, 5 (1951), 10-13; F. Grimaldi, *La Storia della chiesa di S. Maria di Loreto*, Loreto, 1993, pp. 171-175; *Loreto: Ordini e Congregazioni Religiose*, Loreto 1997, pp. 13-14

The visit of St. Therese

An interesting text regarding Loreto is that written by St. Therese of Lisieux during a pilgrimage with her father and others to Rome in November 1878 in order to visit Pope Leo XIII.

"....I was happy to be on the road to Loreto. I am not surprised that the Most Holy Virgin chose this place to transport her blessed house....I was delighted with Loreto. What can I say about the holy house? Oh, I was deeply moved to be under the same roof as the Holy Family, to gaze at the walls on which Jesus fixed his divine eyes, treading the ground on which the sweat fell from St. Joseph's brow, where Mary had carried Jesus in her arms, after having carried him in her virginal womb.... I saw the tiny room where the angel descended at the side of the Holy Virgin....I put my rosary beads in the little bowl of the Child Jesus ....These memories are wonderful!" (*Manuscript* A f. 59v).

In the medieval liturgical texts proper to the Order, we find the themes of the divine Maternity, the Mediatrix of graces, and a consideration of the mystery of Mary from the Immaculate Conception and the Annunciation through to the Assumption. The various themes show a solid theological base of spirituality sustained by the liturgy.

In particular the themes of the divine maternity and Mediatrix are affirmed and held up as clear references to the patronage of Our Lady. As well as the theological data, there is frequent reference to the trust the members of the Order had and their experience of Mary's help and protection in different times of need. In the consideration of the mystery of Mary, there are many texts that express the affection and the beauty of Mary. These texts allow us above all to affirm that the early Carmelites, in their devotion to Mary tended to emphasise her divine maternity, the Annunciation, her Virginity and her Immaculate Conception.

This same tendency is seen also from the 14th century in the theological disputes in which the Carmelites were involved within universities, where they taught and defended these Marian privileges. Henry of Lagenstein in 1385, in a sermon on the occasion of the Annunciation, affirmed, "In this Order there are fervent promoters of the veneration of the Mother of God, the Virgin Mary, and there are many masters of theology who, with great competence, defend her virtues and her perfections."

Finally, there are other less important elements, which nevertheless indicate their Marian mentality. These are the Marian salutation on entering and leaving the house; the writings of superiors on the occasion of affiliation to the Order and in other official circumstances like General and Provincial Chapters; the prescriptions on fast and abstinence on the occasion of the vigil of the principal Marian feasts, a usage that took on a special significance as a part of the scapular devotion from the 16th century onwards.

c) Further reflection

It has already been mentioned that the Carmelite writers, especially in the 14th century,

Marian Greetings

Very early in the Order, the custom of greeting and invoking Mary inside and outside the convent was introduced. The Constitutions of 1294 prescribed that one must salute or invoke the Blessed Virgin, both in the confessional and while seeking alms. The custom of saluting Our Lady was then introduced at the beginning of documents and letters. There are whole series of examples of this custom, The Prior General, Gerard of Bologna, writing in 1300 to the "beatas" of Venice, wished that through the intercession of the Blessed Virgin, they might live in communion with all the blessed spirits. The Provincial of the Roman Province, in a letter dated 6th March 1341, addressed to a confraternity, wished the members "health in the Blessed Virgin". The Prior General, John Grossi, writing to the religious of Avignon, wished them, "Health in the Son of the Virgin with whose title our Order is honoured."

Also in the official acts of Chapters, it is usual to find at the beginning or the end a marian salutation or invocation. For example in the acts of the Provincial Chapter of Lombardy of 1333 and in the Constitutions of 1369, we read, "To the praise of God and of the blessed Virgin Mother of God and our mother".

As well as the above, in the official acts of the general chapters of the Order, the following salutation was used: "Jesus in the heart and Mary on the mind" (chapters of 1434 and 1440). The same idea is expressed in other capitular acts (1513), in which we find the name of Jesus entwined with that of Mary:"JE-MARIA-SUS". Later, in the 18th century, a Carmelite, Richard of the heart of Mary, wrote at the beginning of his book: "De immen-MARIA-sitate Dei" (on the immens-MARIA-ity of God).

Also in the statutes of the Portuguese Province there were norms regarding the marian salutations. From 1748 the religious had to say "Hail Mary" whenever they passed an image of Mary.

Cf: R. M. López-Melús, *Tradición mariana en el Carmelo pre-teresiano*, in *Ephemerides Mariologicae*, 33 (1983), pp. 166, 169, 171, 172, 176-177.

deepened the understanding of the factors involved in the Marian patronage. This happened above all through the controversy concerning the Marian title of the Order. In particular they focused on the reasons for the Carmelites choosing Mary as Patroness; very soon they began to consider the particular characteristic or nature of her patronage. The understanding of the Order as having been founded for the honour and service of Mary was clarified. Furthermore, it was affirmed that such honour and service are an essential part of Carmelite life.

1) Conformity of life

John Baconthorpe in his Speculum de institutione, applies for the first time to Carmel's relation with Mary, the prophecy of Isaiah "the glory of Lebanon will be given her, and the splendour of Carmel and Sharon". (Is. 35,2) Baconthorpe's argument in this and his other works can be summarised in the following three affirmations:

- To Mary is given the "beauty of Carmel" and "in order to continue the veneration of Blessed Mary in her Carmel, the Order of the brothers of Carmel came into being". Therefore the Carmelites must venerate her in a special way as the "Lady of the Place".
- For this reason, everything the Carmelite does, should be done for the honour and glory of Mary, the Lady of the place. The reason for the existence of the Order must bring the Carmelite to the imitation of Mary in all her virtues, because conformity is the best glorification and in the same way the manifestation of love increases love.
- As the Lady of the Place, the Virgin Mary takes care of "the protection and the life" of the Carmelites; "with their actions they honoured the Lady of the Place."

The best way of honouring Mary is to conform one's life to her life and in this way the will of God is always realised. This concept was repeated with insistence by Baconthorpe in his Commentary on the Carmelite Rule: The Carmelites profess "a Rule which in many respects reflects the way of life which the Blessed Virgin Mary sought to follow." He illustrated this with reference to many points of the Rule and their inspiration taken from the life and virtues of Mary. The analysis of Baconthorpe (which for us may appear simplistic), compares biblical phrases and Mary's way of living to the text of the Rule. The dynamic used is that of Lectio Divina with special reference to the texts of the New Testament and apocryphal writings.

Baconthorpe writes for example in his commentary: "in the first place it is established that Mary was perfectly obedient, when she responded to the angel at the Annunciation, "Behold the handmaid of the Lord; let it be done to me according to your word". For this reason the Rule says, "each of the brothers promises obedience to the prior, and, having promised obedience, tries to put it into practice. She gave up her property and was very faithful in chastity… over and above the virtues recorded in the Rule, Mary possessed many more….she practiced all the virtues with great discretion. At the end of the Rule, discretion is said to be the guide of the virtues.

This consonance between the life of Mary and the Carmelite Rule is mentioned again by other authors (in particular Bernard Oller and Egidio Leondelicato da Sciacca, in his "The Carmelite garden", in which we find Baconthorpe's argument repeated.) The tradition is placed in the mouth of St. Brocard in his celebrated spiritual testament: "Lead an upright life, modelled on Elijah and Mary" (the reference to Elijah is in a later text).

It should be noted that the reference to Mary as Patroness depends on the theological truth of the divine maternity. Very quickly reference to the virginity of Mary and her mediation of graces

Our Lady as prioress of the Carmelite community

Choosing Mary and honouring her with the title of prioress is a usage of long standing and rich in symbolism. It goes back to the 11th century with Hugo of Cluny at the foundation of the monastery for nuns in Marcigny, Robert of Turlande at Chaise-Dieu and Robert d'Arbrissel at Fontvrault.

Though it was not adopted throughout the whole Carmelite Order, it can be found in the 15th century in some medieval authors who give the title of prioress or abbess to Our Lady. These authors include John Soreth (+1471), John Paleonidorus (+1507) and Arnold Bostius (+1499) who called Our Lady the teacher with her disciples, the abbess with her monks and lady with her servants. The same expressions can be found in a sermon on the Assumption by a Franciscan, Bernardino de Buste (+1513/1515).

Throughout the 16th century we find a Carmelite legend that Our Lady was the prioress of a monastery of more than 100 nuns. This was a clear reference to the tradition of Marcigny which referred to a certain Abbess Mary, who when the community composed of 99 nuns was beginning, made the Holy Virgin the 100th nun and chose her as abbess. Our Lady was given the first place in every community act.

Important examples in Carmel of naming Our Lady as prioress or abbess are: -
• In 1571 in the monastery of the Incarnation in Avila, St. Teresa of Jesus placed a statue of the BVM in the place of the prioress and called Our Lady "my prioress";

• In 1578 the Carmelite nuns in the monastery of Saint Mary of the Angels in Florence, elected Our Lady as the prioress. This story is told in the chronicles of the monastery: " We, the Prioress and the nuns on the holy morning of the nativity of His most Holy Mother, gathered together in choir, called the choir of the Virgin, together with all the novices and the lay sisters, being of one heart and soul, after holy communion, we elected as Queen, Mother and Prioress for ever of our monastery, the Most Holy Virgin and Mother of our most sweet Lord Jesus Christ. We also took the decision that the nun who would be elected as prioress, in conformity with Our Rule and Constitutions and the Council of Trent, even though exteriorly she would be called Mother Prioress, the principal Prioress would always be Our Most Holy Mother and the nun who served as the Mother Prioress would be her servant." This election was renewed each year.

•The reformed Province of Santa Maria della Vita in Naples, from its very beginning, adopted the usage of venerating Our Lady as prioress, in all the houses of the reform, and considered the local prior as the vicar prior. The image of Our Lady as Prioress was always placed in the choir or the refectory with the following inscription at her feet:

> "If you ask who is the Prior of this house,
> we will tell you that in this place the only Prior is the BVM".

Each year on 2nd Feb, the feast of the Purification of Our Lady - the anniversary of Our Lady's taking possession of her office was celebrated.

In modern times this custom is still kept in some monasteries of our nuns. This happens also in the communities of the Carmelite Sisters of Divine Providence where the image of Our Lady bearing the words, "Here is our Superior", is placed in the community room or in the cells of the sisters.

(Cf. F.C. Costa Ribeiro, *Maria "superiora" na espiritualide da Igreja*, in *Nova Aurora*, 15 (S. Paulo, 1989), pp. 207-216; V. Hoppenbrouwers, Devotio mariana, pp. 169-170, 341).

were added to this theme. From a reading of the authors mentioned above and from other Carmelite authors of the Middle Ages, it can be seen very clearly that Mary was considered as the model for Carmelite life. The concepts that were expressed include familiarity, intimacy, proximity, and a tangible presence of Mary in the life of individuals and communities.

2. The Mother of the Order

Finally after affirming that Carmel belongs totally to Mary, even the birth or the foundation of the Order is attributed to her. The Patroness is transformed into the Mother of the Order.

As regards the Carmelite's growth in virtue in company with "Mary, the Queen of the virtues" (John de Cheminot), the Virgin Mary as Mother of the Order took on importance as well as the Virgin Mary as Mediatrix (cf. for example Michael Aiguani).

- The acts of the Provincial Chapter of Lombardy in 1333 begin: "In the name of Our Lord Jesus Christ and of the glorious Virgin, Mother of our Carmelite Order".
- John of Cheminot defined Mary as "the fount of mercy, our Mother". Referring to the legends of the visits of Mary to Carmel, he underlines her maternal character. "It was right that the Mother of the virtues should enrich by her presence the holy place and her devoted sons".
- We find in a prayer of John of Hildesheim, a unification of the Marian and elijan strands: "Hail, Elijah, illustrious father and guide of Carmel; Hail Mary who from the beginning until now has claimed her rights as Mother".
- John Grossi, speaking of "the Mother of all beautiful things" in his "Viridiarium", presents Mary as mediator and Mother; in a letter of 1400, he calls the Carmelites "the sons of Mary"
- Thomas Scrope or Bradley created the expression "Mother of Carmel"
- The *Vexillum Carmelitanum* of 1499 contained the inscription, "I am the Mother and splendour of Carmel".

The authors of the end of the 15th century often repeated these ideas, e.g. Bruyne, Bostius and Paleonidorus.

- Peter Bruyne desired that Mary "our Mother and sister" could have the joy, like Elijah, of collecting from the garden of Carmel delicate fruits which are pleasing to her Son Jesus.
- Arnold Bostius connects the Maternity of Mary over Carmel with her salvific function as the mediatrix of graces and mercy. He also speaks of her patronage, not only in passive terms, like Oller and Bradley, but also in active terms, relating to the origins of the Order: "Mary is said rightly to be the inspiration for Elijah and the primary founder of the whole company of Carmel". The same idea of Mary as founder of the Order is contained in the bull of Sixtus IV "Dum attenta meditatione" (or Mare Magnum) of 28 November 1476: "By means of an ineffable action of the Holy Spirit, Mary gave birth to a marvellous Flower, incorruptible and eternal, Our Lord Jesus Christ, and also she gave birth to the sacred Carmelite Order"
- Paleonidorus (John Ouderwater) also speaks of the active influence of Mary in the Order but gives more attention to the passive patronage.

The same Paleonidorus, building on the thought of Arnold Bostius, wrote,

"O venerable affirmation of Carmel:
(Mary) as well as being Mother of all,
is in a special way your Mother!
What a phrase worthy
of being pondered upon: Here is Your Mother.
Her heart is touched by any need of yours;

she is deeply moved by all
and each of her sons and brothers;
therefore your response is to love her
and venerate her as always present,
taking her into your home
so that She brings you into her glory."

In the 17th century various authors, referring to the Blessed Virgin as the founder of the Order, usually affirmed that Mary is the final cause, exemplar and source of the merit of this Order. Among others who shared this opinion were, John Baptist Lezana, Daniel of the Virgin Mary, Matthias of St. John, and the Prior General, John Feyxoo of Villalobos, who wrote, "The institution of the Carmelites had its origin in the prophet Elijah who contemplated in the little cloud the Virgin Mother of God, as the true final cause, exemplar and source of the merit of this monastic institute."

The authors avoided putting too much emphasis upon Mary as the final cause, because this could clash with the primary cause, which is the search for intimacy with God. Everything that they affirm expresses the intimate nature and eminently Marian character of the Order, according to the expression, "Carmel belongs totally to Mary"

Pages from the Anthology

1. FROM ELIJAH TO MARY (A JUSTIFICATION OF OUR NAME)

Text from Philip Ribot, *Institution of the First Monks*, Bk.VI, ch.1,1-5 (extracts); ed. Daniel of the Virgin Mary, *Speculum Carmelitanum*; Also in E. Boaga, *Nello Spirito e nella virtù di Elia. Antologia di documenti e sussidi*, Roma, 1990, pp.76-78).

Those (the Carmelites) who professed this Rule, after having been baptised and instructed by the Apostles in the doctrine of the Gospel, understood that the mystery of God, which had been revealed by God to the Prophet Elijah on Mount Carmel, had reached fulfilment. In the book of the Kings, we read, "Elijah went up to the top of Carmel. He bowed down upon the earth and put his face between his knees. He said to his servant, 'Go now and look toward the sea.' He went and looked and said, 'There is nothing'. He said, 'Go seven times'. At the seventh time, he said, 'Behold, a little cloud like a man's hand is rising out of the sea'. (I K.18,42-44)

The distance from the place on Mount Carmel to the summit from where the servant looked out over the sea was ten paces. The servant went to observe the sea once and then returned according to Elijah's command. He had to repeat this seven times. The seventh time that he returned, which was in fact the eighth time that he had looked out over the sea, the servant saw, "a little cloud as big as a man's hand", rising from the sea in the direction of Carmel. Elijah then said, "Go and tell Ahab, 'Prepare your chariot and go down lest the rain stop you'" (I K.18,44). Having said that, in the time that he went from one place to another, the sky darkened with large storm clouds and torrential rain fell.

The secret of future things contained in that vision, apart from the historical fact, is the great mystery which God revealed to Elijah when he was prostrate on the ground and which was communicated by the Prophet, not publicly to everyone, but in a private way to his disciples. From these, we know from the handing on of tradition that God revealed to Elijah, in this symbolic vision, four great mysteries which I will mention in order:- 1) that a little girl would be born, who would emerge from the womb untouched by any stain of sin; 2) the time at which this would happen; 3) that this little girl would embrace perpetual virginity after the example of Elijah; 4) that God, taking on human nature, would be born of this Virgin.

Through the fact of Elijah's servant seeing the little cloud arising from the sea, God revealed to Elijah that a woman, that is the Blessed Virgin Mary, symbolised in this vision as the small, humble little cloud, would be born from human nature which had fallen because of sin. Human nature was symbolised by the sea. That girl would be born pure from all stain of sin, just as that little cloud arose from the bitter sea, without any bitterness. The cloud came from the same source as the sea but it had another condition or quality. The sea is heavy and full of salt; the little cloud was light and sweet. So also in every human being, nature just like the sea, is marked from its very beginnings by the consequences of sin and by the weight of vice. It must be recognised that, "My sins cover my head and exceed my strength like a heavy burden." (Ps. 38,5).

Blessed Mary, on the contrary, is born from this sea, that is from human nature, in a different way, because, from the very moment of her birth, she was not subject to the oppression or bitterness of sin. Like the little cloud, she was free and gentle because of her immunity from sin. She was sweet because of all her gifts. She was that cloud about which the book of Moses symbolically affirms, " The glory of the Lord was manifested in the cloud". (Ex. 16,10).

The Blessed Mother of God, before leaving this earth, was often seen in Nazareth, in Jerusalem and in other places by the followers of this Rule.

The followers of this Rule handed down that God had revealed, as a special privilege, to those who had gone before them, by means of the vision narrated above, the birth of a little girl who would be free from every stain of sin from the moment of her conception, and in line with their rule of life, would profess voluntary virginity. From this virgin the God-Man would be born. Considering then that all these things had been fulfilled and that the human race had received from the Son of God through this virgin, the desired benefit of the rain, that is to say, grace, they decided to serve this Virgin with great devotion. She had been revealed to their predecessors long ago, hoped for by them and now manifested to them. They decided to choose this Virgin as their special Patroness because they recognised only in her the one who had been shown to conform to their ancient plan to profess voluntary virginity. Just as voluntary virginity for the love of God was practiced and introduced for the first time among men by those who from ancient times had professed this Rule, so also, it was practiced and introduced for the first time among women by the Mother of God as we have already mentioned. Just as the Carmelites are the first men to practice voluntary virginity, so Blessed Mary is the first among women to do so because of a vow. This similarity between the Mother of God and the Carmelites in the matter of virginity, contemplated in ancient times and fulfilled in her, was the reason that from ancient times, Carmelites called the Virgin Mary their sister. Because of this conformity, they called themselves the brothers of the Blessed Virgin Mary.

In memory of the vision regarding the birth of this Virgin, prophetically shown to Elijah under the form of the small cloud which arose from the sea and moved towards Carmel, the aforementioned monks, in the year 83 of the Incarnation of the Son of God, destroyed their ancient "Semnion" and built a little chapel on Mount Carmel, near the spring of Elijah, in the place where the prophet had seen, while he was praying, that little cloud, like a man's hand, arising from the sea towards Carmel. From that moment, the members of this Order, had the habit of gathering together in this chapel each day (at the time of the seven canonical hours), to offer assiduously to the Virgin, their Patroness, and to her Son, prayers, supplications and praises. In this same place they began the habit of gathering to exhort one another to listen to the Word of God, to avoid sin and to have a care for the salvation of their souls. For this reason, people outside their own number would call them for ever "brothers of the Blessed Virgin Mary of Mount Carmel…".

2. INTIMACY WITH MARY, MOTHER AND SISTER

Text from Arnold Bostius (1445-1499), *"De Patronatu et patrocinio B.mae Virginis Mariae in dicatum sibi ordinem*, ed. Daniel of the Virgin Mary, *Speculum Carmelitanum*, 1, n.1533-1537

1533. The humble Carmelite friar can rejoice and sing for joy: Here is the Queen of heaven, my sister. I can go about my business with absolute trust and no fear; in the midst of a thousand enemies and in the heat of the struggle, my heart will not fear; my strength, my liberation, my rock, and refuge, my praise, Mary, my sister and mother; in her bosom I will find refuge and salvation. Rightly he can rejoice that he has such a worthy and holy sister as Mother and Patroness.

1534 You, brother of Carmel, show to her that you are a good brother. Never forget her generosity and affection that will always remain and never fail. Think with what tenderness you should embrace and love her who loves you so much and who has made you great.

You will tire first because the graces she pours out on you come from her love that has no equal. She is sweet with an inestimable sweetness; she is ineffably beautiful. To the one who contemplates her, she offers a great miracle of beauty. The Creator of the whole universe used all his colours in creating her beauty and wants to demonstrate his art ……

This is the most beautiful woman in body and soul. The Mother of fair love loves you most tenderly. It will seem to you that you will hear each day a beautiful voice saying to you, "Who gave you to me as my brother? He desires that I feed you as your Mother, o my brother."

You in your turn will be enflamed with love. Who would not want to return an ardent love to the one who is full of all the graces? Certainly there is no one who has failed to experience her loving and gracious sweetness, her faithfulness and her charity. I believe and I am convinced that it is much easier with a healthy and an open eye not to see a very visible object than to fail to desire her with the light of understanding. One cannot even speak her name without being enflamed; neither can you think of her without experiencing the affections of those who love her. She does not enter into a religious person's thoughts without bringing with her the sweetness that she has received from God. Her dear name is sweet in the heart and on the lips. Repeating her name often is a wonderful stimulus for renewing the soul. Reserve a special place in your heart for her. Show to her your fraternal charity in order to sincerely respond to that dialogue of love, "You wounded my heart, my sister, my love, you have wounded my heart." (Sg. 4,9).

May you sing with enflamed heart
I want to respond to your love with love,
I never want to live without you,
I want to love once more she who lived on earth and now in heaven.
How many forget her, replace her with deceiving loves
And pervert their morals.
She has no equal,

Nor will any be known in the future.
She has no equal in the present time.
She knows no equal.

1535. St. Jerome says that those who imitate the works of saints are their sons and brothers more than those who merely live with saints or are related to them.

You, offspring of holy Mary; you, child of Elijah, do not diminish their glory or lessen their praise.

At each instant meditate on the word of Elijah your Father, a word that marked his life, "The Lord lives in whose presence I stand" (1 K.17,1). Remind yourself of this every time your mind is distracted, negligent or taken up with what is not right. If you do this, you will become each day more perfect in the custody of your heart, in interior quiet and in every virtue.

Do not go far from such a good Mother and Sister. Noble blood is proof of one's origin. The brother, faced with the splendid dignity of Mary the Queen, is ashamed to behave unworthily towards such a wonderful sister. By the similarity of your way of life, you show how close you are to her.

1536. To love her is the highest virtue; to be loved by her is the greatest happiness. Run fast and seek after every virtue in order to make up for lost time and you will obtain the joy of greater success in your work.

Invoke her assiduously and go with trust to the throne of grace. Greet her often because she is worthy of every praise and desires to help you much more than you desire help. She, the beloved one, loves always; When she is not loved, she loves more tenaciously and, by her love, she encourages us to love.

Repeat often to Mary the message of the Most Holy Trinity, a word from the heavenly treasure, rich in the mystery of salvation, at the same time as you greet her Son. Repeat also Gabriel's greeting, which is the bearer of a saving invitation. St. Bernard affirms that you can embrace such a loving Mother and kiss her, even though you cannot reach her with your arms, but you can do so every time you greet her with the sweetest and gentlest, "AVE MARIA".

1537. Do not let any day or night, any journey, any research or discussion, any joy, effort, or repose go by without an affectionate remembrance of her. Let her always be in your memory.

Say to her often, "Open to me, my sister, my beloved, my dove, perfect one" (Sg.5,2), love of my heart, my very heart and soul, O Virgin Mary.

Add also this beautiful phrase of Esdra:" O Mother, embrace your children, hold your disciples tightly, do not let their steps falter, guide them with joy." Also use the phrase of Genesis, "Say you are my sister, that it may go well with me because of you." (Gen.12,13).

With such a beautiful name, with such a loving relationship, with such ardent charity and such a strong union, you will ensure that Mary will share her abundant gifts with you.

Each day seek to be greater, more noble, stronger, more transparent, pure and better. She is the Mistress of divine wisdom.

3. PRAYER TO OUR LADY

From the *Works* of Sr. Maria Perpétua da Luz (+1736), in *Analecta Ordinis Carmelitarum*, 12 (1943-45) p.115.

>   My Mother, my light and my consolation, be always my way and my light. Teach me and help me to do what would be most pleasing to Your Most Holy Son and to You. Deliver me from myself and from all my enemies. Give me courage against them in order to destroy them. Take away from me all my faults so that in all things I will give honour and glory to God. I promise to observe perfectly all that He desires and is pleasing to you. From this day forward, I want to give to you a new and total obedience, with profound respect, and the greatest veneration for the dignity that the Most High has placed in you as the Mother of His Only Begotten Son. O Queen and Lady of heaven and earth, as I ponder on your greatness and recognise that it is fitting for noble ladies to have slaves, I want always to be yours despite my foolishness, fearfulness, lack of learning, lack of talent and complete unworthiness.
>
>   However, I also see that with all your dignity, you are also the Mother of sinners and you always have mercy on them. Look kindly on me then so that I may be useful in your service as your perpetual slave. It is only you with your love who can teach me to be strong. Oh how wonderful if it could be thus. Most Holy Mother, grant then that in your sight and in the sight of Jesus Christ, I may receive the grace to give you thanks and to honour you as both of you deserve.

4. THIS IS HOW WE HONOUR MARY

Text from A. Mastelloni, *Sermoni Ascetici*, III, p. 450-452, in V. Hoppenbrouwers, *Devotio mariana*, pp.152-153.

>   To her (Mary) we make our vows, we celebrate all her principal feasts with an octave, seven throughout the whole year. We prepare for all her solemnities with fasting; we recite the little office and we sing Mass in her honour every day. Two days of each week, Wednesdays and Saturdays, we particularly dedicate to her memory. One Sunday of each month is for giving thanks for all the graces we have received through the miraculous scapular. Seven times every day, on our knees, we greet her with the Salve, as we end each canonical hour. Our habit is her insignia; our white cloak is a declaration of her pure and immaculate Conception; our rule is a synthesis of her life. Our Order, which is spread throughout the world, carries her name to every corner. Our preachers are obliged by the Constitutions to proclaim her glories; our theologians, in the matters that treat of her, follow the most pious opinions and those that are most likely to give glory to her. Each one of us loves her so much that we try with all our might to serve and follow her and promote devotion to her.
>
>   I could not relate all that the Carmelites, calced and discalced, men and holy virgins, do to honour Mary who is the mother we have in common. I want to recall what the brothers in this house do to honour her. Even though you are aware of all this, I am sure it will bring you joy to be reminded of it.

Above and beyond the general acts of devotion that are common to the whole Order, we venerate her in some particular ways. On the vigil of her feasts, many of us fast on bread and water since these are days of celebration and her solemnities are for us like the days of Easter. We use more devout psalms, more solemn offices and whatever other way we can and know to honour her, leaving out nothing.

We recognise her as our immediate Superior and her venerated image presides in choir. A miraculous picture of her has the place of honour in the refectory.

It is not only the church that bears her name but our whole house belongs to her. Everywhere one can see and venerate images of her: in the sacristy, in the choir, in the cloister, on the stairs, in the dormitories, in the principal offices, in the novitiate, in the oratories and the various chapels and in other places in the monastery. As a sign of the position she holds, once a year, on the feast of her Purification, we carry a statue of her (the one which is presented in the church once a month for public veneration) in procession throughout the whole house, to bless the offices, the cells and all the religious who, prostrate at her feet, solemnly renew their profession.

We celebrate all her feasts, but with particular solemnity the feast of the title of the church, the solemnity of Our Lady of Mount Carmel. We also celebrate the presentation in the temple and the feast of her birth, which is preceded by a solemn novena.

Every Wednesday and every fourth Sunday of the month we preach a special sermon to extol her praises. Each day in choir we say litanies in her honour. After mental prayer and each Wednesday and Saturday, we solemnly sing in front of her image in church.

We teach our pupils to grow in devotion to her. To sum up in a few words, we continuously study ways to honour her and we seek to win the hearts of those Christians who frequent our churches and talk with us, so that they will love her. We preach her as most worthy of love among all creatures.

For further study.

I Bibliography

- N. Geagea, *Maria, Madre e Decoro del Carmelo*, pp. 123-592;
- V. Hoppenbrouwers, *Devotio Mariana*, pp. 95-153
- L. Saggi, *Santa Maria del Monte Carmelo*, pp. 6-20
- AA.VV., *La dimensione mariana del Carmelo*, I, pp. 11-39, 57-67

II For personal and/or group study

1. Read the basic texts and look at the inserts on the various themes.

2. Try to discover the experiences and the marian values present in the life of the Carmelites of the Middle Ages.

3. Look at the insert on the Marian title of the Order in the preceding chapter, and look for facts and events associated with the various changes in the title.

4. What did medieval people understand by calling Mary, Patroness, Lady of the Place, Mother of the Order? How did this understanding influence their daily life?

5. Seek in the pages from the anthology the various nuances surrounding the theme of Mary's patronage of the Order and the facts and events in the life of the Order that relate to them.

III. Prayer and life

1. Pray with the Word of God:
    Lk.1,39-55;
    Jn.2,1-11;
    Lk.11,27-28;
    Jn.19,25-27.

2. How do we understand conformity with Mary today and how do we put it into practice?

3. What does devotion to Mary mean for us today in relation to the life of the Church?

4. In what way can the exhortation of Arnold Bostius on "Intimacy with Mary Mother and Sister" help you?

3

MOST BEAUTIFUL SISTER

O Mary most pure
I am lost in the contemplation of your unsurpassable beauty and purity.
So I invite you, blessed spirits, together with all my advocates
To come and contemplate Mary
And to give her thanks on my behalf
For the knowledge which has been given to me
Of the most pure and most simple divine love.

(St. Mary Magdalene de' Pazzi, *Probatione*, Part 1, 190).

3 MOST BEAUTIFUL SISTER

Most Pure Virgin

In the 14th and 15th centuries Carmelite authors reflected profoundly on the virginity of Mary. This reflection was based on a search for a connection between Our Lady and the life of the Carmelites. The basis for this reflection was a profound spirituality, which made the Carmelites understand the relationship to Our Lady in a living way. They came to see her present in their lives as their Sister accompanying them on their journey and they praised her purity and understood this as the demanding attitude of total self-abandonment to God and of conformity with the divine will.

1. Sister

a) Harmony in virginity

The reflection mentioned above on the relations between the Order and Our Lady brought out the similarity in the living of virginity. In particular the authors, basing themselves on the texts of the Fathers of the Church (e.g. St. Jerome), affirm:
- The same family. Elijah (the founder of the Order) and Mary (the Patroness and later founder) are from the same family of Aaron. Therefore the passing of the title from Elijah to Mary is justified. This affirmation is from John de Cheminot (1337) and repeated by other authors (Ribot, 1370; Hornby, 1374). John of Hildesheim (1370) repeats this idea and speaks of a symbolic consonance between the names of Mary and Elijah, indicating an affinity between them.
- The argument from virginity. Elijah, Elisha and the sons of the Prophets preserved their virginity (John of Cheminot, 1337). In Mary virginity flourished and became fruitful, prefigured by Aaron's rod (Nm. 17,3-8; Is. 11,1 and Jer.1, 11). This was taken up in the teaching of the Fathers. In Mary, virginity was fruitful! Mary, who was from the race of Elijah and Aaron, generated others who lived a fruitful virginity, as well as being the Mother of the Redeemer (John of Cheminot).
- Elijah and Mary are virgins (John of Hildesheim, John of Malines). Elijah was the initiator of perpetual virginity among men and Carmelites refer to him in this way; Mary introduced it among women, following the example of Elijah; in this way through Elijah, Mary is the sister of Carmelites "in the first fruits of spontaneous virginity". This conformity was the reason for following Mary as their special patroness (Ribot, 1370).

John Baptist de Lezana (+1659) held a different opinion. It was not Mary who followed Elijah but Elijah who imitated Mary in her virginity. When he saw her prefigured in the little cloud, he began to honour her, by preserving virginity and by founding the Order that would also live in her honour. This notion was taken up by many other authors, among whom was Matthias of St. John (1600-1681), formed in the school of John of St. Samson and Dominic of St. Albert, eminent figures in the reform of Touraine. In his treatise on the history of the Order, de Lezana notes the anachronism of Elijah founding the Order to honour Mary prefigured in the little cloud. This difficulty was overcome by arguing in the opposite way, with a tract on the eternal predestination of

Mary to be the Mother of the Redeemer and with Him the co-redeemer.

Among the authors who speak of the virginity of Elijah in relation to that of Mary, we find indications of the mutuality of their relationship from the anthropological perspective of the inter-relationship Man-Woman. This would be a good point for further study in our own day.

Having said that, there are authors, like Arnold Bostius and Daniel of the Virgin Mary, who see in the relation between Elijah and the Virgin Mary a similarity of 12 privileges and nothing more. Generally this similarity has implications for a consideration of the exemplarity of the Carmelite life.

b) The theme of Sister

The theme of Mary as Sister of the Carmelites is later taken up and developed above all by Flemish and Belgian writers (in particular Arnold Bostius and John Ouderwater or Paleonidorus).
- Arnold Bostius: with great insistence he writes about Mary, not only as tender and sweet Mother, but also as Sister of the Carmelites, in order to indicate a more familiar and close relationship. The affinity and likeness between Mary and the Carmelites, by means of voluntary virginal purity, establishes between them a profound fraternal relationship. This author indicates as a practical consequence of this relationship, the dignity, the trust and the tenderness between a Sister and her brothers. From this comes the characteristic of intimacy of life with Mary "wonderful sister".
- Paleonidorus: as well as repeating the same points as Bostius, adds the fact - without foundation - that Elijah chose Mary as his sister and his followers did the same.

Above all in the argument followed by Bostius, the feeling of familiarity with Our Lady is increased and one is encouraged to imitate her in her availability and docility to the Word of the Lord.

Paleonidorus wrote: "If, according to David, it is a wonderful thing to be of the family of an earthly king, just think, o mortal, what it must be like and how you must esteem, being and being recognised as the brother of the Queen of heaven! She, much more than Esther, asks without ceasing that her people be devoted to Him. Now turn to her and say: I ask you to say that you are my sister so that everything will go well for me because of you, o Mary, and my soul will live by your favour."

It should be pointed out that not all the writers of the Order recognise Mary as the Sister of Carmelites. For these authors the term "brothers of the Blessed Virgin Mary" does not indicate a fraternal relationship, but rather a juridical form equivalent to being a religious. Examples of this approach are Baconthorpe, John of Cheminot and John of Hildesheim.

John Baptist de Lezana, a famous Carmelite jurist in the 17th century, invited moderation in the use of the word "Sister" as applied to Our Lady. John Silveira seems to have been of the same opinion. He was a great Carmelite exegete of the same century. In the following century, Andrew Mastelloni, in his numerous Marian sermons, only twice refers to Mary as Sister and each time without reference to the tradition of the Order.

Daniel of the Virgin Mary, the famous editor of the collection called Speculum carmelitanum, even though he was a great admirer of Lezana, did not follow his position in this regard and indeed helped to spread the use of the term "Sister" for Mary among later writers.

In the Marian tradition of the Order, Mary was considered as Sister because of the connection between her virginity and that of Carmelites. For Carmelites to call Mary Sister was the same as calling her Most Pure Virgin and the two titles proposed the Mother of God as the example of Carmelite life.

The white cloak as a sign of the Immaculate Virgin

The cloak of the Carmelites in the Middle Ages was highly symbolic with several meanings. The first to offer a Marian meaning was the Carmelite John Baconthorpe at the beginning of the 14th century. He called the white cloak "Mary's mantle". For John of Hildesheim, Philip Ribot and John Grossi (14th century) the white cloak symbolised the purity of Mary. For Ribot to use the white cloak means "to conserve the purity of the mind and to guard chastity of the body. God has not called us to impurity, but to holiness." After these authors, others spoke expressly of the Marian symbolism of the white cloak.

In the monasteries of the nuns of the Mantuan Congregation, the white cloak was considered as a sign of the Immaculate Virgin and as a stimulus to live in chastity. At profession, each religious was reminded that our standard "is that of the Queen of heaven, the Mother of God, under which you wish to serve and make allegiance with spiritual weapons. It is therefore necessary that you write and swear fidelity, making your profession also to Our Lady". Also the nuns were exhorted to live with great dignity so that "the white cloak of the glorious Virgin and the honour of the Brides of Christ be kept without suspicion".

In his sermon on the feast of the Immaculate Virgin in the Carmelite church in Avignon, Bishop Richard Fitzralph, said, "This holy and ancient Order of Carmelites, which celebrates this feast with special solemnity, underlines it and relates it, prudently and devoutly, I believe, to the whiteness of the cloak." (1342).

In 1370 John of Hildesheim justified the whiteness of the cloak applying Is 35,2: "Lebanon is interpreted in terms of purity because men of the future dressed in white (the followers of Elijah) must glory in their title and more than others must praise Mary...Also it seems probable that the Virgin used the white cloak in order to be like the angels, who always appear with white clothes and because the clothing of her Son, in the Transfiguration, was changed to be as white as snow..."

On the symbol of the Carmelite cloak, see E. Boaga, *Come Pietre Vive*, Roma, 1993, pp. 57-59

c) The Carmelite Virgin

The reflection on Mary as Sister leads not only to the affirmation that Carmel belongs totally to Mary but that she herself was from Carmel. This idea is made explicit in the title "Carmelite Virgin", as if Mary was in fact a member of the Order. This title occurs not only in the notable work of Nicholas Calciuri (+1466), "*Fioretti del Monte Carmelo*", and in the writings of Bostius, but also it appears often in iconography. In many pictures, Our Lady is represented wearing the Carmelite habit. It is interesting to observe that in some representations, Our Lady is pictured with the habit proper to the theologians of the Order, that is, pleated (e.g. in a fresco in the Carmelite church of San Martino Maggiore in Bologna).

Also in the liturgical rubrics of the era, we find the term "Virgin Mary" substituting "Holy Mary".

2. Purity

a) The beauty of the Virgin

In connection with the theme of the virginity of Mary, we also find the idea of the greatest purity being found in Mary. The medieval Carmelite authors consider her virginity, not so much in the physical sense, but as the necessary condition for union with God. It refers to a state of interior integrity that excludes all sin and distance from God and makes the person conform to the divine will. There were two developments from this idea:
- In relation to the figure of Mary, attention was given to her conception and sanctification in the womb of St. Anne (Immaculate Conception).
- With regard to the Order in its relationship with Mary, attention is given to the concept of "*Virgo Purissima*" and to purity and its connection with the interior life.

b) Immaculate Conception

The facts that bring light to bear on the Immaculate Conception are the following:

- At the end of the 13th century (1296) the first signs of this Carmelite interest are seen in the indulgence that 15 Italian bishops granted to those who visited the churches of the Order in Germany on the occasion of the various Marian feasts, among which was mentioned the feast of the Immaculate Conception.
- In 1306 the liturgical feast of the Immaculate Conception was introduced in the Order. This was the official or patronal feast of the Order in Avignon during the residence of the Popes in that city (1309-1377). This feast retained its status within the Order until at least the 15th century.
- In 1342, the bishop of Armagh, Richard Fitzralph, invited to preach at the celebration of the patronal feast of the Order in Avignon in front of the Pope, referred during the sermon to the Marian devotion of the Carmelites with special reference to the Immaculate Conception. His sermon is of great historical importance because it was remembered and referred to later by many authors and theologians in the Order.
- When the patronal feast of the Order was changed to the Solemn Commemoration in July, the liturgical feast of the Immaculate Conception continued to be celebrated. The General Chapter of 1609 declared that all religious of the Order should celebrate this feast in a very special way.
- There are signs of devotion to the Immaculate Conception with the insertion of the word "Virgin" in the title of the Order in the middle of the 14th century and with the reference to "ever Virgin" in 1478 in the same title.
- The basis for the devotion to the Immaculate Conception was encouraged by the diffusion of the texts referring to the Marian interpretation of the "little cloud" of Elijah (Cheminot, Hildesheim, Ribot), as well as the texts which referred to the legend of

the convent in Jerusalem, constructed in the place where the conception of the Virgin was said to have taken place. Also important were the references to the person and work of St. Cyril of Alexandria (Oller).
- Marian devotion in Carmel to the Immaculate Conception throughout the centuries, assumed two forms which are bound up with each other:
  - The virginity of Mary and the Immaculate Conception are related to the nature of the Order, its habit and its title. This connection has its roots in the mystery revealed to Elijah in the "little cloud" and is justified by the same symbols that connect it with the divine maternity.
  - The theme of purity and the interior life will be developed later
- The theme of the Immaculate Virgin is found often in Carmelite statues and paintings (in Corleone, Catania, London, Bergamo, Frankfurt). In the iconography there is an evolution of the theme towards the image of the ImmaculateVirgin seen in the Woman of the Apocalypse.
- In the context of the dispute among theologians over the Immaculate Conception, it can be said regarding the Carmelite position, that generally they defended the privilege of Our Lady. The most important Carmelite theologians in this area were: John Baconthorpe with his sermons on the Immaculate Conception (even though previously he had been against it); Michael Aiguani with his treatise which was widely diffused in the north of Italy (particularly Bologna); and Francis Marti with his works which were well known in Spain. There were some who were against this privilege: Gerard of Bologna, Guido Terreni and Paul of Perugia.

We will cite the arguments of John Baconthorpe and Michael Aiguani who, for their theological authority, especially in relation to Marian doctrine, are considered "masters of the Order", respected and studied up until the 19th century.

- The argument of Baconthorpe was to support the view that Mary had a unique position in the realm of grace because of her predestination to be the Mother of God. In order to be the habitation of the Son of God, Mary was destined to be holy and without stain of sin. In particular, Baconthorpe elaborated the biblical argument of the proto-Gospel (Gn. 3,15), a text that, in his time, was not frequently used nor interpreted in this sense.
- The argument of Michael Aiguani presents 16 considerations taken from the writings of St. Augustine, St. Anselm and other authorities. His fundamental idea has a basis in the explanations of the time that presented the conception of a human being as an act in two parts. These are the material conception (conceptio seminis) and the infusion of the soul (conceptio hominis). The first conception is the material cause of sin and the second the formal cause. Original sin therefore is contracted in the infusion of the soul because it is a fault and as such is proper to the rational soul. For Aiguani, there exists a moment between the two conceptions. However, Mary was subject to the law of original sin "causaliter" and not original sin contracted "formaliter" because she was "purified and sanctified before the infusion of the soul, in the first moment of her conception".

After the Middle Ages up to the 18th century, the cult of the Immaculate Conception, and the defence of this Marian privilege, were very important.

The Carmelites of the Iberian Peninsula made a promise to defend this Marian privilege in sermons and scholastic debates.

In Defence of the Immaculate Conception

Manuel de Sá writes about a usage in the Portuguese Province which illustrates very well the intention to defend the privilege of the Immaculate Conception:

"On the eve of this day (solemnity of Mary), all the religious gathered in choir for a spiritual exercise or a solemn renewal of the vows which they made at their profession to God and to His Most Holy Mother. The Blessed Sacrament was exposed and, beginning with the eldest, they all renewed their vows. They concluded this act, promising to defend the Immaculate Conception of the Virgin Mary, Our Lady."

This custom was established as a law for the whole Province in the year 1617.

The Carmelites of the Aragon Province, having met in Provincial Chapter in the year 1624, in the city of Valencia, made this oath: "I Brother...promise, swear and commit myself to defend always, in the public schools, by means of oral teaching and writing, in each public sermon and private conversation, that the Blessed Virgin Mary, patroness of our holy Religious (Order), was by her Immaculate Conception, immune, free and preserved by divine power, from all stain of original sin, with the full acceptance of what the Church may establish."

In 1662, the formula of profession in the Betica Province stated:
"I Brother... make my profession and promise obedience, poverty and chastity to God, Our Lord and to the Blessed Ever Virgin Mary of Mount Carmel, conceived without stain of original sin (and I swear to defend her purity) and to our Most Rev. Father.... until death."

From 1760, after making vows, the brothers added:
"I make another vow and promise to bear witness to and defend for the whole of my life that the Virgin Mary, Mother of God, was conceived without stain of original sin, from the first instant of her existence."

In the 17th. or 18th centuries, among the devotees of the Immaculate Conception, there existed the practice of making "an oath of blood", or a vow to defend with one's own blood, this marian privilege. This type of vow does not appear directly among Carmelites, but it seems to be present in the writings of Maria of St. Teresa (Petyt):

> "At each moment, I am ready to defend and confirm this truth
> with my blood and my life."

Cf.: Hoppenbrouwers, *Devotio mariana*, pp. 242-243.

- In 1617 Portuguese Carmelites renewed their vows on the day of the Immaculate Conception, making also a promise to defend this privilege.
- In 1624, the Carmelites of the Province of Aragon in Spain swore an oath to defend the privilege.
- In 1662, in the Betica Province (Spain), they made the same promise and from the year 1758, they introduced the 4th vow to defend the Immaculate Conception.
- Also, in Spain and Portugal, lay Carmelites and members of the confraternities of the Order, were encouraged in their devotion to and defence of the Immaculate Blessed Virgin Mary.

From the 17th century, among the communities of the Congregation of Mantua, there was a federation of 15 monasteries, whose focus was the honour of the Immaculate Conception, with their own frequent spiritual practices. These spiritual practices were extended to the faithful, with spiritual exercises and sermons delivered to the devotees of Our Lady.

The references to the "sanctification" of Mary, tended to give great emphasis to the beauty of the Virgin, who was called the beauty of Carmel ("Decor Carmeli") and adorned with every virtue ("Mary, Queen of Virtues", an expression coined by John of Cheminot). The medieval "via pulchritudinis" (way of beauty) finds here a great wealth of content in relation to Carmel. All this content had a pastoral thrust, with prayers and popular practices through which the Marian devotion reached the people.

c) Purity and the interior life

The above-mentioned conformity of the Carmelites to Mary in relation to her virginity or purity, took on greater emphasis with the consideration of Carmel as a "*scientia circumcisionis*". This is understood as everything that circumcises concupiscence in the mind and in the heart, guarding against every form of sin, in particular, sins of the flesh. Nicholas the Frenchman and Philip Ribot identified this with celibacy and the renunciation of the works of the flesh.

The Carmelite writers, by means of this interpretation of the name of Carmel, affirmed that Carmelites are "scientes virginitatem", or simply, virgins. Therefore to climb Mount Carmel means to embrace voluntary virginity, offering to God a holy heart, purified from all stain of sin. By her conformity with Elijah "in the first fruits of free virginity", Mary became the model of the perfect Carmelite who desires to adhere to God with the greatest purity. Ribot expresses these ideas. Before him, there can be found similar allusions in the writings of John of Cheminot and John of Hildesheim.

The white cloak is understood in relation to the Immaculate Conception, considering it as the symbol of her purity.

- Baconthorpe calls the white cloak "Mary's mantle".
- The bishop of Armagh, in his sermon before the Pope (14th century) understands the white cloak in relation to the Immaculate Conception.
- For Philip Ribot and John Grossi (14th century), the white cloak is the symbol of the purity of Mary. For Ribot, wearing the white cloak means to guard purity of mind and holiness of body.
- After Ribot and Grossi, the authors write even more explicitly of the white cloak as a symbol of the purity and virginity of Mary.

All of this, according to the custom of the times, understood purity as having to do with union with God. This led to the connection of the Most Pure Virgin to the characteristic Carmelite way of understanding the interior life.

Carmelites thought of the Immaculate Virgin as "tota pulchra" (all beautiful), "Virgo virginum" (Virgin of Virgins), the Woman of the Apocalypse, and the one who was totally available for union with God.

This devotion to the Most Pure Virgin is the continuation of the remembrance of the Annunciation, in the sense that it was purity, which united Mary to God in the Annunciation. The Carmelites were very aware that they could not imitate Mary in this singular privilege, but they could, however, imitate her in her union with God by means of prayer and the faithful listening to the Word of the Lord.

St. Mary Magdalen de Pazzi (+1607) uses the word purity in connection with the symbolism of the cloak, thus widening its meaning: in the purity of the Virgin her beauty shines out which attracts God to her. An important aspect of purity is the capacity to be available for God by means of an ascetical-mystical journey that begins with the recognition of one's own nothingness and reaches out towards participation in contemplative union with God. For St. Mary Magdalen de Pazzi, Mary the Most Pure Virgin, is the example of this mystical purity. She presents Our Lady as recommending purity, inviting us to live a pure life, being for all a transparent witness to purity. She speaks of Mary as purifying and washing the nuns with the blood of Christ and feeding them with her milk so that they might always be available to choose and accept the divine, transforming them into white doves that fly to the heart of Jesus.

In this ascetical-mystical dimension, the human being learns a lesson: availability for God, conformity with His will, spiritual fruitfulness, bearing witness and prophecy. This ascetical-contemplative panorama goes well beyond a mere physiological fact. It is a mystical adventure that tends to develop within the mystery of the Church, fed with hope in the incarnation. The prophetic function of virginity within the Church consists in living in a situation of availability and fruitfulness like Mary, the Most Holy Virgin.

In the 17th and 18th centuries, the cult of the Immaculate Conception was carefully developed in Carmelite churches and in the Third Order throughout the whole Order. Among the members of the confraternity of the scapular, there was the recommendation of observing "chastity according to one's own state in life". Eventually the following terms become synonymous:- Mary Immaculate, Most Pure Virgin, Virgin of Virgins, Maria Purissima. These had an effect on litanies of Our Lady.

From the 19th century up to the early part of the 20th century, the wealth of the Marian theology contained in the term "Most Pure Virgin" seems to be less present in writings and sermons. In more recent times, after the contribution of Albert Grammatico and the return to and deepening of the Carmelite Marian tradition of the Most Pure Virgin by Valerius Hoppenbrouwers, Claudio Catena and Ludovico Saggi, once again within the Order, there is a rediscovery of this aspect of Marian devotion as a stimulus towards union with God.

"You are my brothers"

In the city of Chester in England, there were some people badly disposed towards the Carmelites. These people claimed that the Carmelites had no special reason, over and above other Religious Orders, to call themselves "Brothers of the Virgin". This provoked divine indignation, so much so that almost all of them died very suddenly. In the light of this punishment, Thomas, the abbot of the monastery of St. Werburg in Chester, gave an order for a penitential procession. To the north of the choir and at the head of the sepulchre where lie the remains of the venerable hermit St. Gostald, there was a miraculous statue of the Virgin. At a certain point during the procession, when the Carmelite friars passed in front of the statue, accompanied by many other people, they bowed, and greeted Our Lady. The holy statue pointed to the Carmelites and said in a loud voice so that many heard, "These are my brothers. These are my beloved and chosen brothers".

Text from Thomas Bradley, *Chronicon*, ch. IV, in *Speculum Carmelitanum* 1680, I, 179, n. 790. The miracle is also recorded by Baconthorpe cf. A. Staring, *Medieval Carmelite Heritage*, p. 241

A Royal Decree to Spread Devotion to the Immaculate Conception in Spain

Philip IV, King of Spain, on 23rd April 1662, responding to an apostolic constitution of Pope Alexander VII of 8th December 1661, regarding devotion to the Immaculate Conception, issued a decree. This decree laid down that in his territories, all preachers, before any sermon, should recite with the people the following prayer: "Praised be the Most Blessed Sacrament of the Altar and the Immaculate Conception of the Virgin Mary!"

When this document reached the Carmel in Cagliari, the brothers were surprised that the King had acted so late…..Fra Carlo Fadda, the secretary of the convent, transcribing the royal decree in the community register, noted, "..this order is already practiced by Carmelites in all sermons .. and has been done for a long time.." (General Archive O.Carm, II Sardinia 2).

Pages from the Anthology

1. SPEAKING TO YOU, MY SISTER

Text from Arnold Bostius, De *Patronatu*, ed. Daniel of the Virgin Mary in *Speculum Carmelitarum*, n. 1704

"Oh, through your union with Carmel
you call yourself my sister,
and you attract in your wake
legions of brothers;
beyond all hope and merit,
you have nourished me.
I beg you to receive from this brother the first fruits.
As the flowers are the glory of the field,
So you are the beauty and glory of Carmel.
We find in you
The seed of all the virtues
As a garden is decorated with abundant flowers,
Give me always, I beg you the fullness of life.

Come down, o beloved sister, frequently
To the garden of Carmel
Surrounded by lilies
Of snow-white purity.

Oh, Mother, nourish new Carmelites,
Bring them to your breast
Which is like the mountain range of Carmel.
I am obliged to give you worthy praise and this I do.
O my Sister,
take me in your arms and embrace me,
and I will respond with all my being.
O most loving Mother, graciously accept my promises.

2. RAISED UP WITH MARY

Text from St. Mary Magdalen de' Pazzi, *Probatione*, Part. II.

Lightness in the body, joy in the heart, freedom in the will, transparency in the intellect, the remembrance of good things in the memory, truth in the will, simplicity in all actions, veracity in one's words, mortification in the feelings; in this way, one can rise up with Mary.

In order that the heart be prepared to receive these gifts, it is necessary that one be pure, transparent and strong. Pure in the integrity of one's habits: for lay people, this means observing the commandments and for religious, the commandments and the counsels, even the smallest. Transparent by the peace that must dwell in him, by the memory of the Blood of the Word which is received in Baptism. Be strong in such a way that one does not desire anything else except God and even if one had to confront a thousand demons and a thousand hells, nothing could stop him from desiring God alone. In a heart that is pure like this, transparent and strong, Mary can spread her gifts and graces. Purity can be arrived at by human self-abasement in the presence of God and of creatures and also with humble confession. Transparency can be acquired by conformity with the will of God and of superiors. Strength comes from hope and trust in God and continuous prayer.

Oh! How many gifts and graces Mary wants to give to creatures. Oh! Who does not desire to have in oneself all the virtues that a creature must have in order to receive these

gifts of Mary? If perseverance in seeking these virtues is lacking, the beloved Mother does not give such a precious gift to her children if she sees that they esteem them little, rejecting them and causing disgust.

Oh Mary, you want to give us your gifts, but I deprive myself of them, mixing them up with my own. I desire the grace, but from my own point of view and in such a way that in fact I do not actually receive it. I would like to have your love but along with the love of creatures which is just not possible. I would like to possess more of your love, along with mine but that cannot happen. I would like to live under your mantle, but at the same time under the mantle of my own complacency; but as your Son said, it is not right that soft members be under a head crowned with thorns. It is not right. It is not at all right that your daughters, with their own comforts, remain under the mantle of the one who forgot herself totally. I want to feed at your breast, but the desire is lacking – in many people the desire is there but they want to feed at your breast and at the same time be nourished by the things of the earth. O sweetest Mother Mary, what is beyond my understanding is that they want to attach themselves to the most vile thing on earth, which is the world itself, and at the same time they want to make themselves servants of that which is given to serve them.

O Mary, what can I give you or what can I offer which will be pleasing to you? My will? I fear that you will reject it because it is not conformed to yours. My intellect? It is not enlightened. Memory? It forgets the good things received. Affection? It is not pure. I will offer You the heart of your only Son and who can offer you a greater gift than that?

Mary desires to sanctify the body and the soul so that what was said of her can also be said of us, "Holy and immaculate virgin". The glory of the mother is the greatness, wealth and beauty of the daughter. If we receive glory from Mary, and not express it through the virtues in our lives, then her glory would be lost on us. On the contrary, if we could increase her glory, acquiring the virtues that are so pleasing to the Word, we would truly increase it. O sweetest Mary, this is the grace most to be desired.

How pure and beautiful you are, Mary! With your glance you move the Word, give joy to the angels, comfort sinners, help the pilgrims. With your glance, you make the Son of the most High become the most base and abject of creatures. In heaven, with your gaze, you make God not to be God, as it were, because you so mitigate His anger that creatures here on earth wonder whether God is really so powerful and just, since they see how great is God's mercy that if someone turns towards Him, He is there waiting. In such a way God, who is just and most pure, does not show Himself thus but shows instead His mercy.

In the beauty of your eyes, o Mary, the whole of paradise delights and the throne of the most holy Trinity inclines towards you.

Being assumed into heaven, paradise remains on earth. Taking Mary away from heaven and earth, heaven would no longer be glorious and earth would not have trust. Going to heaven, Mary left paradise on earth because she left an unheard of example of chastity and virginity, which, in comparison to other states, is a paradise on earth. Just as in heaven, there is the fullness of perfection, grace, virtue and glory, so also the state of virginity includes every perfection of virtue, which can be attained here on earth. It is not that virginity is the perfection of all the virtues, but it is the most apt instrument for acquiring the perfection of virtue.

3. FAITHFUL VIRGIN

Text from Elizabeth of the Most Holy Trinity, *Scritti*, 620-630.

"If you but knew the gift of God" (Jn.4,10) Christ said to the Samaritan woman. What is this gift of God if it is not God Himself? The beloved disciple tells us that "he came to his own and his own did not receive him" (Jn.1, 11). St. John the Baptist could say to many souls, "In your midst, within you, there is one whom you do not know" (Jn. 1,26). "If you but knew the gift of God!"

There was a creature who knew this gift of God, a creature who lost not one single drop, a creature who was so pure and luminous that she seemed to be the light itself. "Speculum iustitiae" – a creature whose life was so simple and lost in God that it is almost impossible to describe. "Virgo fidelis" is the faithful virgin, she who "kept all these things in her heart" (Lk.2,51).

She kept herself so small and focused on the presence of God, in the secret of the temple that she brought down on herself the gaze of the Holy Trinity. "The Lord has been pleased to gaze upon the lowliness of His handmaid. All generations will call me blessed!"

The Father inclined towards this most beautiful of creatures, who was unaware of her beauty. The Father desired that she become the Mother of the One of whom He is the Father from all eternity. The Spirit of love, who presides over all the operations of God, intervened. The Virgin pronounced her fiat: "Behold the handmaid of the Lord, let it be done to me according to your word." (Lk. 1,38).

The greatest of all mysteries came to fulfilment. By the descent of the Word, Mary became forever the possession of God. It seems to me that the attitude of the Virgin, during the months between the Annunciation and the Nativity, should be the model for spiritual people, those whom God has chosen for an interior life, in the limitless depths.

With what peace, with what recollection Mary approached all things and did all things! She made the most banal things divine. In everything and through everything the Virgin remained in adoration of the gift of God. This did not prevent her from spending herself outside in everything that had to do with the exercise of charity.

The Gospel tells us that Mary went in haste to the hill country of Judea in order to visit her cousin Elizabeth.

The ineffable vision that she contemplated within herself never diminished her external charity. According to a pious author, if contemplation goes towards praise and towards the eternity of its Lord, it possesses unity and cannot be lost. An order comes from heaven and charity turns towards human beings, has compassion on all their needs and inclines towards all their miseries, shedding tears for them in a way that leads to good. Charity illuminates like a lamp, burns like a flame, absorbs and devours, sending to heaven what it has devoured. When it has completed its work here below, it rises up and takes again the way towards heaven, all aflame.!"

4. THE GATE OF HEAVEN

Text from Elizabeth of the Trinity, *Scritti*, 650-660.

After Jesus Christ, there is one who without a doubt bridges the distance between the infinite and the finite and who also was the great praise of the glory of the Most Holy Trinity. She responded fully to the divine election of which the Apostle speaks. She was always "pure, immaculate and without fault in the eyes of God, three times holy."

Her soul is so simple, its spiritual movements so profound that they cannot be perceived. She seems to reproduce on the earth the life of simple Being. Within time, she is so transparent and luminous that she seems to be light itself. However, she is only the "Mirror" of the Sun of justice, "Speculum Iustitiae!".

"The Virgin kept all these things in her heart" (Lk. 2,51). The whole of her life can be summed up in those words. She lived within her heart, at such a deep level that no human gaze can follow her.

When I read in the Gospel that Mary "went in haste to the hill country of Judea" to go to fulfil her work of charity towards her cousin Elizabeth, I see her passing by very beautiful, very calm and majestic, recollected within herself with the Word of God!

Her prayer, like his, was always this, "Behold, here I am!" Who? "The handmaid of the Lord" (Lk. 1,38), the least of his creatures, she, his Mother! She was always true in her humility because she always forgot herself and was free from self so she could sing, "The Almighty has done great things in me. All nations will call me blessed." (Lk. 1,48-49).

This Queen of Virgins is also Queen of Martyrs but it is her heart that the sword passes through (Lk. 2,35). In her everything happens within. How beautiful it is to contemplate her in her long martyrdom. She is so serene in her majesty that she inspires at the same time strength and sweetness. She had learned very well from the Word how those whom the Father calls to be victims must suffer. Those whom the Father has decided to associate with the great work of salvation, those whom he "has known and predestined to be conformed to his Christ", crucified by love, must suffer.

She remained there, standing beside the cross, strong and heroic and the Master says to me, "Behold your Mother" (Jn.19,27). In this way he gave me her as a Mother, now that he has returned to his Father and he has put me in his place on the cross, because "in my body I must make up that which is lacking in his Passion, for his Body, which is the Church". The Virgin is still there to teach me to suffer like him, to tell me, to let me hear those last songs of his soul which no-one, outside of her, could perceive.

When I will have said my "consummatum est", it will be she, the "Gate of heaven" who will introduce me into the eternal halls, whispering to me the mysterious words: "I rejoiced when I heard them say, let us go to the house of the Lord." (Ps.122,1)

5. THE BEAUTY OF MARY'S PURITY

Text from St. Mary Magdalen de' Pazzi, *Colloqui*, p. I, p. 345-346, and *Probatione*, part. I, p. 106.

"Oh Mary, your eyes shine with the splendour of purity!

Oh purity! Oh purity! Oh purity!

Without humility there would never have been such purity and without purity there would never have been humility. You gave birth to the one who introduced purity to us, its creator and the one who rewards it.

Blessed are the pure in heart. Purity is such a wonderful thing, so great, so incomprehensible that no creature is capable of understanding it......The stars, the sun and the moon lose their brilliance in relation to the purity of Mary.

Purity remains in the most hidden places of the soul as something so sublime and wonderful, impossible to be acquired by a creature's own power. It is only possible to receive it from God and only He can pour it into the soul. Oh purity! Oh purity, how beautiful you are! In you the Father, the Son and the Spirit rejoice! In you, Mary, the Father is well pleased, the angels rejoice and the saints encounter blessedness.

For Further Study

I. Bibliography

- V. Hoppenbrouwers, *Virgo purissima et vita spiritualis Carmeli*, in *Carmelus*, 1 (1954), pp. 255-277
- Idem, *Devotio Mariana*, pp. 225-277
- L. Saggi, *Santa Maria del Monte Carmelo*, pp. 28-39
- C. Catena, *Il Culto dell'Immaculata Concezione nel Carmelo*, in *Carmelus*, I (1954), pp. 132-215.
- C. Catena, *La dottrina immacolatista negli autori carmelitani*, in *Carmelus* 2(1955), pp. 132-215.
- A. Martino. *Il Culto dell'Immaculata nel Carmelo*, in *La Madonna del Carmine*, 8 (1954), pp. 18-20; 38-42; 72-73
- E. Carroll, *La "Virgo Purissima" y el Carmelo*, in International Marian Congress, pp. 51-74
- A. Costantino, *Maria, sorella nel Carmelo*, in *Maria, icona della tenerezza del Padre*, Palermo, 1992, pp. 63-72
- S. Possanzini, *La "Virgo Purissima", Maria, icona della tenerezza del Padre*, pp. 73-82

II. For personal or group study.

1. Reread the text in relation to the historical insertions and original texts.

2. What elements are decisive in the formation of the idea of Mary as "Most Pure Virgin"?

3. What kind of relationships between Carmelites and Our Lady are suggested by the concept of Mary as sister?

4. What does the concept of the "purity" of Mary offer to Carmelites for their spiritual lives? How do Carmelites bring devotion to Mary Most Pure to the faithful?

5. Reread the explanatory texts and draw out from them the values they have to offer.

6. Do you know any texts from modern authors (Carmelites or otherwise) that touch on these themes?

III. Prayer and life.

1. Pray with the Word of God.
    Lk. 1,26-38; 2,15-19.51
    Lk. 2, 27-35
    Is. 7,10-14

2. Contemplate the "Virgin Most Pure" in her interior beauty, trying to learn from her the way to union with God.

4. Discover personal ways to communicate to others this part of Mary's life.

4. Read the Pages from the Anthology and starting from the feelings that rise up in you, write your own page and perhaps use it for your prayer.

4

LIFE HIDDEN WITH YOU

Mary is the spring made pure by the Eternal Word,
who declares her to be virgin and mother, mother and virgin.
It pleased the Holy Trinity to make this source fruitful.
The whole of heaven watered the earth.
This fount must now irrigate heaven and rejoice in God's everlasting presence.

Mary is the *walled garden* in which the Giver of Life dwells.
God lives in her and therefore all the heavens and all creatures.
By means of the blood taken from Mary, the whole world is saved.
If there had been no Mary, for me there would have been no Paradise.
If there had been no Mary, for me there would have been no God.

Mary desires that there should be in us all that she possesses.
We can have God whole and entire through union.

(St. Mary Magdalene de' Pazzi,
Probatione, Part II).

4 LIFE HIDDEN WITH YOU

Mystical Presence of Mary

In the Carmelite Order in the Middle Ages up to the modern times, there were many figures notable for their experience and their teaching about Mary. In terms of theology, there are also authors who give serious thought to the mystery of Mary. At the end of the Middle Ages and in the following years, a real Mariology began to be worked out by some Carmelite authors, putting great emphasis on the mystical presence of Mary in the spiritual life of the individual Christian.

1. Contemplating the mystery of Mary

Among early Carmelites, we find theologians in the various medieval European universities, who gave particular attention to questions relating to the co-redemption and mediation of Mary. Such topics are generally found within a larger context of theological thought, connecting the figure and role of Mary to the mystery of Christ and the Church. There are a number of treatises or smaller works on the much-debated theme of the Immaculate Conception. The theologians of the Order, with some rare exceptions, are numbered among the defenders of the Immaculate Conception. In their arguments, they follow the opinions of the great masters of the Order, Michael Aiguani (+1400) and John Baconthorpe (+1348).. Therefore it was not strange to see the influence of the marian interpretation of the "little cloud" of Elijah, which had a patristic origin, and was taken up and appropriated by the tradition of the Order, especially in the work of Philip Ribot (+1391).

Throughout the 15th to 17th centuries, in theological courses and university debates, students, readers and masters of the Order returned frequently to marian themes, e.g. the predestination of Mary, her perpetual virginity, her marriage to St. Joseph, the merit of the Incarnation and of the divine maternity, the vision of the divine essence in the earthly state of fullness of grace, the cult of hyperdulia and above all, the Immaculate Conception.

In the 16th century, authors like Pedro Padilla (+1600), Amador Arrais (+1600) and Christopher Silvestrani Brenzone (+1608), developed teaching on the excellence of the marian privileges and the figure of Mary, especially on the great dignity of the divine maternity. In later times, other theologians returned to such themes as the mediation of graces through the intercession of Mary, developing their ideas on authentic patristic sources. All of this theological reflection came under the influence of the general tendency in the Church to enlarge the sense of marian privileges. There was a proliferation of books and pamphlets containing, alongside the theological arguments, various other sources from history or legend.

At the beginning of the 17th century, Paulo Antonio Foscarini (+1616) contrary to the current trend of isolating Mary from the rest of theology, put forward the idea of treating all the theological arguments on the marian privileges as a unity and in strict relationship with Christology. He claimed that it was necessary to examine the mystery of Mary in the context of the Incarnate Word.

Among Carmelites, the first to write a specific and distinct mariological treatise, i.e. distinct from other parts of theology, was Camilo Vischi, whose very modest work, was published in Rome in 1645. More profound was the "Theologia mariana" by the Portuguese, Francisco da Natividade, which appeared in Rome in 1668. Other mariological treatises were published later by notable Carmelite authors e.g. Matthias of St. John (+1681), Alexander of St. Teresa (+1686), Valentine of St. Arnando (+1697),and Matthias of Corona (+1676). A case apart is the interesting work written by the Spaniard, Eliseus Garcia, published in 1679. The author proposed a distinction between reflection on the knowledge of God that Mary had and the theological reflection on Mary. In the first case he spoke of marian theology and in the second case, "Theotocology". For Garcia, Christology and Theotocology pertain to theological discourse that is based on the knowledge that comes from the Holy Scriptures and Tradition. In a similar way there can be "Eliology" on Elijah, in reference to what is known from Scripture and Tradition. The author proposed a new study – "Marieliogia" uniting the doctrine on Mary with that on Elijah.

Valuable contributions for the evolution of theological thought on the mystery of Mary come also from sermons, especially in the 18th century. In this century we find an important contribution in the sermons of Andrea Mastelloni (+1722), with his homilies centred on the universal mediation of Mary and on her spiritual maternity and the contributions of Jacinto de Arenas and of Manuel of the Mother of God Bulhoes (+1738). In these and in other preachers of the modern era there is frequent consideration of Mary as co-redemptrix in the mystery of salvation.

2. With Mary on the pathways of God

From the first generations of Carmelites it was always understood that a true marian devotion cannot be limited to words. In order to be effective, it must involve one's whole being and way of life. The most relevant aspects that strongly influenced Carmelite life up to the 15th century are based on the affirmations that were founded on the mystery of the Incarnation and the virginal and divine maternity of Mary.

Among these aspects, we can note the following:

- Mary is completely attentive and dedicated to God, immersed in the divine mystery (theocentric and christocentric dimensions which were dominant in the life of Mary). From this idea comes the concept of Mary's glorification.
- Mary is for the Carmelite "the Lady of the Place". This means that the relationships between Mary and Carmelites are reciprocal, close, attentive, respectful and lovingly dependent.
- Mary strongly marks the spiritual structure of Carmelite life with her presence. The cult of the "Lady" led to consecration to her in the following of Christ. This presence led the Carmelite to an assimilation of her attitudes and virtues, giving a special quality to the journey towards holiness. In this way, Mary orients the Carmelite towards Christ, the beginning and end of life.

At the end of the 15th century and following, Carmelite authors continued to elaborate more and more their own Carmelite Mariology, placing special attention on the presence of Mary in the spiritual life. The writings of Arnold Bostius (1445-1499) are particularly beautiful. His treatise, "De Patronatu et Patrocinio Beatissimae Virginis Mariae in dicatum sibi Carmeli Ordinem", written in 1479, is a gathering together of the tradition on Mary. He specially refers to the ascending/descending aspects of the Patronage of Mary, explaining and deepening this theme.

Bostius emphasised the need for recourse to Mary in the necessities of life as a sign of confi-

Preaching about Mary

On the feasts of Our Lady it was the custom, for the Fathers to preach sermons about Mary to the people. Apart from this custom, when they had to preach on another topic, they always made several references to Our Lady. This is a custom that reflected norms, which were confirmed several times.

The first norm that is known is from the Prior General John Baptist Rossi. In 1568, in his Compendium of the Constitutions, he ordered under obedience, that all the preachers of the Order, in sermons on the Saturdays of Lent, apart from preaching on the particular doctrinal theme, must also say something about the "Lady of our Order" for the edification of the people. The same General, during his visit to the Mantuan Congregation in 1575-6, spread this norm.

Very early, in the General Chapter of 1575, held in Piacenza, that norm was enlarged upon to cover every Saturday of the year. Each sermon, in whole or in part, whenever possible, must be about Our Lady.

This norm was continually repeated up to and including the Constitutions of 1625. In 1660 the General Chapter ordered that there be a sermon on the scapular in the churches of the Order on the days reserved for the Confraternities.

In Portugal, in the year 1748, the custom of making reference to Our Lady in all sermons began. The Priors General, during their visits, exhorted all the communities of the Order to follow this practice.

The sermons of Frs. Bartholomew Lantana (+1573) and Andrew Mastelloni (+1722) were often taken as models. In Portugal this practice was highly praised by Fr. José Pereira (+1759).

There is also the norm of the General Chapter of 1575, which laid down the custom of invoking Our Lady by praying a "Hail Mary", before beginning any sermon.

Cf.: Hoppenbrouwers, *Devotio mariana*, pp. 101-102, 103, 105, 108, 128-129, 152.

dence in her maternal love and he affirmed that this gave joy to the Virgin Mary, who gladly receives the petitions of her children as any mother would. In order to respond fully to the plan of God and the divine will, he invites his readers to contemplate Mary, Mother and Mediatrix of all graces. For this he recommends –" no day, no night, no activity, no conversation, no joy, no work, must be without the remembrance of Mary. Each day you will become greater, more interior, stronger, more illuminated, purer….. you will be better because Mary will teach you the path to God."

Bostius observes that, through this habitual recourse to Our Lady, who "takes care of the affairs of her brother", the offering of one's life becomes more acceptable to God because "all that God receives through the most pure hands of Mary, is more pleasing to Him than if it were offered by our own hands."

The proposal of a true Marian life led Bostius to affirm its nature as a constant imitation and permanent contact with Mary as Mother and Sister. She is the "Most sweet Mother", full of mercy, on whom one depends totally, and the Sister who participates in the destiny of her brothers and she is the first Carmelite who with her brothers shares the journey on the pathways leading to God.

With reference to devotional practices, the author lists and proposes various things but goes beyond them, laying as a foundation the spirit and mentality of total consecration to the Patroness: "the love of the Mother must be always and in every place and moment an inspiration for the works of the Carmelite".

3. At the summit of love

Some authors of the 17th and 18th centuries who treat of the Marian life, use expressions which reveal the intensity and fidelity of the Carmelite towards Mary. His life is "in", "for", "through" and "with" Mary. Among these authors, we note: Christopher Silvestrani Brenzone, Ludovico of the Presentation, Andrew Mastelloni and Matthias of St. John. The last of these expressed his conviction in the following way: "Whoever leads a Marian life, in a brief time will make great progress in holiness".

Michael of St. Augustine (1621-1684) merits particular attention with his celebrated work on "The marieform and Marian life" which proposes a life of intense union with Mary "as a new manner of living in God". This Marian life is difficult to describe and so the author underlines the necessity to experience it in order to know it and he has recourse to symbolic and mystical language.

The marieform life is no obstacle to the centrality of Christ on the spiritual journey of each Christian. On the contrary, it is an aid and a stimulus because "the Reign of Mary is in no way contrary to the Reign of Jesus, but is totally ordered towards it". The deiform life, explains our author, is a life that conforms exactly to the will of God. The marieform and Marian life is that which conforms to the will of Mary which is completely identified with the will of God. In order to live the divine life, grace is necessary and this comes from Mary. It follows then that the divine life and Marian life are at the same time the work of God and of Mary, that is a solicitous and joyful dedication to the fulfilment of the theological life.

It is possible to live in and for Mary. Life in Mary means "make an effort ……to conserve and grow in a filial relationship, affectionate and pure of soul and directing a loving gaze towards Mary….in such a way that the love for her and through her for God has a delicate inflow and outflow". To live in Mary is equivalent to penetrating the spirit and the intentions of Mary, and with her to go to God and from God to return to her. A life lived for Mary is a total dedication "with the view that Mary be honoured, glorified and loved in all things and that her Reign consist in promoting, bringing about and spreading the Reign of Christ". The marieform and Marian life reaches its fullest expression when we allow ourselves to be penetrated and animated by the spirit of Mary up to the point where we are transformed in her. In this way one learns to live only for God and for Mary. The tender and filial love towards the heavenly Mother brings us to contemplate and to enjoy her presence together with that of God. In this context, it can be seen that perfect consecration to Mary, in its pure form, is the same as consecration to Jesus.

Michael of St. Augustine based all his Marian doctrine, not on particular visions, but on the doctrine of the Church, especially the mediation and spiritual maternity of Mary. He insists on the contemplation of Mary in her union with God, affirming that this contemplation leads us necessarily to unite ourselves with Mary and through her with God. "Mary serves as the means to the strongest link of the soul with God". There comes about a wonderful fusion in which God, Mary and the soul seem to become one thing.

This form of spirituality of "union with Mary and with God", is characterized by the decisive mystical and contemplative orientation which is the high point of the Marian doctrine of Carmel. Michael of St. Augustine, in proposing this doctrine, had before him the wonderful example of the mystical life of Marie Petyt (1623-1677), a Carmelite tertiary and his disciple.

The mystical union with Mary, according to the experience of this tertiary, is not a corporal, imaginative or intellectual vision of any particular thing, neither something that results from one's own efforts. It refers to a union given freely by God. Therefore it is a special grace, which is not common in the spiritual life.

One commentator writes in this regard, "this mystical grace is not to be considered as the normal crowning of Carmelite Marian devotion. It is a grace outside the normal development of the spiritual life. We can certainly say that the Marian life as it is lived in Carmel, can provide the remote disposition and so, in a certain sense, this mystical experience is in fact its crowning".

According to the experience of Marie Petyt, we can see three grades or forms of mystical union with Mary:
- Perception of the presence and assistance of Mary;
- God perceived in Mary and Mary in her union with God;
- Intimate and profound adherence of the soul to God and to Mary.

Comparing the experience of Marie Petyt with some other Carmelite mystics, we find the form to which all of them most frequently refer is "a sense of the presence of Mary" in one's own spirit. This gentle experience can last for some time. Most often, it seems that this particular grace is the experience of the Holy Virgin bringing about in the soul a mission that "assists" the work of God. In this phase, the person does not yet associate this presence of Mary with the presence of Jesus and of God.

Ven. Serafina of God (1621-1699) and Maria of St. Peter (1816-1848), as well as Marie Petyt and her director Michael of St. Augustine, all relate similar experiences. We can also understand analogous texts in the same light e.g.. Balduino Leers (+1483), St. Teresa of Jesus (+1582), and St. Thérèse of Lisieux (+1897).

The second form is more rare. This is the mystical vision of God and the Blessed Virgin united in one's own spirit. As a consequence there is a perception within oneself of the presence of God in Mary and of Mary in God. Our Lady and God appear united: the Creator and the creature in the closest embrace. This is a very clear experience to the one who receives this grace. Other than Marie Petyt, we also find this experience described in the writings of the Ven. John of St. Samson (1571-1636).

The third grade is of the shortest duration. It is the most elevated and perfect state of mystical union with Mary. The mystic feels enflamed, absorbed and lifted up in this union. At this stage there is a unification, which excludes all dualism of consciousness. This phenomenon is described uniquely by Marie Petyt, who experienced it personally. Michael of St. Augustine quotes his disciple in his well-known Marian treatise.

Apart from this, many times in the writings of the mystical Carmelite authors of the medieval and modern eras, Mary is present as Mother and as model for the spiritual journey. The same reference to familiarity with Mary can be found in the interior experience of figures closer to us, like St. Thérèse of the Child Jesus (+1897) and Elizabeth of the Trinity (+1906) up to St. Teresa Benedicta of the Cross (Edith Stein +1942) and Bl. Titus Brandsma (+1942).

In St. Thérèse of the Child Jesus, the most significant Marian experience which penetrated her soul, is the smile of Mary which restored joy to her at the end of a period of suffering and pain. In the experience of the saint, it seems that this has a parallel in the biblical sense of "the smile of God" who protects the little ones and the simple and offers them joy and hope. The Saint in her works often makes reference to this smile. Her familiarity with Mary is such that it reaches the point of experiencing her proximity as a companion for the journey, who with her shares the attitudes of faith, openness to the Word of God, silence, humility, joy, love, and seeking Jesus in the night of faith.

In the experience of the indwelling of the Trinity, Elizabeth of the Trinity saw in Mary the habitation of the Trinity as the mirror of the beauty of God; as a reflection of the tenderness and mercy of God towards human beings. Mary is the living model for all those who allow themselves to be transformed by the action of the Trinity. In this perspective, in her own words, "the soul of the Virgin is the place where one must adore the Most Holy Trinity" because it is sublime to contemplate in it the acceptance of the Word as an immersion in the life of the Trinity, the result of which is love and faithfulness.

Edith Stein considers Mary in the context of women's issues and women's education. She presents Mary as the type of the feminine "the woman Mary at the side of the man Christ". In this model comes together the "Mother-Virgin" and the "Spouse of Christ". In other words, Mary, as Mother and Virgin is the type of those who live for others. As Spouse, Mary is the type of the woman who is dedicated totally to God, the Church and the community. In the life of women the "Mother-Virgin" and the "Sponsa Christi" take on a concrete form. Imitation of Mary, prototype of genuine femininity, helps women to express in a feminine way the image of Christ.

Finally Titus Brandsma exhorts us "to strive to be like Mary" because the goal of true devotion to Our Lady is to become "theotokos or another Mother of God: God must be conceived also in us and by us be offered to the world."

This idea of Titus reproduces a thought that we find in the famous monk, Guerrico d'Igny (+1157). His loving contemplation of the reciprocal love between Jesus and Mary and idea of the mystical awareness of Christ in a pure human heart in imitation of Mary, had a great influence and was part of the reflection within Carmel from the medieval era.

4. Reproduce and Continue the Love of Jesus for Mary

It might appear that there is no more to be said on this topic, however, not so. There is still another aspect, which is very much present in the Marian life of Carmel. The Church, as the Mystical Body of Christ, of which the Christian is a member, prolongs Christ's life on earth until the end of time. In this context the devotion of the Church to Our Lady becomes a manifestation in space and time of the love that Jesus had for Mary, His Mother.

What can be affirmed of the Church can also be affirmed of all Christians. As members of the

Day by day with Mary

In the Directory for the formation of novices of the Touraine Reform (ed., Paris, 1650-1651), there is mention of customs for honouring Mary and offering one's daily actions to her. Among others, we can note the following:

- The one who is to take care of cleaning the convent, can pray while he is working: -

> "Most holy Virgin,
> I desire to apply myself to cleaning your house with care and love.
> I ask for the help of your intercession."

- The one who has the job of waking the community for the night office, prayed,

> "Most holy Virgin, this monastery is consecrated to you
> and therefore is yours and the religious who live here
> form your own family. We are servants consecrated to your service. I bind myself with all my strength
> to guard the splendour of your Order and care for it.
> I ask you, as the Mother you are, obtain for me, your son, this grace."

- During meals, the religious prayed,

> "Holy Virgin, beloved Mother and singular Patroness,
> because we are consecrated in a particular way to your name,
> we receive this food as a gift .
> However, the bread we eat is yours. With it you sustain your children. Do not permit that we fall into the temptation of gluttony or offend God.

In other manuals destined for formation, the professed were encouraged to practice daily the use of these marian aspirations. For example, before spiritual reading, there was the custom of saying to Our Lady:

> "Most Holy Virgin, give me your sweet devotion
> with which you read the Holy Scriptures
> when you lived in the temple of your house."

Mystical Body, they live by the Spirit of Jesus, which they received in baptism and confirmation, and continue to receive in abundance, as they mature in faith. Under the action of the same Spirit, Christians, reproduce in themselves Jesus Christ, expressing one or other aspect of the infinite perfection of the Divine Master.

Approximately in 1370, the Carmelite, John of Hildesheim took this concept and applied it to religious Orders each of which has its own way of imitating Christ. Among the religious Orders, Carmel, the author confirms, has the mission of imitating the love of Jesus for Mary. This thought had great significance for the Marian devotion of many generations of Carmelites. However, their love for Mary, no matter how ardent, could never equal the love that Jesus had for his Mother.

A long time later, Michael of St. Augustine, affirmed that, through the imitation of the love Jesus had for his mother, this love is continued, in the sense that we, "participating in his spirit and living by it, are filled with his life and so Jesus continues living in us. Therefore, through us, Jesus continues to love His mother on earth and at the same time, makes her happy by His love in heaven."

Mary, Model of Carmelite life

The Directory of the reform of Touraine (ed., Paris, 1650-1651), clearly reflects the influence of the thought of Baconthorpe, as also that of Bostius, with regard to the imitation of Mary. This reveals how these two medieval authors were appreciated despite the great distance in time.

"It seems that all the points of our Rule are founded on and inspired by the virtues of Mary most holy. For this reason, all of us, sons of Carmel, have an obligation to have a special zeal for her service, for the conservation of the Order and for the imitation of such a tender Mother …As religious and true sons of the Blessed Virgin Mary, we love and honour her with singular tenderness. We recognise her as our liberator, who withdraws us from the misery of the world, receives us into the Order which is dedicated to her, and above all, gives us the privilege of calling us to the Order whose members make special profession to serve her. We offer all our works through her intercession; we place her before us when we practice any virtue, with the desire to imitate her. Our religious will not truly be sons of Mount Carmel if they do not profess a special devotion to the Blessed Virgin as all the saints of our Order have done."

Pages from the Anthology

1. GOD AND THE VIRGIN MARY

Text from John of St. Samson, *Les Excellences et prerogatives de Notre Dame*, ed. Hoppenbrowers, *Devotio mariana*, pp. 356-360.

There is nothing on this earth which represents so well your majesty, whether in relation to divinity or in relation to humanity, as does the Virgin Mary, internally and externally, with her conduct, with her words, with her gestures and with the whole of her life. By such a vivid representation, she comes to be like You. We discover this in her and in this way we discover You; your goodness in hers, your life in hers, just as in You, her love and her goodness. We are moved then to contemplate her just as we contemplate You. We are moved to contemplate her, above and beyond all our thoughts and speculations, as the one who is most pure, simple, unique and most fruitful.

What can we say or think about a creature who is so perfect and so confirmed in grace and nature above every grace and nature? What should we say about a soul who, even in this life, enjoys always this condition to such a eminent degree? Without a doubt, my love and my light, we will be eternally in awe of this subject and delight in speaking and thinking about it as we admire your choice of her among creatures, if we may so speak.

In this sublime contemplation, we can easily see that she is similar to You and that in You she is above every other creature. There is no other difference between You and her, apart from the fact that she is your creature, though an excellent creature. The limits of her glory and magnificence cannot be Yours. We do better comparing her greatness and her perfections to a great sea, which in its flowing in and out, carries with it all that it meets in its passage, returning to enter into the sea from where it emerged, as its unique centre and its own place of repose. Such is the flow back and forward of the greatness and perfections of Your most holy Mother, which by the movement of its impetuous and rapid current carries us off to her and keeps us united to her."

2. TO JESUS THROUGH MARY

Text from Michael of St. Augustine, *Institutiones Mysticarum*, Bk.1, tr.1, ch.18, ed. Antwerp, 1671, pp. 31-32.

I cannot remain silent for long without recommending with all my strength and most warmly a true devotion and a very tender affection to our loveable Mother Mary. This is a unique and efficacious way to acquire a devoted life in Christ. Each day we greet the Mother of grace and the Mother of mercy, grace and mercy being absolutely necessary for a devoted life. With even more reason, then, we may have recourse to Mary in order to obtain grace and mercy and to take refuge with the Mother of grace and of mercy. With the Apostle I exhort you: "Let us go with faith to the throne of grace whenever we need help".

Because we have been permitted to go with trust to this throne and to the Mother of grace, we should seek to earn her love. All those who profess to be her servants, sons or brothers, must conform their lives with zeal to the demands of their profession, trying to become like their Patroness who is all Holy, to the Mother, who is so loveable and to the Sister who is so good, imitating her perfection and learning from her character.

So, if you love her as a Mother, imitate her humility, her poverty, her obedience; imitate her love for God and for her neighbour and all her other virtues. It is right to practice the virtues, which belong to such a Mother, so that you are not rejected as a spurious son. If she is your Mother, where is your honour? Where is your filial love towards her? At least, where can be found in you her most kind, most pure and most gentle character?

So that you can show her the required honour, each day after you have offered yourself and everything you have and do to the Blessed Trinity, with the intentions of Christ and in union with his merits, offer yourself and all that you have and do to this your most lovable Mother, in union with her Immaculate Conception, with her irreproachable motherhood, her inviolate virginity and her sublime holiness. The offering should be made in union with her honour that is offered to her beloved Son. Just as you do everything the Word of God requires, so do everything that Mary desires and in her name, in imitation of our St. Peter Thomas, patriarch of Constantinople. Imitate him by imprinting on your heart the most sweet name of Mary and having it very often on your lips like sweet honey. Raise your mind frequently night and day to her with very tender affection, saying: Show yourself to be my Mother.

Above all, in every temptation and in every adversity and anguish, turn to her with trust and love, just as little children run to their mothers when they are frightened in any way. Rest in her arms and sleep on her merciful breast. In all circumstances act freely as a little child full of love with its most kind mother. Even if you have many saints and patrons to whom you are devoted, you do not have many mothers. She brought you to birth in Christ and she fed you. When you are looking upon her image in some place, venerate your Mother with joy. When you are writing, write first her most beautiful name. In every circumstance, at every moment and in every place, seek to reflect well on such a lovable Mother in your words, actions and thoughts.

Entrust yourself totally to her and turn to her as to a wonderful Teacher. Consult her as the Virgin most prudent. Look forward to and celebrate her feasts with special honour and devotion. In a word, behave as a good son should and experience that she is the Mother of love and of hope, in whom will come to you every grace and hope. She never ceases to send you the graces that are necessary for you to persevere in true piety. She will be for you like a well of living water. At the hour of your death, she will not refuse to say that she is your sister as well as your Mother so that in that moment you will receive salvation and your soul will live because of her. Thus, ending this life as her devotee, you will merit to be carried through the gate of salvation in her maternal arms. At the final moment all will be well for the one who loves Mary.

3. THE MYSTICAL LIFE WITH MARY

Text from Michael of St. Augustine, *The Marian and Marieform Life*, chaps. 2 and 13.

In order to live in God in all things, it is necessary in what we do, in what we omit and in what we undergo, to put up with whatever is painful with a respectful spirit and with love. This is the case for that which is painful in body or soul, for that which comes from within or from outside, from people or from evil spirits. We must live in a spirit of sincere conversion, and be recollected, our spirit inclined gently towards God, almost breathing in the divine essence. In this way one imitates the Saviour, in whom the Father dwelt and accomplished all things. Christ Himself, in union with the Father, acted with great love, reverently inclined towards His heavenly Father.

In the same way, we can live in Mary, our most beloved Mother. We can seek in everything we do or suffer, in what we accomplish and in what we omit, in our pains, sorrows and afflictions, to conserve and to increase in ourselves a loving aspiration towards Mary. She is our most loving Mother and is the beloved of God. Between her and us and through her, between God and us can be established a gentle inflow and outflow of love. It seems that this is brought about from time to time by the action of the Holy Spirit in our souls by means of the diffusion and overflowing of the love of God for Mary and of her love for God.

For greater clarity we can use these words of the Apostle: The proof that you are sons and daughters is that God has sent into your hearts the spirit of His Son who cries out, "Abba, Father". We understand by this that the Spirit of Jesus lives in the children of God and within them exercises a tender love for God the Father in conformity with the capacity of people. Just as the Spirit of Jesus brings forth from him a filial love for his Eternal Father, so also the Spirit brings forth filial affections and all sorts of signs of affection for his dearest Mother and he does this throughout all eternity.

We should not be surprised, therefore, that the same Spirit of Jesus brings forth tender movements of love for the Father in the hearts of the children of God and cries out, "Abba, Father". In these same hearts, the Spirit cries out, "Hail, Mother", arousing filial love, reverence, intimate exchanges and all sorts of innocent and tender demonstrations of love towards Mary, the most beloved and most worthy Mother. The same Spirit of Jesus who operates in all these souls, arouses at the same time love for God and love for Mary, neither of which lessens the other. Consequently, just as such souls live the divine life by the love of God in God and for God, so also by the same Spirit of love, which extends to their beloved Mother, they also live a marian life in Mary and for Mary. One and the same Spirit works these things in these souls. The same Spirit of Jesus makes them love God the Father and the Virgin Mary and makes them live in God and for God and in Mary and for Mary. The divine life and the Marian life operate at the same time.

4. INTIMACY WITH MARY

Text from Marie of St. Teresa Petyt (1623-1677), *Het Leven*, (4 t., Gand, 1683-1684), II, ch. 214.

From what has already been said and from similar clear knowledge and illumination given to my soul, there grows even more esteem and respect, reverence and love towards the lovable Mother. There is also greater stability, simplicity and purity. My soul seems inseparable from her and I feel my heart all aflame with love for her. This fire of love is violent and what great power seizes the soul, carrying it on high into a loving absorption. By means of a new revelation of the secret marvels which God has placed in her or the love which takes God towards her etc …, my soul is attracted each time to a profound and sublime admiration, contemplating her with ardour and remaining almost absorbed in her. The intelligence is incapable and insufficient to understand those marvels manifested in this majestic and loveable Mother.

Love is not content with these manifestations that rise up in the intimacy of one's heart. In an excess of wonder, love cries out and tries to find words in some way to express the greatness, the dignity and the excellence of this my most sweet Mother. I desire to make her known and praised, to magnify her and to exalt her. The soul thus proclaims the greatness and the marvels of what it experiences and, loving her so much, praises her and magnifies her and exalts her like someone who is madly in love. Such a person does not know what to think, how to express what is within, or what words to use in order to praise the beloved, etc …

I also perceived another ray of light with which my Beloved made me understand that God is well pleased with this loveable Mother and has for her a love greater than for all the saints taken together.

5. GOD IN MARY AND MARY IN GOD

Text from Marie of St. Teresa Petyt (1623-1677), *Het Leven*, (4 t., Gand, 1683-1684) II, ch. 217.

It seems that it is customary to receive the loving Mother in the soul and in the heart in the above-mentioned ways. My spirit comes alive and is possessed by the spirit of Mary, who directs me in all things either to do or not do something. It is as if the spirit of Mary, living in me, acts through me. It is the same as before when the spirit of Jesus seemed to direct me, enliven me and possess for me for a time. It was as if the spirit of Jesus, living in me, completed all my actions through me, keeping me passively under his direction. It was an experience of Jesus living in me.

So also now, almost in the same way, it seems that the spirit of Mary lives in me and directs all the powers and the operations of my soul. She directs and leads me in whatever I must do or not do. In this way my soul lives in God in a new way, up till now unknown and never experienced before. It seems that Mary is my life. She is the gentle air that I breathe and that keeps me alive. In this way I live in God in an even more wonderful and sublime way than before.

6. LIKE MARY WE BRING FORTH CHRIST

From a talk given by Bl. Titus Brandsma to the Marian Congress at Tongerloo, August 1936.

From all eternity God has chosen us, has loved us and has predestined us to live in intimate union with Him. God desires to live in us through grace. This union is sublime, like that of the divine maternity of Our Lady. Rightfully, we also can be called "God bearers". God sends the angel also to us to ask us continually to open our hearts to the light of the world in order to bear it like a lantern…

We too must receive God in our hearts; we must carry God within our hearts, nourish him and allow him to grow in us in such a way that he will be born of us and live with us as God-with-us, Emmanuel.

7. AT THE FOOT OF THE CROSS OF CHRIST

Text from St. Teresa Benedicta of the Cross (Edith Stein), ed. in: Teresa Renata dello S.S., *Edith Stein*, Morcelliana, Brescia 1952, p. 135

Today I have been with you at the foot of the cross and I understood with clarity never before experienced that there you became our Mother. With what fidelity even an earthly mother would seek to fulfil the last wish of her son! But you were the Handmaid of the Lord. The very Being of the Incarnate God was fully inscribed in your being and in your willing. So you hid within your heart those who were already yours. To give to each soul new life, you paid the price of the bitter agony of your suffering heart. You know each one of us. You know what our hurts and wounds are like. But you also know the heavenly splendour that the love of your Son desires to pour into us in the glory of eternity. With maternal care, you guide our steps. In order to lead us to the goal, there is no price you would not pay. Those you have chosen for your crown, those who will surround you one day before the throne of God, must remain with you here on earth at the foot of the cross. The bitter agony of their suffering hearts will be the price paid to obtain the eternal splendour which will be given to those beloved souls who have been given to you as your inheritance by the Son of God.

8. MARIAN DEVOTION: A CALL TO THE INTERIOR LIFE

Text from Gabriel of St. Maria Magdalena, OCD, *Intimità divina*, 2ª, Roma 1956, pp. 1313-1314.

Devotion to Our Lady of Mt. Carmel is a call to the interior life, which is in a very special way the life of Mary. Our Lady wishes us to be like her, more in heart and in spirit, than by wearing an exterior habit. If we penetrate Mary's soul, we see that grace flourished in her and that her interior life was immensely rich. She lived a life of recollection, of prayer, of uninterrupted self-giving to God, of continuous relationship with God and of intimate union. The soul of Mary is a sanctuary reserved for God alone, where no human creature has left an imprint, where there reigns love, zeal for the glory of God and for the salvation of people.

Those who wish to have a full and deep devotion to Our Lady of Mt. Carmel, must follow Mary in the profundity of her interior life. Carmel is a symbol of the contemplative life, a life wholly dedicated to the search for God, wholly turned towards divine intimacy. The one who most fully fulfils this high ideal is Our Lady, Regina *Decor Carmeli*. "In the desert equity will live and on Carmel justice will preside. Peace will flow from justice and from justice silence will flow and security forever. My people will live in peace, in a strong fortress." These verses taken from Isaiah (cf. 32, 16-18) and used for the proper Office for Our Lady of Mt. Carmel, set out very well what is the contemplative spirit and at the same time are a beautiful sketch of the soul of Mary, who is a true "garden" (in Hebrew "Carmel" means garden) of virtue, oasis of silence, of peace, in whom reigns justice and equity. She is a stronghold surrounded by the shadow of God and filled with God. Every soul called to the interior life, even if living in the midst of this noisy world, must seek to arrive at this peace and at this interior silence that makes possible the continuous contact with God. The passions disturb the peace of our soul and interrupt the intimate conversation with God. Only the soul which is completely detached and which has completely dominated all passions can, like Mary, be a solitary, silent "garden" where the Lord finds delight. This is the grace, which today we ask from Our Lady, choosing her as the patroness and mistress of our interior life.

For Further Study

I. Bibliography

V. Hoppenbrouwers, *Devotio mariana*, pp. 154-224

N. Geagea, *Maria Madre e Decoro del Carmelo*, pp. 367-438 (under Arnold Bostius)

AAVV, *La dimensione mariana del Carmelo*, I, pp.40-50; II, pp. 5-60.

O. Steggink, *Mistica mariana carmelitana*, in *Congresso Mariano Internacional*, pp. 63-74

R. Valabek, *Mary, Mother of Carmel*, 2 Vols, Roma, 1988.

Ildefonso de la Inmaculada, *La Virgen de la contemplación*, Madrid, 1973

AAVV, *Maria, icona della tenerezza del Padre*, Palermo, 1992.

S. Possanzini, *La dottrina e la mistica mariana del venerabile Michele di Sant'Agostino carmelitano*, Roma, Edizioni Carmelitane, 1998

P. Garrido, *La Virgen de la Fe. Doctrina y piedad mariana entre los Carmelitas españoles de los siglos XVI and XVII*, Roma, Edizioni Carmelitane, 1999

II. For Personal or Group Study

1. Read the basic text and make an outline of it.

2. Analyse the values for our life, inspired by Mary in the pages from the anthology.

3. Discover in a Marian legend the symbols which are used and the message transmitted through them.

4. According to the perspectives of the authors whom you know, what role does Mary exercise in the mystical and spiritual life?

5. In the Carmelite life and in pastoral work, what are the most relevant aspects of the life of Mary?

6. Examine the mariological doctrine of one of the saints of our Order. (See bibliography).

III. Prayer and Life

1. Pray with the Word of God
   Lk.1,46-55; Eccles. 24,23-25; 1 Sam. 2,1-10; Acts 1,12-14; Gal. 4,4-6; Lk. 2, 15-19

2. What values, among those discovered above, are most helpful for my own spiritual life?

3. In what aspects is a change necessary to reproduce and continue in my life the love of Jesus for Mary?

4. How is my affective relationship with Jesus and Mary expressed in practice?

5. Read and interiorise the aspects that seem to you most significant in the pages from the anthology. Write down your own thoughts.

5

MOTHER OF THE SCAPULAR

Salve, Flower of Carmel
Salve, blossoming vine
Splendour of heaven
Virgin, Mother, Singular Rose

Mother, tender and beautiful
Guide your children, Star of the Sea
Keep far away all dangers
by the power of your Scapular

Life giving root
bring forth the Saviour
come, help me in my sorrow
let my prayer reach you.

Mother, tender and beautiful
Guide your children, Star of the Sea
Keep far away all dangers
by the power of your Scapular

A white lily among the thorns
guard the mind and the heart
of this most fragile of your children
from the guile of the serpent

Mother, tender and beautiful
Guide your children, Star of the Sea
Keep far away all dangers
by the power of your Scapular

The blessed habit
in the midst of the struggle
is the breast's strong shield
my fortress and defence

Mother, tender and beautiful
Guide your children, Star of the Sea
Keep far away all dangers
by the power of your Scapular

Let the traveller
hear your guiding voice
Let the sufferer
know the comfort of the Cross

Mother, tender and beautiful
Guide your children, Star of the Sea
Keep far away all dangers
by the power of your Scapular

On the beautiful day that is yours
the soul faithful in pain
the shackles of sin now broken
will come to live with you in eternity

Mother, tender and beautiful
Guide your children, Star of the Sea
Keep far away all dangers
by the power of your Scapular

The children of Carmel
bathed in the love of your heart
will sing Glory to you in the heavens
in the choir of the blessed.

A song taken from an Italian collection, *Lodiamo il Signore, Raccolta di preghiere e di canti*, Roma, 1953, pp. 117-118

5 MOTHER OF THE SCAPULAR

Our Lady of the Scapular

From the 15th century onwards, in Carmelite devotion, thought about Our Lady in relation to the scapular became widespread. That relation did not eliminate but rather encapsulated the earlier reference to Mary as Patroness and Mother, Mary as Sister, the Most Pure Virgin, and the mystical presence of Mary in union with God.

As early as the 13th and 14th centuries lay people were asking and being allowed to share in the spiritual benefits of the Order, while maintaining their state in life. A sign of this condition and of their affiliation to the Order was first of all the white cloak and then the Scapular from the 15th century onwards. The motivation for the desire for affiliation was provided by talk of "visions and privileges" connected to the use of the sign of the Carmelite habit, and then the Scapular, through which Mary preserved those devoted to her from hell and freed them from purgatory after their death.

It is really impossible to talk about Carmelite Marian devotion without referring to the Scapular, because, after several centuries, the Order sees its devotion as bound up with this symbol, and linked to the venerable tradition of the Order (the vision of St. Simon Stock) and the so-called Sabbatine Privilege.

These two questions, namely the historical nature of the vision of Simon Stock and the validity of the Sabbatine Privilege, have been discussed often over the years and still are today. Here we will examine these two questions and offer some suggestions for further reflection.

A. The life and vision of Simon Stock

According to a venerable tradition Our Lady appeared to Simon Stock in a vision, in the 13th century. She put the Scapular in his hand and said: "This is to be a sign of salvation for you and for those who belong to you. Those who are wearing it when they die will be saved". In other words, those who become part of the Order (those who receive and wear the habit as a sign of belonging) will be saved for ever. What can we say about the historical value of this vision?

a) The life of St. Simon Stock

In order to get a proper understanding of the vision of Simon Stock, it would be helpful to know something about his life, through a reading of the source documents. What do they tell us about who the real Simon Stock was?

1. Information from the sources

In order to get a better knowledge of the life of Simon Stock we will have to take a look at what the experts call the "first hand" documents, i.e. those documents which relate (de visu or de auditu) for the first time the events that occurred. The first documents later become the basis for other documents which repeat them, interpret them, copy them or add to them, sometimes without any historical basis at all. Therefore, it becomes necessary to make a critical and scientific examination of the sources. In regard to St. Simon Stock the first hand sources fall into three categories:

1) The account given by Geralde de Frachet, O.P. (+ 1271)
2) The Catalogues of the Priors General of the Order (up to the 14th century)
3) The Catalogues of Carmelite Saints (at the beginning of the 15th century)

1.1. *The account given by Gerard of Fracheto*

In his book, titled Vita fratrum, Geralde de Frachet, telling the story of the Dominican, Blessed Jordan (+ 1237) who was the successor of St. Dominic, referred to the temptation of a "friar of the Carmelite Order" to leave the Order. Blessed Jordan appeared to the friar in 1237 and helped him to overcome the temptation to leave the Order. Geralde also relates that "this event was told to our brothers by the same friar and by Friar Simon, a truly religious man, the Prior of his Order."

The elements we find in this account refer to:
• a Carmelite friar suffering from temptation
• his Prior, whose name was Simon.

Could this latter be Simon Stock? The document itself does not say and there is no other document from that period which would prove the identity.

The first person in the historiography of the Order who identified this prior Simon with Simon Stock was Arnold Bostius (at the end of the 15th century). Other authors later repeated this affirmation without getting into any kind of critical discussion.

1.2. *The Catalogues or lists of the Priors General*

The most ancient catalogues or lists of Priors General are:
a) the catalogue found in the Florentine necrology (end of the 14th century)
b) the catalogue of John Grossi (end of the 14th century) in two editions (Avignonian and Italian)

We get the following information from these catalogues:

• the name: Simon Stock (Flor. Nec.) and Simon Stock (Grossi)
• the nationality: English
• the religious province to which he belonged: the Carmelite Province of England
• office: Prior General (Grossi, in one of the editions lists him as the 5th Prior General, and in the other as the 6th)
• distinguishing features:: a holy man, known for miracles
• date of death: 16th of May – there is no indication of the year.

1.3. *The catalogue of Carmelite Saints*

The catalogue of Carmelite Saints (beginning of the 14th century) exists in four different editions:
• BR = Very short (the earliest edition)
• B = Short
• L = Long
• LP = Long Parisian (the latest edition)

Some parts of each edition could have been taken from earlier writings: the shorter texts have a common origin. The longer texts are more recent.

The catalogue contains the lives of the saints, following a literary genre of the Middle Ages based on exempla (examples), with a concept of history which is different to ours.

The elements that are common to all four catalogues (BR, B, L, and LP) are:
• the name of Simon
• the English nationality
• his great devotion and holiness
• the fact of his prayer to Our Lady and the apparition of Our Lady with the Scapular (privilege and pledge of salvation).

The details of each edition are:

- BR: in the list of the various Carmelite saints, there is no chronological order but rather one of importance: Prophets, Popes, Patriarchs, Archbishops, Martyrs, Confessors, Priors General, Religious priests, Religious brothers, Women. In this list Simon Stock is classified among the Confessors and not among the Priors General. (Therefore, the BR edition excludes the possibility that Simon Stock was Prior General).
- B: this puts Simon Stock as the 6th Prior General, and adds the following information:
  - the text of the Flos Carmeli, the prayer of Simon Stock to the Blessed Virgin (the most ancient edition of this prayer comes from the beginning of the 15th century and contains the words esto propitia (be merciful) to the Carmelites and not the words da privilegia (grant favour)
  - angels surrounding the Blessed Virgin when she appears to Simon Stock
  - the place of his death and burial, Bordeaux, France.
- L: this edition also adds:
  - the explanation of the surname Stock as coming from the word tree trunk, in which he lived, while waiting for the Carmelites;
  - The saint joins up with the Carmelites after the opening of the houses in Alnwick and Aylesford. This happened in 1241-1242:
  - His election as Prior General at a chapter celebrated in England;
  - His term of twenty years as Prior General. During this time St. Louis IX, the king of France, brought the Carmelites to that country. It was also the time of the interventions by Pope Honorius III (1226), Gregory IX (1229) and Innocent IV (1247) in favour of the Order.
  - The reputation for miracles, which included changing water into wine and the return to life of a fish which was already cooked;
  - The statement that some English nobles, after the vision, asked to receive the Scapular;
  - Simon was 100 years old when he died.
- LP: contains the same information as L, but in a longer form, and with the variant that Simon was Prior General for 50 years.

2. *Reflection on this information*

What we have seen above are the elements that the historians must bear in mind in speaking about the life of Simon Stock. At the moment there is no other information that is not simply a repetition of what we have seen.

In this information we can see a variety of elements, sometimes contradictory, which make it difficult for us to get a clear understanding of who Simon Stock really was. Some observations are necessary.

2.1. *Simon Stock's entry to the Order*

- The L edition of the catalogue of saints states that Simon Stock joined the Order after the beginning of the foundations of Alnwick and Aylesford, which, we know from other sources, took place in 1241-1242.
- If this information in L were true:
  it does not correspond with what the same text says about the period of Simon Stock as Prior General which it puts at an earlier date, based on its association with other events (the intervention of Honorius III in 1226, Gregory IX in 1229 and Innocent IV in 1245 and 1247). There is a contradiction in that the L text would have us understand that Simon Stock was Prior General before he joined the Order.
  In addition to that, if the information in edition L is true, it becomes impossible to identify the Prior Simon mentioned by Geralde de Frachet with Stock. In this case these would be two distinct people.
- If the information in edition L is not true:
  - it puts an end to a chronological reference, calculated by the traditional position of the Order, and at the same time

there is no solution for the other contradictory information in the sources.
- Also the identification of Prior Simon with Stock could be valid, but in this case we would have further complications that arise from a consideration of some questions regarding his period as Prior General.

2.2. *Period as Prior General*

We may observe
- the possible date of the election of Simon Stock has to be placed in the context of what we already know about the Priors General in the 13th century. This date could not possibly be 1249 (when, in all certainty, the Prior General was Godfrey), and it cannot be after 1266, because from 1266 onwards the names of all the Priors General are known, in a list complete with names and dates). It may be supposed therefore that the date of his generalship was either between 1249 and 1266 or before 1249.
- The traditional position affirms that Simon Stock was elected Prior General in 1247. The source of this is edition L of the Catalogue of saints, where, however, there is no indication of the year, but simply a statement that he was elected at the General Chapter celebrated in England. If what L says is true we have to look at the chapters which were celebrated in England and about which we have information from other sources: the chapters of 1247, 1256 or 1281.
- That he was elected in 1281 has to be excluded because that chapter was celebrated under the leadership of Peter of Millaud who was Prior General from 1277 to 1294.
- We have a strong doubt that he was elected in 1247. If the date of his entry into the Order around 1242 is accurate, that means that Simon Stock became Prior General after only five years of religious life and the contradiction in edition L regarding the period of his generalate becomes obvious. Moreover, the naming of 1247 as the date of Simon Stock's election excludes the possibility of identifying him with the "Prior Simon" recalled by Gerard de Fracheto in 1237. And how could Popes Honorius III and Gregory IX be moved by the saint to intervene in the Order's favour if he was not yet a member of the Order?
- There are greater possibilities in relation to 1256. In this case we would have to exclude the identification of Simon Stock as "Prior Simon" as quoted above as well as every reference to events that took place during his time as General that we find in edition L of the catalogue of saints.
- The duration of the mandate of general from 20 to 50 years indicated in the editions L and LP of the catalogue of saints cannot be upheld. In fact, if Simon Stock was the Prior General between 1249 and 1266, this duration is not possible. If Simon Stock was elected Prior General before 1249 the duration of 50 years cannot be true (we have the names of other Priors General during this period, even though the dates may not be exact) and the duration of 20 years involves some complex questions.
- Simon Stock was the 5th or the 6th Prior General according to Grossi's catalogue. Historical criticism today tends to place him 5th in the list of Priors General, but this is still only a probable opinion because of the shortage of data about Priors General up to 1266, after which the full sequence is known.

2.3. *The place and date of his death*

Notable facts:
- The 16th of May as the date presents no difficulty.

- It is much more difficult to establish the year of his death. L and LP maintain that he died at the age of one hundred years. Some writers, without any proof, say that would have been in 1295 approx. This date is probably not true. If the year of death had really been 1265, as others maintain, that makes things even more complicated, because it would be almost impossible to prove the hundred years of age of the saint.
- The place of death can be proven by the location of the grave in Bordeaux (France). The relics (cranium) from Bordeaux are now in Aylesford.

So, as we can see, regarding the life and the chronology of Simon Stock there are numerous contradictions in the data contained in the sources: the truth of one fact denies the possibility of others and vice versa. This gives rise to a number of questions. We may find a solution to these difficulties in an approach based on the "chronological calendar of the Passion" (one of the chronological forms of the Middle Ages) which, however, is not fully satisfactory.

The examination of the sources referred to above, clearly demonstrate the existence of two people with the name Simon: one was the Prior General, the other was not. These two people were merged into one, because of the transfer of information from the Catalogue of Priors General to the Catalogue of Saints (editions B, L and LP) with the addition of other less reliable items of information. No one knows what criteria the authors followed at that time for making this transfer.

3. *Liturgical veneration*

The liturgical veneration of Simon Stock appears for the first time in Bordeaux in 1435; in Ireland and in England in 1458. For the whole Order the feast was introduced through a decree of the General Chapter of 1564.

In the reform of the calendar of the Order after the Council of Trent in 1584 the feast of Simon Stock was withdrawn. It was put back there, along with some feasts of the Discalced Carmelites, in the 17th century.

In the reform of the calendar of the Order in the year 1972 after the Second Vatican Council the celebration of Simon Stock was abolished by the Congregation for Divine Worship. The celebration continued however in places of pilgrimage dedicated to the saint. Finally, it was reintroduced into the calendar of the whole Order in 1978.

b) *The vision of Simon Stock*

A further question connected with the Scapular is the vision which Simon Stock had. Here we need to examine:
1. The information from the sources.
2. The historicity of the vision.
3. The meaning of the vision.

1. *The information from the sources*

The information from the primary sources is as follows:
- The narration of the vision is contained in the Catalogue of Saints (from the beginning of the 15th century), but there is no reference to it in the Catalogue of Priors General (up to the 14th century). Besides that, John of Hildesheim and John Hornby in the 14th century, even though they talk about the "intimate relationship" which exists between Mary and Carmelites, still do not mention the vision. We find the account of the vision in every edition of the Catalogue of Saints from the beginning of the 15th century onwards.
- The explanation of the vision in these sources can be reduced to,
  - the prayer of Simon Stock to Our Lady, the Flos Carmeli (which is not to be found in the BR edition);
  - the apparition of Our Lady to the saint (there are variations in the various accounts, but the sense is always the same) "hoc tibi erit

The Flos Carmeli

The tradition of the Order places in the mouth of St. Simon Stock what is a very beautiful prayer to the Virgin Mary, the "Flower of Carmel". The oldest known text is to be found in the manuscript Misc. Lit. 120 (written at the beginning of the 15th century) in the state library in Bamberg. With the passage of time, the text was added to and adapted for singing in the Liturgy of the Solemn Commemoration.

Flower of Carmel
Tall vine blossom laden
Splendour of Heaven
Childbearing, yet maiden
None equals thee.

Mother so tender
Whom no man did know
On Carmel's children
Thy favours bestow
Star of the Sea

Strong stem of Jesse
Who bore one bright flower,
Be ever near us
And guard us each hour,
Who serve you thee here.

Purest of lilies,
That flowers among thorns,
Bring help to the true heart
That in weakness turns
And trusts in thee

Strongest of armour,
We trust in thy might:
Under thy mantle,
Hard pressed in the fight,
We call to thee.

Our ways uncertain,
Surrounded by foes,
Unfailing counsel,
You give to those,
Who turn to thee.

O gentle Mother,
Who in Carmel reigns,
Share with your servants
That gladness you gained,
And now enjoy.

Hail, Gate of Heaven,
With glory now crowned,
Bring us to safety
Where thy Son is found,
True joy to see.

et cunctis carmelitis privilegium quod in hoc moriens aeternum non patietur incendium, id est in hoc moriens salvabitur" (this will be for you and for every Carmelite a privilege: anyone who dies wearing this will not suffer the fires of hell, that is, anyone who dies with this will be saved)
- No one knows where the vision took place, nor the day nor the year. In 1642 the Carmelite John Cheron published two fragments which he said came from Peter Swanington, Simon Stock's secretary. In both of these writings, Cambridge was indicated as the location of the vision and the date was the 16th of July 1251. Historical criticism today is able to show that the fragments mentioned above are false and cannot be taken seriously. Besides this:
  - In what year during Simon Stock's period as Prior General could the vision have taken place? The answer is not easy because it implies another question: Was the Simon who had the vision really the Prior General? The BR edition would exclude it, other editions would affirm it. In this last case the year of the vision could be set before 1249 or after 1254 (the generalate of Godfrey): in which case it could not have been the year which was stated: 1251
  - the date July 16th was chosen as the date for the vision in the 17th century by Cheron to make it coincide with the liturgical feast "The Solemn commemoration of Saint Mary" the patronal feast of the Order. In settling on this day Cheron was not aware that the solemn commemoration previously was celebrated on the 17th of July and that in the beginning, in the 14th century, it was instituted in order to give thanks to the Virgin Mary for two essential things which would allow the Order to survive (the approval of the Order on the basis of the decision taken by the II Council of Lion and the victory in the Cambridge debate relating to the Marian title of the Order). The connection of this feast with the scapular was made in between the 16th and 17th centuries.
  - Cambridge as a location cannot be affirmed because it is based on the false document of Cheron. Aylesford as the location was suggested only in our own days (in 1948 to be precise) but there are no proofs

2. *The historicity of the vision*

When it comes to the historicity of Simon Stock's vision the opinions of the experts are divided. Indeed, an analysis of the information from the sources shows that the question of historicity is a complex one and from the point of view of intellectual honesty we may agree with Ludovico Saggi, "it has to be said that it is not possible to prove that the vision is false, but at the same time the proofs offered for its historical validity are not sufficient".

3. *The meaning of the vision*

We must take into account that in the middle ages visions and statements like those pertaining to Simon Stock were very common, even in relation to the scapulars and habits of other religious orders. We are sure about this in relation to Cistercians, Premonstratensions, Augustinians, Dominicans and Servites. In each of these cases it was said that the faithful wearing of these habits was bound to a promise of eternal salvation. The clearest meaning of this is that religious life, in accordance with the state professed and symbolised in the religious habit, leads to eternal salvation. This promise of salvation linked with the wearing of the habit, before Simon Stock's vision in the case of the Carmelites, is part of the story of the visions of the founders or of Our Lady, with regard to the habit of the Benedictines, the Dominicans and the Franciscans.

In this type of vision we find another set of elements:
- The founding of the Order by the will of the

Blessed Virgin (Dominicans, Servites and Mercedarians);
- the protection of the Order from the threats and attacks of the opposition (Cistercians, Dominicans, Servites and Carmelites);
- the habit of the Order is worn or pointed to by Our Lady (Cistercians, Premonstratensions, Dominicans, Carmelites, Servites, Augustinians);
- the continuity of the Order until the end of time (Franciscans, Carmelites)
- the liberation from Purgatory granted by God, through the intercession of Our Lady or of the founder, who personally descend into purgatory from where they extract the souls of the religious and associates of their own Orders, all of this ratified by the Pope with an official document (Franciscans, Carmelites).

Also in the year 1470 the Carmelite Gerald of Edam, in referring to Simon Stock's vision of Our Lady stated that the Virgin Mary appeared to the saint and gave him the Scapular so that the Carmelites might be equal to the Friars Minor and to the Dominicans by having the same privilege.

The vision of Simon Stock therefore is to be understood in the context of a medieval mentality that saw religious life as a pathway to eternal salvation. If we are to understand its full Marian significance we must look at it in the context of the patronage of Our Lady.

B. The Sabbatine Privilege

A reflection on the Sabbatine privilege must begin from the distinction between
 a) the Sabbatine Bull, (attributed to Pope John XXII which mentions privilege) and
 b) the content of the privilege.

a) the "Sabbatine Bull"

The most ancient document containing the Sabbatine Bull appears for the first time in the third decade of the 15th century. It was an authenticated copy made in Agrigento (Sicily) on the 6th of August 1430. This copy reproduces the text of a document which claimed to be an "act of a public notary" made in the city of Majorca (Spain) on the 2nd of January 1422 which reproduced the Bull of Alexander IV (which in fact should have been Alexander V since Alexander IV livedbefore Pope John XXII) given on the 7th of December 1409 confirming another bull by John XXII dated the 3rd of March 1322. Other copies of the Majorca document, which were to be found in Sicily up to the XVI century, were made by public scribes or otherwise, and are still extant today. There is no trace in the papal registers of the bulls attributed to Alexander V or John XXII.

Fr. Ludovico Saggi reconstructed the Majorca document, using the twenty or so transcriptions authenticated by notaries, four in Sicily and the others based on these, in other locations: in Sicily itself, Valencia, Barcelona, Rome, Genoa and Lisbon. An analysis of the structure of the Majorca document and also of the bulls that are transcribed in it presents insurmountable difficulties and errors in the system of dating, the indication of the place and other internal elements. Therefore Fr. Saggi concluded rightly that the Majorca document is false and the Sabbatine Bull contained in it cannot be accepted as authentic.

It is very likely that the so-called Sabbatine Bull came into being in Sicily sometime during the 15th century. The text shows some affinity with stories coming from Franciscan circles in which people preached that perseverance in the habit was a pathway to heaven. The Franciscans themselves used to say that Saint Francis went down to Purgatory once a year and set free all those he found wearing the habit. Also the text of the so-called Sabbatine Bull could have been inspired by papal documents confirming the Rule of the Franciscan Third Order: by Nicholas IV dated 17th of August, 1289, and later by Clement V (30th of August, 1309) and Martin V (3rd of May, 1428).

b) The content of the "Sabbatine Privilege"

1. *The content of the "Sabbatine Bull"*

In the so-called Sabbatine Bull, Pope John XXII refers to a vision of the Blessed Virgin that he had before he became Pope: In it he received a promise of help by the Virgin against his adversaries. In exchange for this, once he became Pope, he would have to help the Carmelites by granting them a new approval. In this same vision Our Lady promised, among other things, eternal salvation and liberation from purgatory for every member of the Order and every member of the Confraternity of the Order on the Saturday immediately after their death. For the members of the Confraternity of the Order it would be necessary, to receive and wear every day for the rest of their lives the "sign of the habit" (i.e. the white cloak and not the Scapular), live in chastity in accordance with their state in life, recite the canonical hours, or, if they did not know how to read, fast on the days established by the Church and abstain from meat every Wednesday and every Saturday except on Christmas Day. Freedom from Purgatory would be brought about by the visit of Our Lady to Purgatory in person.

The central meaning of the "Sabbatine Bull" seems to have been aimed at the members of the Confraternity of the Order. The idea was to secure for them that, through their association with the Order, they would share in the privilege of religious life as a pathway to salvation. At the same time the reference to the conditions for obtaining this privilege fit very well into the Carmelite ambience of that time, i.e. the idea of association with the Order of which Mary is Patroness and Most Pure Virgin in order to honour her through a life of chastity, in accordance with each one's state.

We might make some observations in relation to this content:
- It is unusual for a papal document. A Pope never referred, in official acts, to private visions in order to grant indulgences or any other type of favour.
- It is curious to observe that John XXII before he became Pope and during his time as Pope denied, as a theologian, the existence of purgatory and only as his death was approaching (1327) did he accept this doctrine. Therefore the reference to purgatory (if the Bull was written in 1322) is strange from a theologian who denies its existence.
- Besides that, this Pope, just like the Bull, would have been granting this plenary indulgence without revoking the decree of his predecessor Clement V who forbade people from preaching about the liberation of certain souls (for example, one's relations) from purgatory through a plenary indulgence. The contradiction is very clear.
- In the references to the "Sabbatine privilege" we find some expressions that are not exact from the theological point of view (the indication of the Saturday after death and the descent of Our Lady into Purgatory are applications of criteria of space and time to eternity.

2. *The History of the Sabbatine Privilege*

The Bull of John XXII is not authentic and in relation to the Sabbatine privilege there are problems arising from some of the expressions contained in it. Therefore, in order to grasp how we are to understand this Bull and the so-called Sabbatine privilege contained in it, it will be useful to look at the historical facts relating to the confirmation of this privilege by the hierarchy.

The General Chapter of 1517 recognised the need to take steps in order to arrive at the official approval of the Sabbatine bull by the Holy See. The motivation for this position can be found in the fact that the Order was displeased with the absence of a mention of this "bull" among the graces and indulgences recommended by Sixtus IV in Mare magnum (1476 and 1477), a papal document which brought together and reconfirmed all the graces and indulgences granted to the Order.

Marian Legends

In the middle ages a type of literature known as legend, from the Latin word *legenda*, began to be popular. This type of literature offered information about saints and their lives, intended for private reading or for use in the liturgy of Matins.

One particular kind of legend is the "exempla" or the "miracula". As well as being intended for private reading, these were used also by preachers. In this kind of legend we find some historical details alongside fictitious information in short and concise writings. The purpose of this type of literature was always spiritual, with a view to passing on certain values. The understanding of these legends and medieval "exampla" demand a certain deciphering based on the means and the literary forms being used, the symbols etc.

In the Carmelite Order too at this time we find "exempla" and "miracula". We find them in the writings of many authors such as John of Cheminot, Felip Ribot and others, but most of all in the *Collectanea* (Collections) of Baldwin Leersius and in the *De Patronatu* of Arnold Bostius.

The principal examples of this kind of 'exempla" and "miracula" in the Carmelite collections are:

• Elijah, Elisha, and the sons of the prophets who observe virginity (this story or interpretation comes from the time of the patristic writings).

• The origin of Elijah and of Mary, from the one tribe of Aaron (story from patristic literature).

• The dream of Sobac or Sabac, father of the prophet Elijah (a story from patristic literature and from the literature of the medieval ecclesiastical writers).

• The visits of Mary and her virgin companions to Mount Carmel (a story of Hebrew origin).

• The frequent visits of Mary to the religious living on Mount Carmel because of its closeness to Nazareth.

• The founding of a house in Jerusalem, near to the house of Saint Anne, where the Virgin was conceived, beside the Golden Gate.

• The membership of the Order of Saint Cyril of Alexandria and the concession to him by the Council of Ephesus, of the authority to wear the white cloak in honour of Mary.

• Various apparitions of the Blessed Virgin to religious and saints of the Order (St. Simon Stock, St. Peter Thomas, etc.) and to the Popes (Honorious III, John XXII etc.)

•The "miracles" of Toulouse (the conversion of a Jew to whom the Virgin appears and who then becomes a Carmelite) and of Montpellier (where the Carmelites had a house)

• The healing of a young father of a disease of the skin after he had put on the Carmelite habit.

•The appearance of the Virgin protecting the Carmelites with her cloak.

•The appearance of the Virgin to the friars, in choir, to give out gifts (lily, pomegranates, bread)

•The wonders of the Scapular

Many of these "exempla" are identical with or very similar to what other Orders have: for example, a vision of Our Lady who covers the religious men and women of the Order with her mantle is an exact repetition of what Caesarius of Heirsterbach (1223) tells in relation to the Cistercians. Likewise, some of the contents of various visions of Our Lady (listed above) were told by saints from other Orders. Some of the "exempla" however, are peculiar to the world of the Carmelites.

In the deciphering of these legends, it is important to keep some criteria in mind:
- A miraculous or extraordinary happening in the life of the saint or the group as a way of highlighting the presence of God;
- References to the Bible or to the Fathers of the Church are there to help reach a theological interpretation of the life of the saint, situating his mission in the Church and in the history of Salvation.
- Metaphors and symbols used in order to be able to communicate what words alone would not describe.

Among the symbols, which dominate in the literature of the Carmelite "miracula" and "exempla", we find:
- The symbols of house-temple: a meeting place between heaven and earth, the new creation. Applied to Mary they point to intimacy, closeness, familiarity, protection, and the coming of new life. Mary became the archetype of what the Carmelite desires to be.
- Maternity symbols: these express protection, mercy, and tenderness. The theme of Mary who covers her children with her mantle expresses compassion and protection. Mary, the Patroness as a Mother of Mercy reveals the "maternal face of God" to humanity. The theme of Mother-Land applied to Mary appears to be a way of saying that Mary reminds us of our native birth-place (Mount Carmel), who creates a kind of home-sickness for that land and the memory of the Carmelite origins.
- Other Marian symbols: there are various Marian symbols, with references to vegetable, aquatic, sidereal lunar aspects, etc. The "little cloud" which brought the rain is an aquatic symbol of fertility and maternity. The "Flos Carmeli" and the "blossoming vine" are vegetable symbols of fertility, life, regeneration, the beauty of God and harmony. The "star of the sea" is a sidereal symbol, which points to Mary as the point of reference of salvation.

All of these symbols can be examined in an inter-relational fashion among themselves. We can see that the purpose of the "exempla" and the "miracula" is to foster the genuine and authentic meaning of Mary's patronage of the Order, that is, that the origins and the life of the first generations of Carmelites are marked by the presence of Mary, close and familiar (our sister in faith), attentive and caring (Mother of Grace). This is confirmed by the explicit affirmation of Baldwin Leersius who in his *Collectanea* states that Mary the Patroness "nourishes, protects, broadens, exalts, honours and keeps her Order and her brothers every day". Mary the Patroness is the Mother who reveals to Carmelites the face of the mercy and tenderness of God towards humans, which has implications for the life of the Church.

You will find the texts of legends in: *Speculum carmelitanum* (see Leersius, Bostius, etc); A. Staring, *Medieval Carmelite heritage*, Roma, 1989; E. Boaga, *Como pedras vivas* (see pp. 74, 78, 132). See also others in the inserts in this book. For a study of the legends it would be good to consult: E. Carroll, *The Marian Legends of Carmel*, in Marie, no.5 (1952), pp. 13-15; E. Palumbo, *Le leggende mariane di B. Leersio*, in *La dimensione Mariana del Carmelo*, 1, Roma, 1989, pp. 93-97.

In 1527, the Prior General, Nicholas Audet obtained an authentic copy of the "Majorca document" which he presented to the Holy See for the purposes of having the privilege confirmed. On the 15th of May of the following year Clement VII with the letter *Dilecti filii* confirmed the content of the privilege. Within a year this would he superceded by another document *"sub plumbo"* (i.e. the most solemn form of papal document), otherwise the confirmation would become invalid. In the letter however there is no inclusion of the supposed documents of John XXII and Alexander V, but simply of the content: Our Lady, after the death of each member, "in visiting their souls would set them free from the pains of purgatory".

The document "sub plumbo" was issued by Clement VII on the 12th of August 1530 in the bull Ex clementi. The Pope did not reproduce the "sabbatine bull", but he did "renew and confirm" the content of the "privilege" supposedly given by John XXII. The expression "renew and confirm" in the juridical and curial style means a ratification of the content of the "privilege". It is worth noting, in the description of the vision of Our Lady, the Pope adopts a different approach to his previous document: it does not state that Our Lady descends into Purgatory on the Saturday immediately after the death of a member of the Confraternity of the Order, but uses more general expressions indicating that Our Lady would help them after death by her intercession and special protection. In the bull all mention of Saturday is avoided. The bull *Ex clementi* became the basis of subsequent pontifical approvals.

Paul III on the 3rd of November 1534 asked for a transcription of the Clementine bull from 1530 and approved it by another bull Provisionis nostra. Later on, in 1549, the same Pope renewed the privileges, indulgences and graces granted to the Order by Clement VII and other popes.

Pius IV in the bull *Cum nobis* of the 30th of May, 1561 approved for the Carmelites of Portugal everything that had been granted by his predecessors.

At the General Chapter of 1564 a decision was taken to ask for the confirmation of what Mare magnum said about the privileges and of the "Sabbatine bull". Two years later in an official form of the Littera Confraternitatis (the letter the Prior General would write to affiliate a lay person to the Confraternity of the Order) there is a reference to the Saturday after death.

Pius V, in the motu proprio, Superna dispositione of the 18th of February 1566, in confirming the privileges, indulgences and graces for the Church of Traspontina in Rome lists also the "Sabbatine privilege".

The Council of Trent, with some strict regulations re-ordered the discipline relating to indulgences. As a result, Pius V in the decree Etsi dominici of 1567 abrogated all the indulgences for which alms were asked. The Prior General Rossi then asked for a renewal of the approval of all the indulgences granted previously to the Order, taking out the clause about alms. Thus on the 18th of October 1577 Gregory XIII in the letter *Ut laudes* confirmed once again all the previous indulgences, graces and privileges, including the "Sabbatine privilege" in accordance with the tenor of the bull *Ex clementi* of Clement VII. He specified among other things that the help given by Our Lady was "on the Saturday after death, through her continual protection, merciful prayers and merits".

At the end of the 16th century there was protest in Rome against the Sabbatine privilege. The problem was fired by a scandal concerning a prostitute who made statements about being guaranteed salvation even if she did not change her way of life, as long as she was wearing the Scapular. The same happened in the case of a merchant who cheated on the weight of meat sold to a customer and said to those who protested that it was no problem for him because he was wearing the Carmelite Scapular. All of this led in 1603 to the intervention of the noble Baronio and of Cardinal Borghese (afterwards Paul V) the Vicar of Rome.

After a few years the problem was re-ignited in Italy, France and Portugal. On the 16th of August 1603 the Congregation for the Index issued a decree prohibiting the reading of a book that explained the indulgences granted to the Order of Carmel, until such time as corrections were made to it. Besides this book, there was a Summary of the indulgences that included the "Sabbatine bull". In the same year, 1603, the general inquisitor for Portugal, Pedro de Castilha, after consultation with Rome, prohibited that book (and/or Summary) and in 1609 he prohibited all the books that dealt with the Sabbatine privilege, insisting that they be handed over to the inquisitor himself. Some people sent to the inquisitor, not only the book but also their scapular and the letters of affiliation received from the Order. The Provincial of the Carmelites in Portugal then sent a letter to the inquisitor asking for clarification of what was happening. However, the inquisitor in 1610 prohibited also the diffusion of the list of indulgences and preaching about these in sermons. Indeed, this same inquisitor on the 12th of July, 1610 issued a decree to this effect. The negative reaction that this provoked forced him to declare that the edict did not include the Scapular. The problem did not end there.

In the meantime, in 1609, an intervention was made by the doctors of the University of Bologna in favour of the "Sabbatine privilege". On the 29th of June 1609 the Congregation for Sacred Rites gave approval to the reading of the 2nd nocturn of the Feast of Our Lady of Mount Carmel in which there is mention of the liberation from purgatory, as quickly as possible, through her motherly protection, for those who were inscribed as members of the Confraternity of the Order. The readings had been examined by Cardinal Bellarmino.

The Carmelite Order in Portugal sent two priests to Rome: Fr. João de S. Tomé and Fr. Jorge Godinez, to ask the Holy See to intervene in favour of the Scapular and the Sabbatine privilege. Fr. João had recourse to Cardinal Farnese who presented the petition to Pope Paul V. The Pope in turn asked for the judgement of the Congregation for the Holy Inquisition (The Holy Office). In this Congregation the cause in favour of the Carmelites was defended by Cardinal Roberto Bellarmino. This same Cardinal put courage into the Prior General Henrique Silvio with these words: "As long as Cardinal Sfrondati and I are in the commission it will be like as if the two Carmelite Generals are there". The Prior General Silvio had already prescribed that there be prayers throughout the Carmelite Family for the success of the cause.

In addition, in favour of the Carmelites there was the intervention of Phillip III of Spain, who wrote letters to his ambassador in Rome, to Cardinal Mellini, protector of the Order and to the Pope. It would seem that at this time, when the Sabbatine privilege was under discussion, a minister of King Phillip III had a suggestion about forbidding the preaching of the privilege in Spain while the response of the Holy See was being awaited because the practice of abstaining from meat by the wearers of the Scapular every Wednesday and every Friday meant an annual loss of three hundred thousand escudos for the royal coffers. The King responded resolutely "I would rather have subjects who are devoted to the Blessed Virgin that more money in the coffers".

On the 8th of March 1612 Fr. Joao de S. Tomé at a meeting with Cardinal Millini defended the "Sabbatine privilege". He argued in favour of a pontifical approval and the spreading of the devotion world-wide.

At the Congregation of the Holy Inquisition the debate about the "Sabbatine privilege" went on a long time. At a meeting on the 14th of July 1612 there were sharp differences of opinion: the seven cardinals who made up the commission could not reach an agreement. The following day some of the cardinals, among them Sfrondati and Bellarmino, took part in the celebration of the Office of Our Lady of Mount Carmel in the church of Santa Maria della Scala (Rome). Many of them were impressed by the texts of the readings of the Carmelite Office that made allusion to the intercession of Our Lady for the sake of the members of the Confraternity who were in purgatory. That was the solution! They called Fr. João de S. Tomé and they indicated to him that they accepted that solution, but he rejected it because there was no allusion in it to Saturday. On the 5th of September at a general meeting of the Cardinals and the consultors of the inquisition, mainly due to the influence of Cardinal Bellarmino, there was a final and conclusive vote in favour of the Carmelites. Fr. Joao de S. Tomé, in very happy mood, brought the news to the Prior General Silvio who at that time was seriously ill in bed. He died the following week on the 12th of September, 1612.

Finally the Congregation for the Inquisition issued a decree dated the 20th of January 1613, but published on the 11th of February of the same year.

The decree contained the following dispositions:

- the Carmelites would be allowed to preach that the Christian faithful could believe devoutly in the help given to the souls of the members of the Confraternity of the Carmelite Order once they observed the conditions laid down in the privilege, and that Our Lady would free them from Purgatory through her intercession and special protection as soon as possible and especially on the Saturday after death, the day dedicated to the Blessed Virgin by the Church.
- Artistic representations (pictures, paintings, holy cards) should not represent Our Lady descending into Purgatory to set the souls free, or at least not in the midst of the flames. It should be the angels that would take the souls out and lead them to heaven through the intercession of Mary.

Some specific instructions for the Superiors of the Order were added to this decree:

- it was absolutely forbidden to preach or write that the Virgin Mary descended into Purgatory or that the souls would be set free from that same place of purification on Saturday or on any other specific day, on the basis of the bull of John XXII. Therefore the term "Sabbatine bull" and the reference to it were outlawed in preaching as a support and explanation of the privilege. As a consequence the "Sabbatine bull" should have been forgotten.
- It was allowed to say that the Confraternity was greatly favoured by the Popes and that, by the indulgences granted, whatever punishment remained unsatisfied after death in the state of grace would be greatly reduced.
- Given that the Confraternity is desired by Our Lady, and that Saturday is a day of special devotion to her, it was to remain clear that it could be said that the members of that Confraternity would be especially helped and favoured on Saturdays. This would still depend on their living in accordance with the conditions laid down and it would come about "not by means of an indulgence" but rather through the intercession of Our Lady.

As soon as this decree was given to the Order, it was read to the Carmelites gathered in prayer in the choir of the Church of Traspontina (the location of the General Curia), where they gave thanks to God and praise to Our Lady for such a great favour. Fr. João de S. Tomé returned to Portugal. At his arrival on the 23rd of April 1613 he was greeted by the ringing of the bell of the Carmelite church in Lisbon.

In 1648 the parish priests of Rouen (France) asked the University of Paris to intervene to counteract the indulgence of the "Sabbatine privilege", but the eight professors to whom the case was referred decided in favour of the Carmelites. They decided that they could set up a Confraternity and preach the Sabbatine privilege as long as they observed what was laid down by the Holy Office in 1613.

The same decree of 1613 was reconfirmed on various occasions throughout the 17th century and it was included in the Summary of indulgences, edited in 1678 under Pope Innocent XI. Benedict XIV referred to it as a "very wise decree". Finally this decree was faithfully reformulated during the pontificate of Pius X in the Summary of Indulgences of the 5th of July 1908 and in the decree of the Holy Office of the 16th of December 1910.

Pius XII in his apostolic letter Neminem profecto latet of the 11th of February 1950 wrote: "Certainly, this most holy mother, in line with the tradition called the Sabbatine Privilege through her own intercession with God will surely obtain in the shortest time possible, the heavenly homeland for her children who are expiating their sins in purgatory".

In conclusion, it is clear in the thinking of the Pontifical Magisterium and in all that we have been saying that a proper presentation of the Scapular and the privileges attached to it and the content of these has to be based on a good theology of Mary's role in the mystery of Christ and of the Church. Indeed the power of Mary to help those who wear the Scapular is in substance, from the theological point of view, the application of the doctrine of her spiritual motherhood and her role as mediatrix of graces, properly understood. Mary acts in us but we have to be willing to accept what she does and respond fully by coming to Christ, offered to us by Mary. The Scapular devotion then should be understood as a consecration, or, more precisely, an entrusting of oneself to Mary by means of the Carmelite habit and the observance of its conditions. It thus becomes an effective form and means for fostering fidelity to Christ and to a full acceptance of him in our lives, following the example of Mary.

Names given to Mary

With the passage of time the Carmelites thought up tender expressions with which to speak about and to Mary. Here follows a list, somewhat incomplete, of titles found in writings, songs and poetry from various periods and which make specific reference to the Order. The titles which are common to the whole Church have been left out, those such as Star of the Sea, Splendour of Heaven etc.

- The Lady of the Place
- Mistress of the Order
- Abbess of Carmel
- The Lady and the Creator of the Order
- Foundress of the Order
- Virgin Most Pure
- Princess of the Family of Elijah
- Queen of Carmel
- Guardian of Carmel
- Standard-bearer of the Army of Carmel
- Virgin Most Pure
- Mother of Carmel
- Hope of Carmel
- Virgin Flower of Carmel
- Divine Testament
- Merciful Mother of Carmelites
- Most Serene Princess of Carmelites
- Sweet Virgin Mary
- Star and Cedar of Carmel
- Mother of the Carmelite Family
- Prioress of the Order
- Mother of the Order
- The Lawgiver of the Order
- Patroness of the Order
- First Born Sister
- Head of Carmel
- Helper of Carmelites
- Sovereign Queen of Carmel
- Mother and Ornament of Carmel
- Fruitful Virgin of Carmel
- Flower of Carmel
- Sweet and Divine Melody
- Blossoming Vine
- Queen and Mother of Carmelites
- Mother of Mercy
- The Most Beautiful Star of Heaven
- The Cloud of Carmel.

The Salve Regina

From very early on, throughout the Order, we find the custom of singing the "Salve Regina" to honour Our Lady and express love for her. A decision was made by the General Chapter of Barcelona in 1324 that this antiphon would be sung at the end of every one of the Canonical Hours of the Liturgy and perhaps also at the end of Mass. This applied to the entire year. The practice of singing the "Regina Coeli" in the Easter season, was introduced only in 1585.

The "Salve Regina" was sung also in Church, as the grace after meals, except on those days when this prayer of thanksgiving was said in the refectory.

When the Divine Office ceased to be sung the singing of the Salve Regina was also abandoned. Meanwhile in the reforms of the Order in the 16th and 17th century, the friars decided to take up again the use of the antiphon. The Prior General, Nicholas Audet, decided that all the religious, without exception, should take part in the devout singing of the "Salva Regina" at the end of Compline, every Saturday, wearing the white cloak, standing before the altar of the Blessed Virgin Mary. The Prior General Rossi not alone adopted the custom but indeed gave it more weight by providing a solemn ritual for the procession and singing.

In the documents of provincial chapters in the 17th and 18th centuries and in the acts of visitations of Priors General and of Provincials we find evidence of how the solemn singing on Saturdays was recommended.

In the ceremonial of 1616 and again after 1744, there is a reminder of the practice of placing an ornate candle stick at the centre of the choir holding a large lighted candle, as a reminder of the presence of the Mother of God, as if she was visiting her brother religious. Cantors solemnly intoned, to the accompaniment of the organ, this salutation to Mary, bowing deeply to her image at the beginning and at the name of Jesus. This practice was very widespread in Portugal, which in 1658 added that each friar was to hold a lighted candle. From Portugal this custom moved to Brazil.

A charming tradition in 1488 in the priory in Bologna relates that when the friars intoned the hymn, Our Lady appeared in the choir in the midst of the community.

Cf. Hoppenbrouwers, *Devotio Mariana*, pp. 100-101, 106-108, 136-137, 147-149.

Pages from the Anthology

1. HOW TO PREACH ABOUT THE SCAPULAR

Text by Matias de St. Jean, *La veritable devotion du sacre Scapulaire de notre-Dame du Mont Carmel, True devotion of the Holy Scapular of Our Lady of Mount Carmel,* Paris, 1656; also in *Speculum carmelitanum,* I nn. 2236-2243.

First of all we need to pay attention to the fact that Carmel by a singular act of God's providence was chosen to give devotion and veneration to the Mother of God. The Scapular, whose origin is in the Order of Carmel, is the means that the authority of the Church has approved to suitably honour the same Holy Mother of God ….

Besides the seven sacraments of the Church, which signify and convey grace ("ex opere operato") as the theologians say, there are other signs and helps for salvation that are not sacraments but are related to them in a lesser order. It is in this that the Scapular is said to be and truly is a sign of salvation. There are authors who refer to the Scapular as the "sacrament of the Blessed Virgin, Mother of God". In the Sacred Scripture as well, the word sacrament is used to describe something given by God to signify a mystery for the purpose of teaching people. In the first chapter of the Book of Revelation there is a reference to the sacrament of the mystery of the seven stars (Rv 1,20). Therefore, the Scapular, given by the Blessed Virgin, is a visible sign of the spiritual realities, which stimulate the practice of virtue and devotion. Likewise, it is also a stimulus for the sanctification of the soul, having been approved for this purpose by the authority of the Church. In the blessing of the Scapular (the little habit) it says, "God, Lord of all the faithful, let your powerful hand sanctify this habit and all that it stands for so that it may become a reality….etc." Nevertheless, we need to be somewhat prudent in using this term and to avoid using it in order not to lead simple people into error in the way they understand it, by treating it as if it were a sacrament and behaving as if it were so.

The Scapular is also a sign of a special kind of slavery to the Blessed Virgin, Our Lady of the World. Thus in the clothing ceremony when the Scapular is being put on, it says, "Receive the yoke of Christ, whose burden is light and whose yoke is easy". It also exhorts every member to wear the Scapular as the "light and gentle yoke of Mary" on whom we are to fix our gaze as if she were our own Lady.

The Scapular is the stamp that the Blessed Virgin puts on the heart of everyone, for them to bear it always, and to help them in such a way that with heart and mouth, they may pronounce the name of Mary, honouring her, after God, with all their actions. Those who wear the Scapular possess that mark through which the Blessed Mother of God recognizes them as her children.

The Scapular is a memorial of the Blessed Virgin that helps to frequently lift the heart up to her with holy aspirations. As we explained earlier, the Scapular is an invitation to live in the presence of God: it is at the same time a reminder of the presence of Mary for those who are familiar with her and turn to her in what they are doing and in time of temptation.

The Scapular is also a sign of covenant and of an eternal pact between Mary and those who wear it. It is a sign of love and of protection in time of danger. Here it would be useful to recommend the use of this short prayer in moments of danger and temptation: Holy Mary, Our Lady, turn your eyes toward me and have mercy. Give your strength to your servant and save the child of your servant. Give me a sign of your favour! Let my enemies see it and be confused because you, My Lady, help me and console me" (From Ps 85,16-17)

The Scapular is also a sign of her confraternity, a sign also for those who wear it that they are the adopted children of the Blessed Virgin ... As Christ says to everyone, "those who do the will of my Father are my brothers and sisters and mother". So it must be said of anyone who wears the Scapular (not just physically but morally as well) in order to be a better son or daughter of the Virgin Mother and be able to say to her with great confidence, "Show me that you are my Mother" etc. In order to say that with the fullest confidence, we would have to observe what St. Bonaventure says, "Try to imitate the Mother of God, as much as you can in everything, like a good and devoted child, so that she may recognize you and help you". Truly the Scapular is a sign of the obligation to be clothed in the virtue of the Mother of God by imitating her. St. Bonaventure again exhorts us, "Be clothed in Mary, you who love her, and let her shine out in all your actions and be the light of all that you do", that is, through the imitation of her virtues. That is the kind of devotion that is dearest to her and through which you can obtain many maternal favours ....

From all that has been said up to this it may be concluded that the Scapular strongly and gently leads the people who wear it into allegiance to the Virgin Mary. The Scapular's function in unifying is indicated by the two parts of which it is made up as they are placed over the person's shoulders: the Virgin herself seems to say to the wearer of the Scapular, With these bonds of goodness I draw you to me, with bonds of love (Hos 11,4). She leads them to salvation, obtaining for them the help of grace by which they can come to salvation. Equally, from their part, the wearers of the Scapular offer her their allegiance, because love is two-sided.

Finally, the Scapular is a means of more speedy liberation from purgatory; it is a protection in dangers; it is a defence against the insinuations of the devil; and besides all that, through Mary, other benefits come about as well.

2. EXHORTATIONS IN FAVOUR OF A WORTHY LIFE, AT THE RECEPTION OF THE SCAPULAR

Giovanni Taddeo di S. Giovanni Battista († 1743) *Meditazioni per la mattina e sera di ciascun giorno della settimana, Morning and Evening meditations for every day of the week ....* Milan 1732, pp. 343 ss.

The priest says, as he gives the Scapular, Receive this habit that has been blessed, you who are devoted to Mary; let us pray to the Blessed Virgin, that with her help, you may wear it without fault, that it may defend you from every adversity and lead you to eternal life ...."

In the first place, the intention of the prayer is to obtain, through the intercession of the Queen of Carmel, that the wearers will be enabled to wear the Scapular without any stain on their souls. Purity of soul is the first thing to which you must devote your attention, with the same desire that Mary had. This habit has been given by the Blessed Virgin; therefore it will be good to preserve it free from what most displeases her, the offences committed against her Divine Son, the stains that soil the beauty and cleanliness of the livery of our most merciful Lady.

On this point you have to pay great attention the more you desire that these prayers should be heard: that you be preserved from every adversity and that you be led to eternal life, *"Et te ab omni adversitate custodiat et ad vitam perducat aeternam"*. Know the importance of these prayers: but if you do not keep your soul free from stain, then you put yourself outside Mary's motherly protection. Can you imagine how many spiritual and corporal deviations we risk in this valley of tears? The dangers to the body are continuous, and continuous also the deceit played by the infernal enemies, for the destruction of souls. Do you look for the protection of the Queen of Heaven? Wear her garment with such devotion that by its cleanliness and purity it may be recognized as the garment given by the Mother of God. Preserve your soul with that purity which is right for a child adopted by the immaculate Generatrix: and may the demons, finding you clothed in this noble livery fly far away from you.

The Scapular will distinguish you on the outside as one who is devoted to the Blessed Virgin but it is your purity of conscience that makes you truly devoted.

The Scapular reminds you to put the adoption you have received into effect. Your works will declare you to be a child of the Queen of Carmel and a member of her family.

When you join the corresponding virtues and habits with the wearing of the heavenly garment, when you accompany your being an adopted child of Mary with works that are in conformity with that, you can keep the hope that the Scapular will lead you to the enjoyment of eternal life. *"Et ad vitam perducat aeternam"*. Without this accompaniment, hope will degenerate into presumption and the habit will only increase your confusion.

3. A DEVOTIONAL VIEW OF THE SCAPULAR

The Lives of the Saints of Carmel, compiled by Thomas Jansen, Kevelaer, 1930, pp. 149-150.

As a devotion verified by the evidence of miracles, full of promises that on their own are enough to arouse the love of Catholics, and, what is even more important, shown by our Most Holy Mother to one of her most faithful Carmelites, this devotion deserves to receive our particular affection and to be fervently embraced by us. At a time when we are the victims of attacks of all kind, evil and voracious, we have the assurance that it is enough to wear the Scapular devoutly to be saved from eternal fire – it is a treasure that would be mad to neglect.

In the present tumultuous and deafening world, in which even the greatest of surprises, the great surprise of death, is not uncommon, the knowledge that the wearing of the Scapular assures our liberation from purgatory, on the Saturday after death occurs, is a grace of such measure that to ignore or forget it would be folly indeed.

But we do not believe that it is enough simply to wear the Scapular to obtain this great favour. We have, first of all, to fulfill the conditions with which it is given, to honour the Scapular by a holy life, especially in relation to chastity, and observe the other instructions that accompany the reception of the Scapular. These instructions include the observance of chastity and the recitation of the office of Our Lady of Mount Carmel, who grants these favours abundantly.

We, Carmelite Tertiaries, have an extra obligation in this regard. The great favour that has been bestowed on us, in the happiness we possess in wearing the glorious habit of Carmel, makes debtors of us. For this great pledge we have to be rescued from whatever would stand in the way of our reaching complete fidelity to the Scapular devotion.

By cultivating it, we can extend its benefits also to those with whom we live in this valley of tears, drawing them to us, with the prospect of that great treasure which our caring Mother of Carmel has granted us.

And so we will achieve all that our most holy Mother desires, that is, to lead our souls, filled with the greatest joy, to the Holy Mountain of Carmel, allowing us to share her own happiness.

4. THE RYTHMIC PRAYING OF THE FLOS CARMELI

Enrique Esteve O.Carm. (1905-1990) *The Scapular Devotion and the Universal Mediation of Mary*, in *Lo Scapolare*, n.2(1950), pp.77-80.

The rhythmic praying of the *Flos Carmeli* produces a deep and delicate love for the Blessed Virgin. Even before that, however, it offers us, with its two lines of verses with alternating consonants (a,b,a,b, c-d, e,d,e,c) the perfect and distinctive idea that, as the Carmelite Directory says, lies at the base of that deep and delicate love or devotion; this is no different to the idea that comes from the ancient and popular Marian hymn *Ave maris stella* with which the *Flos Carmeli* seems to have several points of contact.

Thus in the first verse we see Mary as she is in herself, in four distinct and interrelated titles: Flower of Carmel, Blossom laden vine, Splendour of Heaven, Singular Virgin and Mother. The last of these, Virgin Mother, which recalls the *enixa puerpera* of Sedulius, or even more, the *Virgo concipiet et pariet* of Isaiah (7,14) points to the central concept: fruitful virginity, supernatural and divine, by which Mary establishes, on her own, as the Virgin Mother of God, an order of transcendent singularity which belongs to her, the one who is singular as the text specifically says. It is in the light of this that we have to explain all the other titles, because everything in Mary has to be understood in terms of her divine maternity, which is the whole reason for her existence and meaning.

There is good reason therefore why she should first be invoked as the Flower of Carmel because by reason of her perfect transcendent virginity or immaculate virginal purity, Mary possesses all the fragrant spiritual beauty that Carmel symbolically represents. Isaiah, in fact, referring to the virgin of Israel, Yahweh's spouse in messianic times, said: she will flourish ..: she will be given the beauty of Carmel (Is 35,2), in the same way that in the Song of Songs we find (7,5) in a parallel text it says: your head, like Carmel. This was verified, in perfect fashion, only in the ever-virgin Mary, to whom, quite rightly, these passages were applied by our writers from John Baconthorpe down to Arnold Bostius.

In the second verse, Blossom laden vine, there is a declaration of the grace of divine fruitfulness, on account of the fact that precisely because of her perpetual virginity, Mary, as the all beautiful and stainless woman, merited to conceive God, who could be born of her only in a way that is divine, in the same way that only the Virgin could conceive God, as we read in the traditional thinking of the Holy Fathers: *Egredietur virga de radice Jesse et flos de radice eius ascendet* (Is 11,1)

The third verse, finally, Splendour of Heaven, sings of the consequent incomprehensible greatness of fruitful virginity, which, rising to the summit of all creation, appears, wrapped in the heavenly glory of the Divinity, in accordance with the hypostatic order of the Son of

God incarnate. Therefore in a literally eminent sense, to the Virgin, as an organic type of the Church, we apply the celebrated apocalyptic text, imaged in the ancient shield of the Order: "A great portent appeared in heaven: a woman clothed with the sun, with the moon under her feet, and on her head a crown of twelve stars. She was pregnant ……"

This is the image, so clear and so dense, of the Virgin in the Flos Carmeli, that recalls the description of divine Wisdom in the Book of Ecclesiasticus (Sir 24). In medieval exegesis, as we can see in the famous notes of Ugo di St Caro (+1263), a contemporary of Simon Stock, this description is commonly applied to the Blessed Virgin in a secondary, analogical way on account of her association with the Incarnate Word, source of all purity and beauty, source of life and light: "I have grown tall as a palm of Engedi, as the rose bushes of Jericho, ….as a fine olive, etc. "(Sir 24,18-23; 6 in the Vulgate).

We can say, however, that the first verse is only an introduction to the prayer insofar as it is there to lift the mind to the very person of the Virgin, by invoking her holy name, as the final object of all Marian veneration, based always on her dignity and singular excellence.

It is in the second verse, rather, that we can find the principal part of the prayer as such: that is the supplication which indicates what the Virgin means to us, in particular for Carmelites. In this sense, the high point, without any doubt, is to be found at the end of the prayer: "To Carmelites, grant your favour": This request is obviously very short, but in its brevity it offers a very clear vision and expresses a very deep faith in the central role that Mary has in the plan of salvation through her universal mediation.

I believe that we can get the general idea if we bear in mind the context that immediately precedes and immediately follows, even though, to see more of the detail, we would have to look not only at the terms themselves, but even more, at the historical situation which lies behind the story of the prayer.

The invocations that precede, "Mother so tender, whom no man did know" is really just a repetition of the verses: "Child-bearing yet maiden, none equals thee." This is in inverse order, like a chiasm, a rhetorical form that was very popular among ecclesiastical authors, to highlight as much as possible the two concepts of maternity and virginity, apparently contradictory in an abstract sense, but not in a superior transcendent order, providing in this combination all that was special about Mary.

The adjective "tender" would seem to suggest the general aspect of salvation and mediation, under which the Blessed Virgin is being thought of here. If it is true that the maternity we are looking at is the divine maternity, by a parallelism, it is no less certain that the grace of divine maternity has a soteriological significance, insofar as it is dictated exclusively by "mercy", as Richard of St. Victor and St. Anselm believe. Hence the divine maternity, would be seen as the root of Mary's mediation, in a way that is analogous to what we find in the *Ave maris stella* where it says, "Show us that you are our mother". That is like referring to Mary in relation to Jesus as Theotokos, referring to the power which was there before the Son.

What in the beginning is merely mentioned, in the end is developed fully in the popular invocation of the Middle Ages in reference to the Blessed Virgin: "Star of the Sea". The popularity of this image is due to the fact that it was thought by St. Jerome to be the etymology of the name Mary (even though it would seem that the Doctor Maximus did not say star (stella) but drop from the ocean (stilla). Today, however, the philologists attribute to the Hebrew word Miryam the meaning of 'heavenly" (excelsa). What is even more important is the real meaning of the title in the thinking of the ancients, gathered faithfully by St. Albert the Great: "Maria –

he says – is called Morning Star because with her virtue she dispelled the cloud of sadness which enveloped the faithful who were longing for the coming of Christ ... She is called also Star of the Sea, because the sailors always look to the so-called star of the sea to find their way back to port, and it is the same for us who try to make our way through this world. Mary shows the way that leads to the port of heaven" (Sermon for the Nativity of the BVM § 2)

In accordance with this, the general direction is the quest for salvation, with liberation from all obstacles. What else could be expected from the Blessed Virgin since, as Irenaeus of St. James notes, "every gift of the Blessed Virgin, as well as those of her beloved Son, tend spontaneously to work for the eternal salvation of humanity".

A more direct exegesis of the text confirms, and makes more clear, this conclusion, if we follow the "da privilegia" reading, (...) The "privileges" in fact that we are talking about here, in literary agreement with "viri nescia" are in reality nothing other that the heavenly confirmation by the Blessed Virgin, as Patron, of the title of the Order, as a Marian Order, recognizing it and thus laying claim to the spiritual value of the title, in other words, the Order as consecrated to her service. Such is the case even though it is in the nature of things that every service given to the Blessed Virgin is pleasing to her and good for salvation, what the Carmelites offer is particularly so.

That is the meaning of the word "privilege" (...) The word "privilege" in fact, or also "benevalete" in late and middle Latin, as can be seen from the Glossary of Du Cange, is nothing other than the declaration by a prince or pontiff of the concession made whereby a church may enjoy official recognition or pontifical status.

That means we can understand perfectly the sense of the promise, as an expression of the value of the veneration that Carmel gives to the Blessed Virgin, whose followers cannot perish, since She is the Mediatrix of all graces.

In relation to this, the comment by Tobia Götz, the German Carmelite from around the year 1600, seems to be exact, when he identifies the link between the double complement, direct and indirect, in the proposition, "To all Carmelites, give privileges", in the following way: "Because to the members of the Sacred Order of Carmel, especially devoted to the Virgin Mother of God and dedicated to her allegiance and service, what we read in the Prophet can rightfully be applied: *To her will be given the glory of Lebanon, the beauty of Carmel and of Sharon*, since the Blessed Virgin is the principal splendour, honour and beauty of the Carmelite Family. With even more reason we are given to repeat what was said of Judith, the figure of the Virgin: *You glory of Jerusalem, you joy of Israel, you the honour of our people.* May we be allowed to say: we glory in having you as mother and carer; you show mercy to your children; to you we come, asking for your help and as you adorned us with royal generosity of the singular grace of making us your children, when you were on the earth, grant that we may enjoy in heaven the inheritance of our being your children, which, through your intercession, may the fruit of your womb, Jesus, Our Lord, kindly grant us ..." (Ms. 458 A., Flos Carmeli, f.59, in the Gen. Archive, O.Carm.)

5. THE PALM-TREE AND THE QUEEN OF CARMEL

João de Sylberia O.Carm. (1592-1667), *Apologia carmelitana*, 2 ed., Lugduni, 1687, p. 485.

It is interesting to note in the Song of Songs the link that the author makes between the two metaphors alluding to the Spouse. After exclaiming, "Her head is like Mount Carmel" he adds, "Her noble stature is like a palm tree" (Sg 7,5-6)

The reason for this analogy between the Blessed Virgin and the palm tree can be seen in the following four characteristics of the palm tree:

1. The palm tree, as St. Jerome notes, is taller than any other tree, plant or flower.
2. The palm tree produces a fruit that is as soft and sweet as honey.
3. The palm tree provides material for clothing
4. The palm is used as a symbol of long duration, of a certain incorruptibility and because its branches are in the form of rays, it recalls the splendour with which the victor vanquishes the vanquished. With branches of palm trees and olives, Christ was welcomed by the children of the Hebrews on his way into Jerusalem, celebrating in this way his triumph over the prince of darkness, according to the interpretation given by St. Isidore.

All of these characteristics of the palm tree, by an admirable analogy speak of the Queen of Carmel.

Firstly, it is said that the Queen of Carmel is like a palm tree, because of her height and sublimity, standing above all the other trees, plants and flowers in the same way the title of the Queen of Carmel stands above every other invocation and title such as Our Lady of Peace, Our Lady of Victories, Our Lady of Holy Hope, etc.

Secondly, the Queen of Carmel is like the palm tree because she leads us to and prepares heavenly food for us.

Thirdly, the Queen of Carmel is like the palm tree because she provides heavenly clothing for us in the form of the Scapular that guards and protects us. The rays that shine so strongly from above neither strike nor injure the palm tree: it is the same with the garment with which the Queen of Carmel keeps us safe from fire. Moses witnessed a great vision: the bush that was in flames but was not consumed. How could the bush be in flames and not be consumed? How was it not damaged in any way by the flames? The bush too symbolizes the Blessed Virgin Mary who gave birth to the eternal Word, Light from light, without any damage either to her body or to her virginal state. Because it was a small sign of Mary, the bush took on the power to resist the flames of fire. That is more or less what St. Germanus of Constantinople said: "it was not on account of its own power that the bush, devoured by the gentle flames, was not burned, but because of Mary who bore the fire of Divinity in her nature that was mortal, subject to corruptibility". St. John Damascene says similarly: "the burning bush remained unharmed because it was a sign of Mary", Now, if being a sign of Mary, the bush was preserved from being destroyed by the fire, we could conclude that by giving the heavenly garment with her own hands (the Scapular) her adopted children will be saved from the fire. This reasoning is strengthened even more if we recognize that in the Scapular there is a portrayal of the Virgin as St. Jerome says, "The Holy Virgin is a very pure wool". In this sense we might read in Psalm 71,6 "He will descend like water upon the grass". The Blessed Virgin is like very pure wool that absorbs the dew of the Divine Word. Just like her, the sacred Scapular, made of wool, in its original colour, without any mixture, made fruitful by the heavenly dew of the Virgin Mary, works many wonderful signs.

Fourthly and finally, as a symbol of victory the palm tree is analogous to the Queen of Carmel, because it is principally through her intercession that victory is won.

For further study and reflection

1. Bibliography

- B. Xiberta, *De visione sancti Simonis Stock*, Roma, 1950
- H. Esteve, *De valore spirituali devotionis S. Scapularis*, Rome, 1953.
- L. Saggi, *Simone Stock, santo*, in Santi del Carmelo, Roma, 1972, pp. 320-323
- Id , *Santa Maria del Monte Carmelo*, pp. 40-44
- Id. , *La "bolla sabatina". Ambiente, Testo, Tempo*, Roma, 1967
- Id., *Lo Scapulare del Carmine oggi*, in Rivista di Vita Spirituale, 28(1974), pp.557-569.- M. Reuver, *Lo Scapolare oggi*, in *Carmelus*, 15(1968), pp. 222-229
- *"Mary, model of Christian life"*, Carmelite Marian Commission, Interim Report, Rome, 1985.
- R.M. Valabek, *A New Vision of the Scapular*. International Marian Congress, Rome, 1986.

II. For personal or group study

1. Read the basic text, picking out its essential aspects.

2. What values contribute to the emergence of the image of Mary as Our Lady of the Scapular?

3. Check in the "Pages from the Anthology" the ways in which people preached about the Scapular in the past and compare that with the texts of the Popes (see "Pages from the Anthology" in Chapter 8)

4. Look into the biblical sources for the *Flos Carmeli*, (see the insert)

III. Prayer and Life:

1. Pray with the Word of God:
    Is 61,10-11,
    Apoc 1,19; 12,1.
    Eph 6,10-18.
    Jn 15,1-8.

2. At the end of this study, how would you explain to a knowledgeable person and also to a person without education the vision of Saint Simon Stock? Also the so-called Sabatine Privilege?

3. Read the Pages from the Anthology and check how the recent Popes refer to Our Lady of Mount Carmel and to devotion to her.

4. What proposal would you make to help people get a better grasp of the Scapular? Would it not be good to experiment, share, and collaborate with others in this regard?

6

IN FRATERNITY

O Mary, Queen and Mother of Carmel
Let my whole life be an expression of homage to you
For the graces that God gives me
Through your kindly hands.
    Your eyes gaze, with so much gentleness,
on all those who wear the Scapular:
I pray with confidence,
let your strength support my weakness
your wisdom enlighten the darkness of my mind.
    Increase in me always
    Faith, hope and charity.
Let your scapular give me strength against sin
And remind me every day of the most important things I have to do:
Think of you,
Clothe myself with your virtues,
    Be united with your spirit
    And offer everything to Jesus
Through you
Divine mediator.
And then one day, I will most certainly be granted
    To exchange my Scapular for the nuptial garments of eternity
    And I will live with you and with my brothers and sisters from Carmel
    in the kingdom of your son.

    (An act of consecration to Mary, on the 7th Centenary
    of the Scapular, with some modifications.)

6 IN FRATERNITY

The Carmelite Confraternities

1. Preface

This topic is rather complex. In order to get a proper understanding of it we need to distinguish between the various kinds of confraternities which in the past were organised in the houses of the Order. Some of these bore a Carmelite Marian title but their origins, evolution and aims came from elsewhere. The various kinds of confraternities linked with the Order of Carmel throughout the years are:
  a) confraternities of the "Laudesi" and "Battuti" type, existing in the 13th and 14th centuries in close proximity to a Carmelite church.
  b) Confraternities, with the "sign of the Order", found close to Carmelite churches between the 13th and 17th centuries.
  c) Confraternities with a Marian title, set up to venerate Mary in the Carmelite churches between the 16th and 18th centuries.
  d) Carmelite confraternities or confraternities of the Scapular, or of Our Blessed Lady of Mount Carmel, more recent than the other three, and found also in churches not belonging to the Order.

Before beginning an examination of each type of confraternity it will be necessary to clarify some terms and concepts in order to avoid misleading interpretations:
- The phenomenon of the association of lay people with the Order exists since the middle of the 13th century. This type of association consisted in a sharing in the spiritual benefits of the whole Order and, also, it was offered by the Order as an expression of gratitude and recognition to benefactors. The form of association with the Order was the *Littera affiliationis* or *Littera fraternitatis* (a letter of association or of fraternity). Besides that, in the question of association, there was also another form, namely, the idea of self-oblation as a desire to be "converted to God", and to live in fraternal communion with the religious. There were also forms of oblation for financial reasons. The whole collection of associates (benefactors, oblates, members of the confraternity, wearers of the scapular etc.) constituted a very varied group, not just from the juridical point of view but also in terms of the level of the spiritual bond and commitment.
- The "signum Ordinis" (sign of the order) in the middle ages was the white cloak which was given to the lay people at the moment of their association. Sometimes people would refer to the "habit of the Order" but not in the proper sense: this generally can be found in the writings of the 16th and 17th centuries referring to previous ages.
- The Scapular, in the medieval period, was considered to be the habit of the Order and therefore worn only by the religious. A norm, up to the end of the 15th century, forbade the giving of the scapular to lay people: for a lay person to wear the habit of an order, as in the case of the Scapular, would have meant changing from the lay state to the religious state with all that meant in terms of solemn profession (which, for example, would have implications for marriage and for property). In order to avoid this situation, the association of lay people did not include the giving of the habit; rather, the new members would be given the sign of the Order (the white cloak). In this same period, it was

permitted for lay associates to be buried in the habit of the Order, the Scapular, because after death Canon Law had no longer any power to bind. We have many examples to support this affirmation in our Order in the 15th century.
- The origin of the vision of Simon Stock is linked at the beginning (the 14th and 15th centuries) to a message given exclusively to the friars: afterwards, in the 15th century, its meaning was extended also to lay people. For reference to the vision and the sabbatine privilege, see the previous chapter.

2. Medieval confraternities in Carmelite Churches

In the churches of the Carmelites during the middle ages there were very many confraternities of the "Laudesi" kind: in Florence (1280), Lucca (1254), Siena (1289) and Bologna (1344); there were also confraternities which fitted into the category of "Flagellantes" or "Battuti"; in Modena (1325) and in Prato (1350), all in Italy. (Cf. Come pietre vive, p.149)

The members of the first type of these confraternities, called the "Laudesi", held their meetings in their respective Churches, generally in the evening, singing hymns in honour of Our Lady followed by psalms and popular canticles; frequently they would have a Marian procession.

The members of the second type of confraternity, called the penitents (Flagellantes and Battuti) held their meetings in the open space in front of the Church and, in the presence of a priest, they would practise the discipline, or corporal penances.

The only bond that these confraternities had with the Order lay in the fact that they used the churches that belonged to the Order and their open spaces for their meetings and activities. They are not confraternities that are affiliated to the Order and have nothing to do with the Marian devotion of the Order as such.

3. The confraternities "of the sign of the Order"

In the Middle Ages those affiliated to the Order were referred to as brothers and sisters and they were organised in groups. There were groupings of varying numbers of people with different kinds of commitment: affiliates or associates (benefactors, converted people, wearers of the white cloak, family members etc.)

Before long the members would meet in their chosen type of confraternity (fraternitas) with the idea of sharing in the spiritual benefits and the suffrages of the Order itself. An example of this type of confraternity is the one which grew up close to the house in Valls (Spain) twenty years after this house was opened. In 1340 a share "in the Masses, prayers, vigils, preaching, confessions, fasting, abstinence and works of the religious was granted by the provincial chapter". The deceased members were remembered in the provincial chapter, in the same way as the religious themselves.

In these confraternities there were people who came from different backgrounds: women and men, single and married. In a short time, these confraternities received a shorter Rule of life and they used some external identification as a sign of their belonging; it was the white cloak of the Order, received in a ceremony. Many of these members wore this cloak on a regular basis. This gave rise to their being called "cloak wearers".

This collection of associations formed the confraternities of "the sign of the Order", called also sometimes the "confraternities of the habit"; there may be some confusion between the "religious habit" (i.e. the Scapular) and the sign of this habit which was the cloak.

In the documents of the time, it is not always easy to understand the juridical standing of this type of association or group. At that time, in the Carmelite Order, the emphasis was more on the life that people led rather than on the juridical standing of any of these.

Carmelite Confraternities around the World.

Up to the present time we do not know the exact number of Carmelite or Scapular confraternities which presently exist or which have existed throughout the years. According to the information available in the General Archives of the Carmelite Order, we have a set of statistics that give us the number of confraternities erected by the Priors General between the year 1850 and the year 1950, in 62 different nations. However for the same period we do not know the number of confraternities that bishops or Priors Provincial erected.

Confraternities between 1850 and 1950:
North America: 598.
Central America: 123.
South America: 288.
Europe: 4.952.
Africa: 30.
Asia: 99.
Oceania: 26.
Total: 6.116

The confraternities erected by the Priors General from 1850 to 1950 in terms of the nations to which they belonged:

Italy: 2649.
Spain: 1.077.
United States of America: 521.
France: 414.
Switzerland: 190.
Brazil: 160.
Portugal: 139.
Poland: 135.
Germany: 101.
Lithuania: 78.
Yugoslavia: 74.
Belgium: 45.
Argentina: 43.
Mexico: 41.
Holland: 35.
etc.

Ancient popular xilography, (XVIIIth. Cent.)

4. Confraternities for devotion to Mary

Sometimes, close to Carmelite churches, from the 14th century onwards, there were confraternities bearing a Marian title (e.g. the Annunciation, the Immaculate Conception, Saint Mary of Carmel) whose aim was to foster devotion to the same titles and to take care of the altar, or the chapel or the church of the confraternity, the organisation of the titular feast, and the picture or the statue of Mary venerated in that chapel, or altar or church.

The activities of the confraternities consisted in collecting alms among their own members and among the people in order to support the devotional aim of the confraternity. This collection had to follow certain rules: it had to be held on a certain day; the collectors wore the emblem of the confraternity or the image that the group venerated; this was painted on the box where the offerings were put and on the banners which served as a guard of honour for the image.

It seems that the members of this kind of confraternity did not have any commitments outside of their devotions, their internal organisation, and the burial and remembrance of their deceased members. Among the devotional obligations very often one could find the obligation to take part in the processions that might be organised in the city: they would carry their own banner in the procession, and wear the uniform of their confraternity.

Examples of these confraternities would be, in the 14th century, the one in Perpignan (1399), Majorca and Camprodón (1367) in Spain. We find another example in Italy, the Carmelite confraternity erected in 1593 in the Carmelite church in Jesi. Its purpose was to promote the feast of Our Lady of Mount Carmel in the month of July, despite the fact that the principal feast of the church was the feast of Our Lady of Graces in the months of April and December organised respectively by the Carmelite friars and by a group of people from the rural areas.

Confraternities of this type went out of existence in the 18th century.

5. The Scapular Confraternities.

In the 15th century, around Carmelite churches Marian confraternities emerged, that take on the distinctive name of the Scapular. In the spreading of this kind of confraternity one can see principally the influence of lay people who had clearly heard the story of the vision of Simon Stock and the Bull of Pope John XXII concerning the "privileges" (eternal salvation and liberation from purgatory on the first Saturday after death).

This new type of confraternity is given the name, Confraternity of Our Lady of Carmel, Confraternity of Our Lady of Mount Carmel, Confraternity of the Scapular, Carmelite Confraternity, Confraternity of Our Lady of the Scapular and other similar titles.

In order to understand how these confraternities began and developed, it is very important to examine the Letters of Affiliation that were written by the Prior General, extending to lay people the benefits and indulgences of the Order, including the "privileges":

- When in 1530 Pope Clement VII in his Bull *Ex clementi* confirmed the sabbatine privilege, extending it to the affiliated members of the Carmelite Confraternity, it became permissible for them to wear the habit. For that reason, the Prior General of the time, Nicholas Audet, imposed as a juridical condition that the members of the confraternity, in order to enjoy the privilege, must wear the habit of Our Lady, even though at that stage there was yet no talk of the Scapular. The law that forbade the wearing of the habit by lay people had already fallen into disuse.
- For the Prior General Rossi (1532-1578) the most important aspect of affiliation was the Scapular. Affiliation was considered by him to be a mediation of Marian devotion, through the wearing of the Scapular, as Mary's garment. Rossi, glories in the fact that in his visit to Spain and Portugal, he

wrote close to 200,000 letters of affiliation and gave the Scapular to a similar number of faithful. During this visit in Spain, some people from outside the Order criticised the behaviour of Rossi and various theologians and prelates made his work difficult. The problem was resolved in Rossi's favour by the University of Salamanca.

- The same Prior General Rossi could see however that it was not a good idea to continue to act in this way. We can see this in some letters of affiliation that he wrote: we find texts that he erased as well as modifications referring to the content of the letters of affiliation. In a particular way, he affirms that the wearing of the Scapular is not enough in itself to obtain the sabbatine privilege. It has to be worn with devotion and commitment. In 1570 Rossi wrote, for the first time: "you will wear the habit in a reduced form beneath your normal clothing " In order to share in the promise made by Mary he prescribed the daily recitation of the Rosary and the observance of chastity in accordance with each one's state in life.
- The constitutions of 1586 unite the sharing of lay people in the spiritual benefits of the Order with the blessing and imposition of the Scapular. The previous Constitutions of 1593, along with this, prescribe that every second Saturday of the month, a procession should be held in honour of Our Lady of Mount Carmel, with a homily on the indulgences, graces and privileges granted to the Order.
- When we come to 1600, changes appear on account of the wide diffusion of the confraternities connected to the Scapular. The letters of affiliation take up once more the original medieval form, that is, a sharing in the spiritual goods of the Order, the Province or the local house; indulgences, including the sabbatine privilege, were not granted. There is no mention in these letters of the use of the Scapular.

With the spread, after the year 1580, of the Scapular Confraternities, the members of these, in order to enjoy the sabbatine privilege, began to adopt the obligations of tertiaries or of the "White Mantle", to whom that privilege was already granted. This phenomenon had enormous repercussions to the extent that the distinction between the members of the two different forms of association became almost imperceptible. Disputes and controversies arose between the confraternities of the "White Mantle" and those of the "Scapular". In 1595 a papal bull speaks of indulgences for the confraternities of Our Lady of Mount Carmel.

Pope Clement VIII, in the same year, 1595, applying the Council of Trent (which had placed under the care of the bishops all pious associations and confraternities) spoke of indults and faculties that would be necessary for the erection of confraternities.

The intervention of Clement imposed the necessity for clarity regarding the state of these Carmelite confraternities, at the end of the 16th century. Therefore the Prior General Henrique Silvio, in 1599, wrote the Chapters and Statutes of the Carmelite Confraternity of San Martino ai Monti (Rome) that had been erected in 1515 as a confraternity of "the sign of the Order". The same Henrique Silvio, again in the year 1599, wrote the Chapters or the first official rule for all the Scapular confraternities.

In the decree *Quaecumque a Sede Apostolica* of the year 1604, Clement VIII prescribed a form to be followed in the erection of confraternities no matter what their kind:

- To have a primary seat in Rome, affiliating with it all the confraternities of the same kind in order to be able to enjoy the corresponding privileges and spiritual benefits.
- The confraternities which already exist have to request affiliation, thus uniting themselves with the arch-confraternities in Rome.

In the Carmelite Order, by way of complying with this decree, the Confraternity of San Marti-

The Carmelite Wednesday Devotion

We find the origin of this practice at the time of the Holy Year 1500 in the extraordinary events that accompanied the journey from Naples to Rome and the return journey by pilgrims carrying the Marian icon known as La Bruna. Because of the endless number of people who were devoted to this image the King of Naples, Federico II of Aragon gave the order that on the 24th of June of that same year all the sick for whom it was possible should be brought to the church of the Carmine Maggiore to pray to Mary for their return to good health. Many cures took place in the midst of the great commotion.

That day was a Wednesday and so Wednesday was chosen as the day of special devotion to the Blessed Virgin under the title of La Bruna. So great was the flow of people that continued to come that Pope Pius V in 1567 gave permission, on the days when the crowds were really big, for the women to enter and leave the church through the door of the great cloister, since the doors of the church itself were far too narrow. This permission was a departure from the rigid rules of the Council of Trent in relation to the cloister.

This devotion to La Bruna spread later on, not only throughout the ancient kingdom of Naples, but far beyond, especially to the churches of the Carmelite Order and those of the Scapular Confraternity. Very soon it developed into the "Devotion Mass". Besides the Mass this included the singing of the Litany and the recitation of the Seven Joys of Mary along with seven Our Fathers and seven Hail Marys. The priest would normally preach a sermon. There would be exposition of the Blessed Sacrament. Confession and Holy Communion were recommended.

Introduced to S. Maria in Traspontina in Rome in 1724 this devotion was granted a series of indulgences by Benedict XIII in the bull *Alias pro parte*: a plenary indulgence on one Wednesday of the month, seven years and seven times forty days on the other Wednesdays. In Traspontina, the Wednesdays between Easter and Pentecost took on a special character: on each of them a sermon was given on one of the seven joys followed by the customary seven Our Fathers and Hail Marys. What became the custom in Traspontina soon spread to other places. In other churches of the Order and of the Confraternities the nine Wednesdays preceding the feast of St. Joseph began to be celebrated in a more solemn fashion. This practice was given an indulgence by Pope Clement XIII in 1765. The Wednesday devotion was only a morning devotion in the beginning. At the beginning of the twentieth century it began to be celebrated also in the afternoon.

After Vatican II this devotion, like many others, disappeared from many places, but it still continues in the place of origin in Naples. In the Basilica Shrine of Carmine Maggiore an annual pilgrimage is still celebrated with great devotion by the people as a way of honouring the Blessed Virgin, Mother of God and of all humanity. Even through the traditional forms have been preserved, it is presented today as a day of prayer and catechesis. Each year a particular Marian theme is chosen. This is backed up by the various services that are offered to the most needy as a concrete expression of the love that comes to us through the intercession of the Virgin, Mother, Guiding Star and Safe Harbour.

Cf.: E. Boaga, *Il Pellegrinaggio de "La Bruna" nel giubileo del 1500*, in *Analecta Ord. Carm.*, 49 (1998), pp. 164-173; C. Catena, *Pie pratiche in onore della Madonna del Carmine*, in *La Madonna del Carmine*, 7 (1953), pp. 202-206; Hoppenbrouwers, *Devotio mariana*, pp. 285-288.

no ai Monti was set up as the arch-confraternity in Rome. Its statutes then formed the basis of the statutes that the other confraternities would adopt at the beginning of the next century.

We must also remember that in 1599 each provincial had the possibility to authorise the giving of the habit, and in 1606 permission was given for the creation of confraternities of the Scapular also outside the churches of the Order. Thereafter, from the middle of the 17th century up to 1917, diocesan bishops also could erect Scapular confraternities.

The controversies between the confraternities of the White Mantle and those of the Scapular continued. In 1606, with the intervention of Paul V (bull *Cum certas*) favour was given to the Scapular confraternities, for whom the privileges of the confraternities of the White Mantle were recognised. There were some conditions attached to these privileges:
- The wearing of the scapular
- The observance of chastity in accordance with one's state
- The recitation of the Little Office of Our Lady, or, if this could not be done, abstinence from meat every Wednesday and Saturday of the year, except if Christmas Day fell on one of these days.

The situation continued to be chaotic in relation to the rights and duties of the confraternities and other forms of affiliation to the Order. Finally, the Prior General, Teodoro Straccio, brought some clarity to the situation with two interventions:
- He joined to the Third Order secular all the confraternities of men and women who made vows (1637)
- He put all the other associations and forms of affiliation to the Order into the Scapular confraternity (1640).

The interventions of the two Priors General, Silvio and Straccio, had important consequences: a person who wanted to receive the Scapular and to practice this devotion had of necessity to be a member of a confraternity, not in any vague or generic way, but effectively in a confraternity erected by the Priors General or by the Bishops and therefore with all the commitments of religious and social membership of the confraternity they joined.

6. Characteristics of the Scapular Confraternities of the 17th-18th centuries.

Here we will deal with the great expansion that the Scapular confraternities experienced, their spiritual more than juridical bond with the Order and practical aspects of the life of these confraternities.

a) *The spreading of the Scapular confraternities.*

The spreading of the Scapular confraternities in the 17th and 18th centuries was rapid and extensive. The principal vehicle for this was the preaching of the Carmelite Friars. The sermons were delivered during the celebration of the liturgy in the parishes, especially in Lent and at Christmas, when the Carmelites would be invited to preach. Normally, at the end of the sermon, a confraternity would be set up which then would become the pastoral means for promoting the Marian devotion of the Carmelite Order. They would receive visits periodically from the friars. As well as this, another factor that would explain the creation of a confraternity was the spontaneous initiative of the faithful who would ask the bishop or the Order itself for the erection.

The writers of this era – the end of the 16th century up to the 18th century – give us a lot of information about the extent of the development of the confraternities, when they refer to the number of people who were wearing the Scapular, bearing in mind the necessity of being properly affiliated and of following the obligations of the confraternity. Here are some examples:
- In 1595, Jose Falcone, compared all of Spain and Portugal to one great Carmelite house.

- A chronicle of the year 1611 states that the Prior of San Martino alone in a short number of years, gave the Scapular to more than 3000 people.
- In 1613, Francesco de Voersio (secretary to the Prior General, Henrique Silvio) recounts that in the Kingdom of Naples, very few people did not wear the Scapular.
- Francesco Mondini, in 1675, recounts that in Venice the members of the Scapular confraternity were at least 70,000.
- An indication of the spreading of the Scapular may be seen also in the large number of people who abstained from meat in Naples, in Germany and in Spain. In relation to the Sabbatine Privilege recall the response of Phillip III in regard to his appreciation for his subjects who were devoted to Our Lady.

There may be some difficulties about the accuracy of these numbers. Nevertheless they are very valuable when looked at along with other sources, leaving no doubt that Carmelite Marian devotion was very widespread at that time.

In the second half of the 16th century and the first few years of the following century, we witness the spreading of the Scapular confraternities in the various Italian states, in Spain and other European countries. In Latin America the Scapular confraternities begin to spread thanks to the work of Discalced Carmelites; in 1620 in Guatemala and Argentina; in 1643 in Chile; 1692 in Bolivia; 1727 in Colombia; 1751 in Uruguay; before 1736 in Peru. In Brazil the spread of devotion goes back to the 17th century thanks to the work, not only of the friars, but also of the Carmelite Tertiaries.

It is practically impossible to offer a complete catalogue of Scapular confraternities: it would demand an enormous amount of work due to the complexity and the dispersal of the sources both within the Order and outside. Some of the sources no longer exist. In the general archive of the Order there is an inventory made in 1950 in which a large number of the confraternities erected by the Priors General are listed, from the 17th century onwards, throughout the world (see the insert on p.123) We have no inventory of the confraternities erected by provincials or diocesan bishops, which we know were numerous. In the case of some nations the lists are complete; for Italy, a survey done in 1975, reveals the existence of 3,532 Scapular confraternities erected between the 17th and the 20th centuries.

b) *The concept of spiritual union with the Order.*

To the concept of juridical union of the Scapular Confraternities with the Order the interventions of Henrique Silvio and the restructuring carried out by Teodoro Straccio in 1640 added the further concept of an effective spiritual union.

This spiritual union with the Order is expressed in the following elements:
- The constant wearing of the Scapular, the Marian uniform of the Order, a sign and means of affiliation with the Order;
- A sharing in the spiritual benefits of the Order, and the indulgences proper to the Order;
- The right to share in the privileges proper to religious life, in accordance with the concept of the Middle Ages (preservation from the fires of hell and speedy release from purgatory, that is, the enjoyment of the "privileges of Carmel").

In the confraternities erected by diocesan bishops generally there is no juridical bond with the Order; indeed, at times, the spiritual bond with the Order was not always fully understood, or fully lived out.

c) *Regulations*

The Scapular confraternities had their own legislation from the end of the 16th century and the beginning of the next. These regulations take their inspiration from the norms written by Henrique Silvio for the confraternities, and in the latter half of the 17th century they develop more or less in accordance with these norms. In the confraternities erected by the bishops, there is some particular legislation that is different from the norms set down by Henrique Silvio.

All of these regulations establish and define structures and commitments for the members – the way that new candidates will be received, the system for electing the officials (the prior, councillors, the care of the sick, the sacristan etc.) and the functions and limits of each of these offices. Besides that, the regulations would always contain indications for the various kinds of commitments of the members: religious, devotional, moral and financial.

d) *Aspects of the life of the confraternities*

An examination of numerous texts of regulations of the Scapular Confraternities erected by the Order, and therefore along the lines that Henrique Silvio laid down, reveals the following elements in the life of the members:
- devotion to Our Lady expressed through prayer, pious exercises in her honour (e.g. Rosary, the Little Office, processions)
- the practice of prayer, (above all, devotions, mainly of the community kind, and occasionally individual) on fixed days (Saturdays, Wednesdays), and oftentimes Mass in the oratory of the Confraternity on feast-days (especially on the 2nd and 4th Sundays of the month), on every Marian feast of the Order and on the principal liturgical feasts of the year.
- a sacramental life (frequent confession and communion) oftentimes with the same frequency as was prescribed for the Mass:
- the penitential practice of chastity in accordance with each one's state and of abstinence on Wednesdays and Saturdays, along with the other penitential practices in use in the Church.
- the obtainment of plenary and partial indulgences on fixed days of the year.
- a life of fraternity in the way that people helped one another and in the practice of the works of mercy. This social involvement was extended to the members of the confraternity and also beyond especially in the form of visits to the sick and the providing of dowries for young girls for their marriage or for their entry to religious life.
- the burial of the members with the appropriate suffrages.

In practice, the confraternities fostered by the Order, through these regulations and structures, turned into the pastoral means of spreading devotion to Mary. In this pastoral outreach the three elements common to all genuine spirituality were present:
- prayer,
- sacraments
- a commitment to charity (known today as the commitment to justice).

The activities listed above are a proof that these three elements were present in the life of the confraternities that followed Silvio's line.

There is a difference in the regulations put forward by the bishops: we will not always find the elements contained in Silvio's approach. Generally, they emphasise the devotional aspects and the burial of the members.

To get a better knowledge of how the confraternities lived it would be useful to look at what is contained in the books and pamphlets written for the confraternities in the 17th and 18th centuries. We find authors who unite the wearing of the Scapular with a truly Marian life, but oftentimes, the authors also refer to the miraculous protection of Mary for her devotees, with an account of the advantages of the indulgences, comparing them to the very undemanding conditions necessary for obtaining them.

The structure of these writings is in general the following:
- a short history of the Order to show how in the past Mary protected the Carmelites;
- the origins of the Scapular devotion, linked to the vision of Simon Stock and the sabbatine privilege;
- the obligations of the members;
- a series of indulgences;

- a description of the miracles obtained by means of the Scapular;
- some prayers and other conditions necessary to obtain an indulgence; these books also offered prayers which were proper to Our Lady of Mount Carmel (novenas, texts for the seven joys of Mary for the Wednesday devotions; special invocations and litanies);
- sometimes also they would offer meditations and reflections on the life of Mary.

With the passage of time, these writings had an ever greater influence on the lives of the devotees of Our Lady of Mount Carmel, by way of devotional orientations. In examining these texts we notice how the dispositions in relation to the Scapular continued to develop.

The most widely used manual in the 17th century was the one written by the Carmelite Simon Grassi. It became the most well-known manual up to the beginning of the 20th century in the world of the Scapular confraternities. By 1885 it was in its 25th edition. Among other well-known works we could mention, the one edited by Pedro Luis Bagnari O.C. (Rome, 1728) and the work of Alberto di San Caetano, a discalced Carmelite of the province of Venice, edited in Naples in 1855, but which in reality was the work of Federico di Sant'Antonio, with Alberto as the editor.

e) *The members of the confraternities*

A study of the regulations already referred to, especially with reference to Europe, reveals interesting things about the kind of people who were members of the Scapular confraternities in the 17th and 18th centuries. The information we have at present leads us to believe that the acceptance or admission of members was not limited to any one category of people. The Scapular confraternities were open to people of all classes: nobles, middle-class, labourers, peasants, artisans, etc. both rich and poor. This situation of mixed classes made it possible in the confraternities to develop a relationship of "inter pares" and a fraternity that could prevent conflict between the classes in power and the subject classes. It was not rare to find in the 17th century as the prior of a confraternity someone from the humble classes, sometimes even illiterate while among the members you could find highly educated people of the upper classes. One example of this may be found at the beginning of the 17th century in the confraternity of Palestrina (Italy) which brought together workers and peasants along with members of the family of the Principality of Colonna, none of whom held any office in the confraternity.

This kind of unity among members from different social backgrounds lasted a long time. It was a characteristic of Scapular confraternities as distinct from other types of confraternities even religious ones. It was only at the end of the 18th century and throughout the 19th century that the phenomenon of having directors chosen from among the upper classes became widespread. It represented an ambition and desire to have among the leaders of one's own group, people from the upper classes. These directors, even though they may have exercised their role in a paternalistic more than a fraternal fashion stayed within the ranks of the confraternity and fulfilled their duties towards the group.

Another factor which favoured the choosing of more educated people as leaders of confraternities was the growing complexity of their organisational structure.

Despite all this, the relationship between the members of the confraternities seems to have remained fraternal and peaceful. There are no signs of conflict of a social nature or of any kind of distance between the members on account of their different social backgrounds. Eventual conflicts arose for other reasons, which had more to do with the character of the individual members.

The situation in Brazil was different. From the first appearance of confraternities there was discrimination between brotherhoods for whites and brotherhoods for blacks. In this context, in the 17th and 18th centuries the confraternities or brotherhoods of Carmel, brought together in the

Marian Devotional Exercises

Here are some of the private devotional exercises in honour of Our Lady which were widespread in the Order

a) The crown of 12 stars

This devotion, which we find from the end of the 15th century onwards came into use among the groups called the "Slaves of Our Lady". In Belgium it was bound up with devotion to La Bruna. (Some authors of the Order hold that it began with Peter the hermit, who lived on Mount Carmel; others hold that it was St. Cyril or St. Berthold. Lezana holds that Bl. John Soreth began it in Belgium. There is however, no doubt about Jerónimo Gracián spraeding at the beginning of the 17th century). This practice was known also in Italy and its daily use spread among the novices and among many members of the reformed province of Saint Mary of Life (Naples). The crown of stars was made up of three Our Fathers, 12 Ave Marias in honour of the twelve privileges or principal virtues of Mary.

b) Devotion in honour of the Child Jesus

This devotion began with the Reform of Touraine, in the novitiates and in the student houses. It spread later to the whole Order. It was linked to a very special devotion to Mary. Every month (or every week), among the novices or the students, lots were drawn to find the person who would keep the image of the Child Jesus and the image of Our Lady in his own room. The one chosen would make a commitment to venerate the images for the whole month and be more dedicated to the life of the community. There was a specific ritual for the drawing of lots and for the transferring of the images from one room to another. In this context, processions were frequently held in the novitiates and student houses, each one with appropriate exhortations.

c) Novena in expectation of the delivery

Besides the novena for the feast of Our Lady of Mount Carmel, with a solemn sermon, a typically Carmelite practice was the celebration of a novena in expectation of the delivery of Mary. We still have a variety of texts from this novena. The practice differed from province to province. It consisted in meditations on the feelings and the events that were part of Mary's life, in the nine months during which she bore the Child Jesus. Each meditation would be followed by a request to be granted the corresponding virtue. Each petition would be accompanied, depending on the place, by a particular number of Our Fathers and Ave Marias.

c) The three Hail Marys

It was customary among the friars to stop in front of the picture of Our Lady, which was placed at the entrance to the house, and say three Hail Marys on their way out. The General Chapter of Piacenza mandated this custom in 1575. Throughout the 17th century, praying the three Our Fathers and three Hail Marys in honour of the virginity of the Mother of God was introduced among the obligations which the friars had to observe. The practice of the three Hail Marys was very widespread in the Order. In the communities of Poland in the 18th century, they added another short prayer in honour of Our Lady to each Hail Mary. In Germany, around the year 1735, the friars at the end of Vespers sang the three Hail Marys.

For more information about these practices see, V. Hoppenbrouwers, *Devotio Mariana in ordine fratrum B.V.M. de Monte Carmelo*, Roma, 1960, pp. 302-319.

beginning nobles and whites, while the Rosary confraternities were for the blacks, and others for those of mixed race, etc.

f) *The Oratory*

Every Scapular confraternity had its own chapel or church, which they took care of with great zeal and attention. Sometimes the chapel of the confraternity would be situated within the cloister of the Carmelite friars in a place that allowed the members to have their own entrance from the street.

Where it was not possible for the confraternity to have its own meeting room, meetings would take place in the chapel and the archives, the members' habits and the objects for worship would all be kept in the sacristy.

g) *Care for the patrimony*

During the 17th and 18th century we see the accumulation of a considerable patrimony, which included rents, land and institutions (hospitals etc.) As a result, the problem of administration became relevant. As well as the normal demands that have to do with the administration of goods and institutions, one has to add the demands of Canon Law after the Council of Trent and the relationship with the local diocesan bishop in this regard. Further questions arose on account of the clericalisation of administration and also the relationship between the confraternities and the community of friars of the Order. In this new situation the confraternities came into conflict with the diocesan structures and they lost a lot of their power as a pastoral mediation. The process of secularisation of the confraternities came about also in other states and outside of Europe as well as through the influence of laicism and masonry.

7. The Carmelite Confraternities of the 19th century up to the present day

The great Marian network of Scapular confraternities was almost entirely dismantled and destroyed as part of the suppression of religious groups in the course of the 19th century. The confraternities that survived very often continued to live their own lives without much contact with the Order. They tended to emphasise the devotional and administrative aspects of their life. The different commitments to the works of mercy almost entirely disappear and what remains is a few cases where work is being done more from a philanthropic point of view than one of Christian Charity.

After the suppression of the 19th century and with the direction given by Canon Law up to the Code of 1917 everything to do with confraternities was re-organised:
- the erection of sodalities
- the appointment and duties of directors
- the habit of the members
- the privileges and indulgences granted to the members
- the general obligations, and the special and particular favours
- the instructions for the priests to whom the faculty of giving the Scapular was granted.

All of this reorganisation changes the confraternities into sodalities with the purpose of ensuring that the members would have access to the spiritual privileges and indulgences, without the effort of a more demanding and charitable commitment. Thus the Scapular devotion developed more and more as a sign of the protection of Mary, forgetting almost totally the dimension of consecration to Mary and the demands of a covenant of love made with Mary.

As a fundamental element, in order to enjoy the privileges attached to the Scapular, it was enough to receive it from an authorised person and to have your name written in the general confraternity register of the Order. This kind of affiliation, to all intents and purposes, nullified the relationship that existed in the past between the devotee and the local confraternity.

In the two decades leading up to the second world war and in the period immediately following it, the concept of the confraternity as a vehicle for spreading Scapular devotion was rediscovered and promoted. This phenomenon did not last long because the structuring of it was not thought out well enough in terms of the needs of the times. It applied only the model of confraternity proposed by the Code of Canon Law, with its accent on the devotional leading to the abandoning of the life-oriented and social aspects which were part of the previous structure in the period between 16th and the 18th centuries. The structure in the mind of Canon Law of a confraternity "ad modum organicum constituta" (constituted structurally like a social body and similar to such) is then something rare and generally without any link with the Order.

Coming to our own age, people who wear the Scapular tend to live in isolation without the help of a specific pastoral structure. At best, those who receive the Scapular are prepared by hearing about the privileges and indulgences and the conditions required for receiving them (prayers, chastity in accordance with one's state in life, abstinence from meat on Wednesdays and Saturdays). Back in the year 1902, the Order granted to all priests who asked for it, the faculty of giving the Scapular, without any connection with the local confraternities. There was merely the obligation to send the names to be included in the general register of the Order. Soon afterwards this faculty was extended to all priests, thus eliminating the character of a "reserved blessing" (that is, the need for non Carmelite priests to request the faculty of giving the Scapular). These and other similar measures (e.g. the abolition of the obligation to keep a register of inscriptions) assumed with all the best intentions of helping more easily to spread devotion to the Our Lady of Mount Carmel, in fact, along with other causes, weakened this devotion and practically annulled any link with the Order.

This evolution of the Scapular confraternities in our time brought with it among other things the need for the Third Order Secular to become an association that would honour Our Lady of Mount Carmel in a more special way and therefore it would receive more attention from the friars, who previously were taken up with the confraternities and their world. This evolution was necessary once it was clear that the Order had lost its influence over the confraternities throughout the world. Within the Third Order certain devotional elements began to develop and the rhythm of the Third Order began to look more like that of the confraternities of previous centuries. All of this had a profound impact on the Carmelite Third Order from the beginning of the twentieth century up to the time of the writing of the Rule in 1948. Some elements endured even up to the post-conciliar period. At present, the Carmelite Third Order has a new rule or set of norms for a gospel way of life (1977). The rule reflects Carmelite values, proposing a commitment to prayer, the sacraments, the works of justice and the building up of the human person in accordance with God's plan.

Pages from the Anthology

1. THE BEST KIND OF DEVOTION TO THE BLESSED VIRGIN

Juan de Jesus Maria, O.C.D. *Treatise on Love and Veneration of the Queen of Heaven*, Bk I, Chap 3.

The devotion that is best suited to the Blessed Virgin and the devotion most desired by her is the imitation of her. Whatever the people who are devoted to her may do, it will be of little worth if they differ from her in their behaviour. Indeed, even though this merciful Queen may have protected at the hour of death more than one criminal, who had no intention of being converted, but who were in the habit of turning to her everyday, we cannot deduce from this that it would be advisable and good, ignoring her virtue, to place too much hope in a prayer or a time of fasting in honour of the Blessed Virgin, because the same Virgin has very little regard for bad behaviour. Therefore, the principal effort of those who wish to receive the favour of the Queen of Heaven should be to imitate her innocent life.

And so that the effort to imitate her, which generally is vague and uncertain, should be more practical, it would be useful to pick one particular virtue, for example, humility or patience, in which the imitators would make a special effort. The purpose of imitation may be understood in the following way:

"Merciful Queen of Heaven, perfect example of holiness
I, N.N., relying on the help of your Son and on your help too,
Purpose to imitate your virtues and customs
So that, by that imitation I may do something that is pleasing to you:
And so that I might do this with greater energy,
I purpose to imitate in a special way Your humility (or your patience, your chastity...)

I humbly ask you,
Most Pure Virgin To help me so that,
fired by the love of such great virtue
I may practise it faithfully
And once I have acquired it, I may in some way be like you.

2. CHILDREN OF MARY

Francisco de la Madre de Dios, O.C.D. *An instruction and method for spiritual exercises*, Valencia, 1774, pp. 244-249.

> When you are desperate, listen to Christ repeating what he said to St. John as he stood at the foot of the cross, Behold your Mother.
> With great love in your heart think how you have as your mother the woman who is the Mother of God, the Queen of Heaven and earth, the revelation of divine omnipotence and the paradise of the Most Holy Trinity, the woman who is before all the angels and the saints as regards her merits (….) The woman who is the instrumental cause of all the favours that we receive from God. How much you should rejoice to have as your mother, the Queen of the World.
> Secondly consider that this Mother loves you with a love that in a certain way is infinite. Out from this love, just like from a spring, inestimable favours flow, favours that are given to you, that no one can receive unless they pass through her hands. She offers everything to the Eternal Father for you, and for you alone she is willing to accept every kind of suffering if God should so desire.
> Thirdly, from this come those ardent affections of the sincere love of the one who desires to love her with the same love with which the courtiers of heaven and the just of the earth have loved and always love her; and if it were possible, the same love with which the persons of the Blessed Trinity loved and love her. Respect her as the true Mother of God …. Try to serve her to the degree that your powers will allow and let your desires extend to everything that is possible; desire that everyone serve and honour her; rejoice often on account of her perfections; keep great confidence in her power to intercede; because to her has been given every power and she loves you so much and she is so liberal and merciful; offer her Son to her often in the Sacrament of the Altar, especially after you have received him in the Sacrament because that is something that is very pleasing to her and gives her great glory. Strive to guard the purity of your soul and body and imitate her in all her virtues; thank her in everything you do, which you will offer to God through her hands, make every effort to honour her on her feast-days … so that your heart may always be grateful.

3. CONVERSATIONS WITH OUR LADY

Text by, Sr. Maria Escobar, ed. in: Roque Alberto Faci, *The Life of Maria Escobar*, Pamplona, 1761. pp. 249-250; published also in Hoppenbrouwers, *Devotio Mariana*, pp. 384-385.

> Mary, most holy and most worthy Mother of God, White star of the morning, Dawn of the day, Shining mirror, Example of humility, My mother, lovable mother, Loved more than all creation, You are the Mother of sinners and the refuge of orphans, Guardian of virgins, Light of the solitary and guide of confessors, Strength of martyrs. Mary, you are our holy Lady. Sweet is your divine name Whose unworthy servant I am, Desiring to be all yours and so to remain from today onwards, I proclaim it and will proclaim it always, wherever I go. My Lady, may I revere your name. May I bless and praise, the sweet name Maria. Mary I rejoice and find consolation in pronouncing your name. May I be a great lover of

this name and so receive your blessing. Give it to me, my Lady and beloved Mother, do not lose sight of me. I am yours and will be so more and more. Keep me safe from the devil, and do not allow that proud dragon to surround me. Keep far away from me all his snares and deceits, so that under your protection and with your help I may be strong against them and go on loving God alone, my Lord. And, embracing his commandments and precepts. I may love him above all else; This is what I feel right now, which I choose to sign. With my own hand and with all the affection of my heart. And so I ask you, Holy Mary, my Lady that on the day of my particular judgment, when I have to give an account to God of my wasted life and of my sins you may be my refuge and protection.

Intercede for me with your holy Son and just judge, that he might pardon me. Give him what I have written here along with the other testaments I have signed and already given to you. By signing them I proclaim my desire to be your unworthy servant, and the servant of God, Sister Maria. A thousand times I beg you to take care of me and to accept me, beyond what I might deserve, on account of the precious blood of your beloved Son Jesus Christ, through whom I make this request and to whom I will belong forever. Amen, Amen.

VIRGIN MARY
I WRITE MY NAME
AS YOUR SLAVE
TODAY AND FOREVER

Sr. Maria Escobar.

For further study and reflection

1. Bibliography

- V. Hoppenbrouwers, *Devotio Mariana*, pp.320-330
- E. Esteve, *De valore spirituali devotionis S. Scapularis*, Roma, 1953
- E. Boaga, *Le confraternite del Carmine"*, in *La dimensione Mariana del Carmelo*, I, pp.68-78
- J. Smet, *The Carmelites*, II, pp. 225-228.

II. For personal and/or group study

1. Read the basic text making an outline of its content.

2. Throughout the years, did the phenomenon of the Confraternities remain always the same or did it undergo changes? Explain your answer.

3. In your region today what shape do the Confraternities take? Are there any similarities between the confraternities of today and those of the past? Are there differences? What are they?

4. Do some research on the Carmelite Marian characteristics that you find in your region or another region in which you have a special interest. What does this research suggest?

III. Prayer and Life:

1. Pray with the Word of God:
    - Jn 2,1-11
    - Hos 11,4
    - Prov 8,32-35
    - Prov 8,21-31
    - Eccles 24,1-2.5-7.12-16.26-30.

2. How do you think you could help your local church community as regards the life of fraternity?

7
THE FEAST OF LOVE

Lord God, you willed that the Order of Carmel
should be named in honour of the Blessed Virgin Mary, Mother of your Son.
Through her prayers as we honour her
today bring us to your holy Mountain, Christ our Lord ……..

> (from the Collect of the 16th of July,
> in the Carmelite Missal)

7 THE FEAST OF LOVE

The Solemn Commemoration of Our Lady of Mount Carmel

1. Marian celebrations in the Order

From the beginning, the Order has celebrated with great devotion the feast days which the Church celebrates, namely, the Annunciation, the Assumption, the Nativity and the Purification. Along with these the most ancient liturgical books of the Order prescribe the feasts of the Visitation and the Immaculate Conception or the veneration of the sanctification of the Blessed Virgin Mary. Carmelites gave special importance to the feasts of the Annunciation, the Assumption and the Immaculate Conception.

With the passage of time other Marian celebrations were added to the Order's proper of feasts. The following in particular are the feasts that were introduced (the indication of the year refers to when the feast was celebrated by the Order as a whole).

- 1393: Our Lady of the Snows
- 1393: The Presentation of the BVM
- 1666: The Most Holy Name of Mary
- 1698: Our Lady of Graces
- 1699: The Marriage of the BVM
- 1730-1733: The Seven Sorrows of Our Lady (Friday before Palm Sunday)
- 1730: The Waiting for the Delivery
- 1730: Our Lady of the Rosary
- 1738: The Patronage of the Virgin Mary (the feast used to be celebrated before this in some provinces)
- 1745: Our Lady of Loreto
- 1814: The Immaculate Heart of Mary (Before this, the feast was celebrated by the Carmelites of Apt in France.)
- 1814: Feast of the Seven Sorrows of Mary (in September)
- 1818: Mary Help of Christians
- 1851: The Maternity of Mary (Since the year 1764 the feast was celebrated in the province of Venice)
- 1851: The Purity of Mary the Virgin (since the year 1767 this feast was celebrated in the province of Venice)
- 1932: Mary Queen and Mediatrix of Graces
- 1935: The Apparition of Our Lady in Lourdes

In some cases the Order celebrated feast days before they were included in the Universal Calendar of the Church, while others came into use after their acceptance for the whole Church.

Among the celebrations of Our Lady there was always a custom to commemorate Our Lady on Saturdays. This practice came into the Order very early. Due to the importance of the Solemn Commemoration as the patronal feast of the Order, we will now deal with its history as well as its significance and briefly analyse the content of the liturgical texts.

2. The Solemn Commemoration

Contrary to what some people think today, the Solemn Commemoration of the Blessed Virgin Mary of Mount Carmel did not begin with the Scapular and the vision of St. Simon Stock. A recent and as yet unpublished talk by Arie Kallenberg throws much light on this question. I will summarise his thought. It is well known that the early Carmelites had no feast of their own to celebrate their founder and patron, as other Orders tended to have. This forced them to celebrate Mary, Lady and Patroness (including the sense of Mater Ordinis, foundress) by choosing from among the most important marian feasts that were celebrated at that time. Thus as patronal feasts we find the Annunciation (even before 1300, and in Avignon

Devotional Exercises in Carmel

With the celebration of the Feast of Our Lady of Mount Carmel on the 16th of July, the practice of preparing for the feast or of having nine days of prayer before the feast or eight days of prayer after it became more widespread from the 17th century onwards. This gave rise in time to the novena and octave of the Feast of Our Lady of Mount Carmel. As well as these two kinds of exercises the people added the practice of the Carmelite Fortnight in the month of August and of the Audience.

a) The novena

This was a solemn moment of preparation. Preachers designated by the Prior General would use the principal pulpits of the Order. Prayers in honour of Our Lady preceded the preaching. Soon texts came to be written down for these prayers. After the preaching, the prayer would continue and the celebration ended with Benediction of the Blessed Sacrament. The people sang litanies, sometimes with special Carmelite references. After the Second Vatican Council, it became more common to celebrate the novena with a celebration of the Word or the celebration of the Eucharist.

b) The Carmelite Fortnight

The most picturesque form of Carmelite devotion is the Carmelite Fortnight, celebrated in Sicily in the month of August. It involved the saying of prayers like the Our Father, the Hail Mary, the Credo and the Salve Regina over and over again each day for a specific intention. These intentions were made up on the basis of events in the life of Mary and of Christ – from the Gospels or from traditions. Each event had a significant number, (e.g. the 20 years of sterility of Mary's parents; the 15 steps of the Temple that Mary ascended; Mary's 63 years of age, etc.) which determined the number of prayers that were to be said in her honour. Mary in this devotion was given an enormous number of titles and the most extraordinary list of attributes.

c) The Audience

This was a typical exercise in honour of Our Lady of Mount Carmel, linked to the celebration of the Wednesdays. It took on different forms, in relation to the place where the practice had spread. It involved a lengthy text that indicated the intention of the prayer and of the intercession being made to Our Lady. It ended with some vocal prayers, like the Our Father, the Hail Mary or the Credo and with a hymn. In this devotion Mary was called, Ornament, Mystical Rose, Lyre, Olive branch, the Cloud, the Star and the Cedar of Carmel.

For further reading see, V. Hoppenbrouwers, *Devotio Mariana in ordine fratrum B.V.M. de Monte Carmelo*, Rome, 1960, pp. 302-319.

from 1306), Mary's Dormition or the Assumption (certainly in the period 1376-1380) and Mary's Conception (in 1306). It is interesting to note how the choice fell upon three celebrations that are closely related to the mystery of the Resurrection, a characteristic of the liturgy of the Holy Sepulchre of Jerusalem, which was used by the Carmelites. Indeed, as Kallenberg points out, two of these feasts (the Conception and the Annunciation) turn out to be closely related to the notion of human existence, in Mary's conception in Anne's womb and the conception of the Word in Mary; at the same time, the third, the Assumption, exalts new life and participation in the Lord's Resurrection. We are dealing here with feasts that highlight the beginning and the end of human existence, in which the redemptive work of the Risen Lord takes effect. In this context, the Annunciation (celebrated on the 25th of March and in Advent) reminded the early Carmelites of the beginnings of Redemption, the Word made flesh in Mary, and was therefore an invitation to them to honour her divine Motherhood, while Mary's conception in Anne's womb was the reason for adding the praises of the Most Pure Virgin. Finally, the Assumption, with its message about the full eschatological fulfillment of human existence in heaven, shows Mary as the prototype for their own life.

With time, by way of analogy with the central place in the liturgy of the Holy Sepulchre that the Solemn Commemoration of the Risen Lord assumed, the daily remembrance and the special remembrance on Saturdays, of the Virgin Mary, the Mother of the Lord, associated with the work of redemption, developed to the point where they became the Order's own feast-day. As the Solemn Commemoration it took the place of all the other patronal celebrations.

As a separate feast, the Solemn Commemoration of Our Lady was being celebrated as early as the middle of the 14th century, especially in England, and subsequently throughout the whole Order (the second half of the 15th century) even though its official recognition as the patronal feast, "Festa Confratrum", did not come until 1609.

A. Date and place of origin

In England the Carmelite Nicholas of Lynn put in his calendar, written before 1386, a feast-day on the 17th of July with the title Solemn Commemoration of Saint Mary. This is repeated in Breviaries and Missals of the Order: the Oxford breviary (1375-93), the Parma breviary (1440-78), the Missal of the British Museum (1357-93), the Missal of Kilcormic (a copy from 1489 perhaps of a manuscript of 1411-25). Therefore, the Solemn Commemoration appears at the end of the 14th century in England and spreads out afterwards to other places: Belgium (the Parma breviary has this origin; but in the Brussels Breviary of 1481 there is still no mention of the solemnity), Germany in 1495 as a "festum duplex" and with its own proper collect; in Ferrara in a breviary of the 15th century and afterwards at the end of the 15th century and the beginning of the 16th in the Order as a whole, becoming its titular feast.

B. The name of the Feast

From the time this Feast was introduced up to the beginning of the 17th century in manuscripts and printed texts we find the following names:

- "Commemoratio beatae (sanctae) Mariae"
- "Commemoratio solemnis beatae (sanctae) Mariae"
- "Commemoratio sanctae Mariae Virginis"
- "Commemoratio gloriosae Virginis Mariae"
- "Commemoratio solemnis beatissimae Virginis Mariae"

In the official Marian title of the Order the specification of "Mount Carmel" is also there. Comparing the names of the feast with the names of the Order (cf. the insert), we note that the former are a reflection of the evolution of the latter.

The Discalced Carmelites, before the separation of the two traditions, having left aside the Order's own rite, adopted the Roman Rite in 1586 and the following year were granted the use of the "Proprium" (ed. Segovia 1589) which they took entirely from the reformed breviary of the ancient branch (1585). We will find there the title of the feast "Solemn Commemoration of the Blessed Virgin Mary".

After the division of the Order, in 1593 and the subsequent division of the Discalced Carmelites in 1600 into two autonomous congregations, the title of the "proprium" of 1589 continued to be used in Spain while in Italy in 1609 the words "of Mount Carmel" began to be used (we do not know exactly when) in breviaries and missals.

C. The day of the celebration

Nicholas of Lynn, already mentioned, placed the date of the celebration on the 17th of July and thus it was put in the breviary and missals up until the end of the 15th century. The date of the 17th of July still appears in Germany in 1495.

The date of the 16th of July appears for the first time (perhaps by mistake) in the 1481 breviary from Venice, and it was used again in the liturgical books edited at the end of the 15th century and the beginning of the following century. Thus we can find it in the breviaries of 1490 and 1495 edited in Venice and again in the Venice missals from 1500, 1504, and 1509, thereby becoming the normal date.

The fact of changing the date from the 17th to the 16th of July, besides the influence of the liturgical books just mentioned, is also supposed to be a result of the fact that the 17th of July was the day dedicated in Europe to St. Alexius, and because of this the Carmelites decided to bring their feast day forward one day.

D. The Rite for the Celebration

The Rite differs from one liturgical text and codex to another. Up to the year 1585 we have the "duplex" rite or the "totum duplex" in accordance with the nomenclature peculiar to each period.

After that we get a "duplex maius" as in the Roman breviary (1585) and Venice (1586) and in the Roman Missal (1587). Among the Discalced Carmelites in the Spanish Congregation the rite is "duplex" in the "Proprium" of 1589. In the Italian Congregation, in the "Proprium" of 1609 it is a "duplex primae classis" with an octave.

In the General Chapters of 1620 and 1625 of the Ancient Order permission was sought from the Holy See for an octave to be celebrated, given that it was the titular feast of the Order. This permission was granted by the Congregation for Rites in 1628.

Could it be said that the request was made by these Chapters just because the Discalced Carmelites were already celebrating an octave? It would seem not. While there was the question of retrieving from the Discalced Sanctoral the saints that had been removed in 1564 as a result of the decisions of the Council of Trent (something that caused great reaction in the Order), those General Chapters treated the question of the octave separately. Most likely the origin of interest in the octave lay in the fact of how the celebration of the Feast of Our Lady of Mount Carmel was spreading outside the Order.

E. The object of the feast

We have already recalled how the Solemn Commemoration in the beginning, in the context of the liturgy of the Resurrection, was linked to the memory of the Virgin Mary, the Lady and Patroness, associated with the work of Redemption of her Risen Son, and the eschatological dimension of human existence. As early as the 14th and 15th centuries however, there is wide interest in this "day of the Order" as a day to remember and give thanks to the Blessed Virgin for the benefits received through her motherly intercession. In time, the notion of Mary's favours will dominate the celebration. We read in the Collect, *Deus qui excellentissimae* and in the reading *Inviolabilis antiquitatis* the great things that the Blessed Virgin did for the Carmelite Order are the

two things that allowed the Order to survive:
- the approval of the Order and its Rule by the Holy See (even if in this regard there was confusion between the approval given by Honorius III in 1226, the decree of the II Council of Lyon in 1274, the interest of Honorius IV and the measures taken by Boniface VIII in 1298, to the point of concluding that the same II Council of Lyon, approved the Order by its decree of the 17th of July 1274)
- the victory gained by the Carmelites in defense of the Marian title of the Order at the University of Cambridge in 1374.

In the 15th century, people added the notion of the Solemn Commemoration as the feast of the Scapular and therefore of all those who were part of the *fraternitas Ordinis*.

From the year 1609 onwards, the feast began to be celebrated by the confraternities, whose number was growing throughout Europe. It began to be known as The Feast of the Scapular, because of its focus on the Scapular, considered to be the greatest gift of Mary to the Order and its devotees. Among the various reasons for this development there is the strong influence exercised on both traditions of the Order by the document *Cum Sacra Pentecostes* (written by the Discalced Carmelites in Italy in 1609). This document in fact opened the way towards a liturgical approach which will be linked more and more to the privileges of the Scapular. This idea remained as a constant theme in subsequent liturgical texts, as for example, in the 1919 Preface. In the years 1950-52 many Carmelites (especially Discalced) expressed the desire to have the name of the feast changed to the Feast of the B.V.M. of the Scapular. Fortunately the idea did not get much attention.

The present liturgical texts offer even greater theological refinement, introducing us to the values of Carmelite Marian life and devotion. The spread of the Feast of Our Lady of Mount Carmel to different parts of the world, especially among lay people, induced Pope Benedict XIII to extend

An exhortation for the devout celebration of the feasts of the Blessed Virgin.

The venerable father Juan de Jesús María, O.C.D. (1564-1615) in his short work on the Love and Veneration of the Queen of Heaven, suggested to the devotees of Mary, how they should live out their life of devotion every day. From this work that springs from a heart that was filled with love for Mary we give you the exhortation for the devout celebration of the Feasts of the Blessed Virgin, taken from the second part, Chapter VII

"The feasts of Mary have to be prepared and organised beforehand in order to do something special in honour of the Queen of Heaven. It would be good, during the novena, that people would kneel down and repeat many times the invocation of the Blessed Virgin, the Ave Maria; people should eat frugally, leaving aside fruit, and give alms to the poor for love of Our Lady, fast or take on some bodily penance, and finally, on the day of the Feast, go to confession and Communion with more recollection and devotion than normal."

it to the whole universal Church with the Bull dated the 24th of October, 1726.

3. The Liturgical Texts

A. The Divine Office

At the beginning the solemn commemoration barely had an "Oremus" that was proper. The other parts came from the common. The proper "Oremus" *Deus qui excellentissime* appears for the first time in the Oxford breviary (1375-93). This "Oremus" thanks God for two reasons: the Marian title of the Order and the defence of this title. In the breviaries of 1575-1579 other proper prayers were added, for Terce, Sext, None and II Vespers. Another proper element is the text *Inviolabilis antiquitatis* which was said between the readings of Matins.

Another element proper to the Carmelite liturgy was the text *Inviolabilis antiquitatis,* distributed over the light readings of Matins (to the exact, the 1st to the 6th ant the 8th to the 9th, the 7th being the Gospel Homily, *Homilia in Evangelium*. The reading *Inviolabilis antiquitatis* recounts the miracles performed by God through the intercession of Mary for the defence of the Order, the death of the enemies of the Order and the threatening appearance of Our Lady to Pope Honorius III, a vision that led to the approval of the Order. We also find in this reading a clear reference to the Marian title of the Order granted by the Holy See through the intercession of Mary, as reason for giving thanks to her.

There was also a rhythmic office that was composed in the second half of the 15th century. Besides the prayer Deus qui excellentissimae and the reading Inviolabilis antiquitatis (and its additions) this office included antiphons, responsories, an invitatory and verses in rhythm, as well as the Flos Carmeli twice, (once with the phrase Esto propitia and once with Da privilegia). There is a question as to whether this office was used as part of the liturgy.

With the reform brought in by the Council of Trent the office of the Solemn Commemoration was reduced to common texts losing the prayer *Deus qui excellentissimae*, and the reading *Inviolabilis antiquitatis*. There was some negative reaction to these changes in the ancient branch of the Order. In 1609 the Discalced Carmelites in Italy were granted the use of the reading *Cum sacra Pentecostes* for the second nocturn of Matins and the prayer *Deus qui beatissimae*, which is in fact the older prayer *Deus qui excellentissimae*. The reading *Cum Sacra Pentecostes* refers to the Marian life of the Order especially to the Scapular and to privileges attached to it. The texts were reviewed by Cardinal Roberto Bellarmino. Soon after that the ancient Order received the permission again to say the prayer *Deus qui beatissimae* in the Office and to use the readings approved for the Discalced.

In 1794 the Discalced Carmelites in Spain obtained a proper office for the celebration of the Solemn Commemoration that then was extended to the Discalced Carmelites in Italy in 1856. This text which is rather poor remained in use up to the reform of Vatican II. The Congregation of Discalced Carmelites in Portugal (1773-1834) had a different text that was somewhat better.

In 1828 the ancient Order was granted a proper office with vigils and octaves but with no proper hymns, which were granted in 1917. The prayer of the Office is *Majestatem tuam*. In this same year they were given permission to use another prayer, *Crescat Domine*. In 1829 the Discalced Carmelites also received permission for the vigil and octave.

With the reform of the liturgical texts provided by Vatican II, we have a text of the office that is the same for the two branches of the Order. The renewed liturgical texts, besides containing an act of thanksgiving to God and singing the praises of Mary as Mother and Queen of Carmel, look at Mary also from the point of view of the spiritual experience of Carmel: Mary is the Virgin at prayer, a model for all Carmelites in receiving, interiorising, living and preaching the Word. Mary is the spiritual mother who accompanies our journey towards the fullness of Christ, from the waters of Baptism to the glory of God.

B. The Mass

In relation to the texts proper to the Mass, we may say that the element which is most typical at the beginning of the Mass is the prayer, *Deus qui excellentissimae*, which appeared in the London missal (1387-93) along with the Sequence *Flos Carmeli*, the Secret, *Familiae presentis* and the Postcommunion prayer, *Da quaesumus*.

In the missal edited in Brescia (1490), the prayers and the Sequence, *Flos Carmeli* are found again (just the first two verses) and for the rest the common *Salve, sancta parens* is used. The *Gloria* and the *Credo* were added in the editions of the missal which came out in Venice in 1504, 1509, 1551 and 1574. In the missal of the ancient Order, reformed in 1587 after the Council of Trent, the text of the *Gaudeamus* Mass appears, taken from the Common of the Blessed Virgin with a reference to "de cuius solemnitate" in the entry antiphon to the Solemnity of the Feast. So the prayer, *Deus qui excellentissimae* was lost and replaced by the prayer *Majestatem tuam*, taken from the Common. In the course of 1663 the collect *Deus qui beatissimae* appeared once again as well as the Flos Carmeli sequence.

In the year 1865 the Holy See responded by way of a "Dilata" to a request by the ancient branch of the Order to use its own texts for the masses: for the Vigil, *Induxi vos*; for the Feast, *Quam pulchri sunt*, and for the votive Masses, *Gaudens gaudebo*. All of this was granted in 1903. The same texts were granted to the Discalced slightly modified and without the *Flos Carmeli* sequence.

Finally, on the 26th of March, 1919 the Holy See granted to the ancient Order its own Preface, and the same to the Discalced Carmelites on the 13th of August of the same year.

With the reform of the liturgical texts promoted by Vatican II we have a new common text for the two branches of the Carmelite Order.

The composition of the celebration is centred on Mary, mother, model and helper for those who seek Christ, the holy mountain of God. In the spiritual typology, the reference to Mount Carmel has a very clear theological significance. Also the reference to the idea of Mary's protection for the Order, as well as the Order's thanksgiving to her for the graces the Order receives, reminds us of the theology and Marian devotion that were typical of the Order: Mary, Mother of Christ, Immaculate Virgin, example of listening to the Word of God in contemplative prayer, hope during life and after death. There are still other elements of the tradition that we find in the text of the Votive Masses.

The Rosary

A very common practice in the Church, the Rosary became widely known among Carmelites. Some of the authors of the Order held that this began with Peter the hermit who lived for a time on Mount Carmel, or with Saint Berthold. This unusual position was explained in these terms by the jurist and historian of the Order, John Baptist de Lezena: Saint Dominic invented the Rosary using 63 or 150 beads: for Peter the hermit the Rosary was a simple and private form of prayer in which people could repeat the Hail Mary as often as they wanted. In the past some Carmelite friars were members of Rosary Confraternities; and the form of the Rosary most commonly used was 6 or 7 decades, or else the Hail Mary 15 or 63 times and the Our Father 7 times.

The reformed province of Touraine and afterwards all the provinces of the stricter observance obliged the brothers to wear a rosary tied to their belt. The practice disappeared between the end of the 19th century and the beginning of the 20th. The practice, however, survived in the Provinces of Holland and of Rio de Janeiro up to the 1960s, surviving also among the womens' congregations and among the cloistered nuns.

For further reading concerning the history of Marian devotion in the Carmelite Order, see, V. Hoppenbrouwers, *Devotio Mariana in ordine fratrum B.V.M. de Monte Carmelo*, Roma 1960, pp.311-315.

Pages from the Anthology

1. WE ARE CHILDREN OF THE MOTHER OF JESUS

Federico de S. Antonio, *Il devoto di Maria del Carmine*, 2 edition, Milan 1882, pp. 564-566 and 572.

There is no denying that on the top of Calvary Christ gave the Blessed Virgin Mary to all the faithful represented by John the Apostle, as their Mother. When he said to the disciple John: "Here is your mother", it was indeed proper that if the first woman received the name Eve, *eo quod Mater esset cunctorum viventium*, the Mother of the second Adam should be given the privilege of being the Mother of Christians, Mater Christianorum.

Nevertheless, since it is the custom for the mothers of many children to favour particular one as in the case of Rebecca, who looked more kindly on Jacob than on Esau, it is very certain that the Virgin has a special way of being mother to those who wear her holy habit (…). Even if she had never given the gift of the sacred garment (the Scapular) she gave such innumerable graces and tender signs of love to her Carmelites. We know that she wants to be for us our good Mother; a mother who is always caring and attentive to our needs. The Church gives us a very beautiful name, Children of Mary, calling us *filius in scapularis societatem relatos* (Reading 6, Office BVM, 16th of July)

Have you ever thought about such an important privilege? I am a child of the Blessed Virgin, that Virgin who is the Mother of the Most High, that Virgin to whom devoted people offer their humble respect and the Angels and the saints as well? What a great dignity we have! If you were a child of an earthly Queen, how great you would think that was! How much more you should feel happy knowing that you are the children of Mary, the heavenly Queen. (…) Stop here to reflect, how great are the reasons you have for honouring Mary and of going confidently to her. You should honour her in special ways, since she honours you with such special favours. Her dignity as Mother and your duty as children mean that you should obey her, honour her and love her. How much benefit you will gain from this, if you fulfill your duties towards this great Mother!

Mary, Most glorious Queen of Carmel not only declares that she receives us as adopted children but even more, she accepts us as her brothers. A clear sign of this is what she said to the beloved Simon Stock, that the Scapular, would be a sign of confraternity, *Meae confraternitas signum*. Who will not be an admirer of the love of Mary? How many new inventions to attract our devotion! How unworthy I am of such a honourable name! The Queen of Heaven declaring that I am her brother! Where are the works that I do that measure up to such a glorious title! That your unequaled goodness, Mary, should deign to call yourself Sister of the poor, no less than of the rich, of nobles and of common people, I can understand; but that you would still want to raise me, sinner as I am, to such a high standing, I can only admire and give thanks for what in you is such an outstanding kindness. But since that is what you want to be for me, let it be so, and this glorious recognition will only increase my confidence in your most powerful protection. Abraham, as he was about to enter Egypt, in fear of being killed by the Egyptians, instructed Sarah, his wife, that she would say that she was his sister, something that was just in the thinking of those times, as she in fact was his cousin (…). You too, say to Mary when you are in need that she be your Sister, so that thanks to her, God may hear your prayer and turn everything to your good.

2. TRUST IN MARY

Texts read in the Liturgy of the Hours on the 16th of July, before the Council of Trent, extracts from, A. Forcadell, *Commemoratio sollemnis B.V. Mariae de Monte Carmelo*, Rome, 1951, pp. 127-129.

Mary! You are the protector of Carmel, full of compassion and attention towards those who turn to you: you are the head and crown of Carmel. Oh, Blessed Lady of Heaven! You are the flower of the virgins, the Queen of chaste souls; you are the pavilion of the truth, the sum of all goodness! Oh Rose of purity! You are the dignity of patience, the first fruits of justice, the violet of beauty. Oh Mirror of prudence! You are the field of strength, the book of temperance, the balance of equity, universal and unwavering hope, fortress of faith, consolation of the afflicted, refuge of sinners. You are the providence of the poor, the joy of the just, praise and honour of women, open gate of life, school of virtue, pearl of salvation, name of morality, sure health of the sick, a door to embrace the shipwrecked, throne full of strength, the cause of humility and the goal of holiness.

Out of a duty towards sacred nobility, dear brothers, we celebrate the festive commemoration of the holy Virgin, whose splendour has no equal in the feasts of other saints. She is the only one who does not refuse the prayers of whoever might turn to her; she alone has reached the perfection both of the Old and of the New Law….., If you repent for your sins stir up your confidence in this Mother. If you feel drawn by virtue, learn the lesson of purity from the Virgin. Flee from the impure deviations of your imagination, put a brake on your carnal instincts and enkindle in your heart a calm movement of holy love, so that , even if you cannot be a worthy preacher, you may at least be the humble servant of this glorious Virgin.

We really can say very little to praise her when we think of the height of her blessedness. In fact, she being the throne of the Father, the temple of the Son, the ark of the Holy Spirit, the glory of Lebanon, the beauty of Carmel and Sharon, she has the regality and she stands higher that the highest court of angels and of the human race. Come then, o Protector of Carmel, come and care for your beloved Carmelite family, and when you see the kind of affection our Carmelite family reserves for you, look even more kindly upon us. If prosperity should come to us, keep pride far away from us; if futilities increase, give us balance; if irregularities appear, stop our insolence; if everything is in order, help us to keep it that way. O Mother, who unites God, the angels and humanity, strengthen in us and preserve our mutual charity. Through your intercession, O Mother of Mercy, we believe that all that is lacking to us will be restored to us; through you we hope to be raised to the degree of holiness that is intended for us.

3. THE CARMELITES AND THE MEDIATRIX

Extracts from a variation on the Office for the Solemn Commemoration, probably from the end of the 15th and beginning of the 16th century.

> O purest conduit
> Through whom, like falling dew
> the Word descends from heaven
> enkindled by the Spirit
> to set the human heart on fire
> like a flame burning inside
>
> We sing a new song to you, Blessed Virgin
> so that by your intercession
> we may receive a viaticum
> for the life of heaven
>
> O Blessed Virgin,
> the most lovable of all
> be for all Carmelites
> the pathway
> whereby we may enjoy
> heavenly blessing
> in the company of all the blessed.
>
> O Blessed Virgin
> flower of chastity and star of glory
> Queen of Virgins and Mother of Grace
> Be merciful to your Carmelites
> and defend us, in your goodness,
> from all sadness.
>
> Salve, the only music that delights the ear of the king
> You are the trumpet of Gideon
> putting terror in the camp of the enemy
> You are the gentle timbrel
> that moves the hearts of the faithful:
> sure salvation and hope of all who suffer.
>
> Wellspring and Mother of Grace
> surround us with the grace that protects us
> from defeat in the battle.

4. IF I WERE A PRIEST

Text by, St. Therese of the Child Jesus, O.C.D. from her *Last Conversations*, August, 21st.

> How I would have loved to be a priest in order to preach about the Blessed Virgin! One sermon would be sufficient to say everything I think about this subject.

I'd first make people understand how little is known by us about her life. (…)

For a sermon on the Blessed Virgin to please me and do me any good, I must see her real life, not her imagined life. I'm sure that her real life was very simple. They show her to us as unapproachable, but they should present her as imitable, bring out her virtues, saying that she lived by faith just like ourselves, giving proofs of this from the Gospel, where we read: 'And they did not understand the words that He spoke to them'. And that other no less mysterious statement; 'His father and mother marveled at what was said about him'. (…)

We know very well that the Blessed Virgin is Queen of heaven and earth, but she is more Mother that Queen; and we should not say, on account of her prerogatives, that she surpasses all the saints in glory just as the sun at its rising makes the stars disappear from sight. My God! How strange that would be! A mother who makes her children's glory vanish! I myself think just the contrary. I believe she'll increase the splendour of the elect very much.

It is good to speak about her prerogatives, but we should not stop at this, and if, in a sermon, we are obliged from beginning to end to exclaim and say Ah! Ah! we would grow tired. Who knows whether some soul would not reach the point of feeling a certain estrangement from a creature so superior and would not say: If things are such, it's better to go and shine as well as one is able in some little corner!

What the Blessed Virgin has more than we have is the privilege of not being able to sin, she was exempt from the stain of original sin; but on the other hand, she wasn't as fortunate as we are, since she didn't have a Blessed Virgin to love. And this is one more sweetness for us and one less sweetness for her!

5. WHY I LOVE THEE, MARY

A selection of verses from the last poem of St. Therese of the Child Jesus (PN 54), translated by S.L. Emerly.

(1) Oh! I would like to sing, Mary, why I love you,
Why your sweet name thrills my heart,
And why the thought of your supreme greatness
Could not bring fear to my soul.
If I gazed on you in your sublime glory,
Surpassing the splendor of all the blessed,
I could not believe that I am your child.
O Mary, before you I would lower my eyes!…

(2) If a child is to cherish his mother,
She has to cry with him and share his sorrows.
O my dearest Mother, on this foreign shore
How many tears you shed to draw me to you!….
In pondering your life in the holy Gospels,
I dare look at you and come near you.
It's not difficult for me to believe I'm your child,
For I see you human and suffering like me ….

(6) O Queen of the elect, you make be feel,
that, step by step, it is not impossible
to follow you by the narrow road to heaven:
you make it easier to see,
by the humble virtues you have.
Walking behind you, Mary,
I want to remain small, the way I am now;
I am all too aware of the vanity of earthly glory.
I learn to act in ardent charity
by looking at Elizabeth who welcomed your visit.

(17) Mother full of grace, I know that in Nazareth
You live in poverty, wanting nothing more.
No rapture, miracle, or ecstasy
Embellish your life, O Queen of the Elect!
The number of little ones on earth is truly great.
They can raise their eyes to you without trembling.
It's by the ordinary way, incomparable Mother,
That you like to walk to guide them to Heaven.

(23) You appear to me, Mary,
standing on the top of Calvary,
standing at the foot of the cross, like a priest at the altar,
making an offering that will satisfy the justice of the Father,
gentle Emmanuel, your beloved Jesus.
Mother of sorrow, the prophet said of you,
There is no other pain like your pain.
O Queen of Martyrs, in your abandonment,
you pour out for us all the blood of your heart!

(24) The home of Saint John becomes your home,
the son of Zebedee takes the place of Jesus;
the last things to be told in the Gospel,
and after that they say nothing more about the Virgin Mary....
But this great silence, dear Mother,
does it not reveal that the Eternal Word himself
wants to sing of the secrets of your life,
to bring joy to your children, all the elect of heaven?

(25) Soon I'll hear that sweet harmony.
Soon I'll go to beautiful Heaven to see you.
You who come to smile at me in the morning of my life,
Come smile at me again … Mother … It's evening now! …
I no longer fear the splendor of your supreme glory.
With you I've suffered, and now I want
To sing on your lap, Mary, why I love you,
And to go on saying that I am your child.

For further study and reflection

I. Bibliography

- A. Forcadell, *Commemoratio solemnis Beatae Mariae Virginis de Monte Carmelo*, Roma, 1951
- Id., *La fiesta del Carmen, Historia y Liturgia*, Onda, 1986.
- E. Caruana, *Marian Liturgical Themes in the Liturgical Life of the Carmelite Order during the 16th Century*, in *De cultu Mariano saeculo XVI*, Romae, 1985, pp. 305-326.
- Id. *Analisi eucologica delle feste Mariane nell'Ordine di Siberto de Beke*, in *La dimensione Mariana del Carmelo*, I, pp. 51-57.
- Id., *Le feste Mariane dal 1312 al 1972*, ibid., I, pp. 58-67.
- J. Castellano Cervera, *La Virgen del Carmen en la Liturgia*, in *Congreso Mariano internacional*, pp. 131-158.
- A. Kallenberg, *Mary and Elijah in the liturgical tradition of the Carmelite Order*. A talk given at the Course for Ongoing Formation, Sassone, November, 2000.

II. For personal and/or group study:

1. In the Proper of the Liturgy of the Hours look up the texts (readings, antiphons, hymns and prayers) for the feast, and see the Carmelite values they contain.

2. Do the same with the texts for the Eucharist in the Carmelite Missal.

3. Check in the pre-Vatican II constitutions what Marian celebrations are treated.

III. Prayer and Life

1. Read the word of God:

    Is 35,1-10; 61,8-11.
    I Kg 18,42-45
    Prov 8,17-21. 34-35.

2. In the constitutions of your group, see what is said about the role, the place and the attention that is to be given to Mary in the personal lives of Carmelites and in their communities.

3. How does your community celebrate the feasts of Mary?

4. What is the basis of your devotion to Mary?

8

IN THE LIFE OF THE CHURCH

O Mary, faithful virgin
mother, always near
    by the light that comes from you
    may we find the surest way
to serve others,
and help them become citizens of God's kingdom.
Help us, let our presence in the community be kind,
caring and attentive towards others, like yours,
at home in Nazareth, and in the Upper Room in Jerusalem.
    for as long as the life of Carmel lasts
    enable us, like you, to look at the world
the way God looks at it
in order to be able to love it
the way God loves it.

May the very special gift of your presence,
our eldest Sister,
make us into true companions for everyone on the journey,
    companions along the road of faith,
    following Jesus Christ.

May your motherly presence,
arms opened wide,
attentive heart,
    gentle gaze, generous hands
    teach us the measure of love,
    the delicacy of service,
the warmth of welcome.

Thus ever more like you,
embraced by the grace that makes us beautiful for God,
    we may be gathered under your mantle
    and with you, already in eternity,
prolong our lives in love and joy.

        (A Carmelite Sister of Divine Providence)

8 IN THE LIFE OF THE CHURCH

The Scapular from the pastoral point of view

1. Popular piety

Before studying the pastoral significance of the scapular we need to look at this devotion in relation to popular piety of which it is a part. We need to have clear ideas about faith, religion, religiosity, and popular piety. In addition to this, in our case, it will be necessary also to identify the sources and the applications of this piety.

a) An explanation of concepts

It is useful to remember the following concepts:
- *Popular religion*: generally this term refers to the religion of the lower classes, as opposed to the religion of the upper classes and an "official" religion. This type of interpretation comes from a Marxist ideology and ignores other elements in the religion of the people.
- *Popular faith*: is a term used to indicate expressions of piety in their relation to faith, understood as the message of salvation and in reference to the person of Jesus Christ. Not always however does what is termed popular faith have this meaning. The term therefore, is sometimes ambiguous.
- *Popular religiosity*: this term is used to signify the practice of faith in the attitudes and behaviour of people.
- *Popular piety*: this is the source and the explanation of all the previous terms. Without this, expressions of religiosity could be reduced to forms of social or psychological conditioning in an underdeveloped culture. In the Synod of Bishops in 1974, Cardinal Pironio defined popular piety as follows, "it is the way in which Christianity is embodied in different cultures and ethnic settings, lived and manifested among the people". This definition makes reference to inculturation and to the various aspects of the life and expressiveness of faith (the way the universal takes shape in the particular).

b) Characteristics of popular piety

As characteristics of popular piety we might list the following:

- *spontaneity*: it springs more from feelings than from the certainties of reasoning and very often finds expression in creative forms more than in repetitive statements
- *festivity*: as a way of overcoming the monotonous routine of everyday.
- *An experience of the transcendent*: does not presuppose but simply offers a vision and an experience of the transcendent outside of every rational discourse.
- *Memory and sharing*: popular piety is a mixture of remembrance, personal experience and a desire for all that one can aspire to. It is based on faith and therefore it is evangelical, as a way of seeking the face of God. All of this has a collective and participatory character.

c) Expressions of popular piety

The expressions of popular piety might be classified as follows:

- expressions of prayer: this appears in prayers, songs, and devotional exercises through which there is an expression of praise and thanksgiving, intercession and reparation
- moments of celebration: feasts and special occasions, extra-liturgical and para-liturgical rites
- sacred actions, penitential pilgrimages, pilgrimages to shrines
- oblation, acts of sacrifice, vows and promises. As acts of faith and as expressions of prayer, invocation and thanksgiving, they are signs of a spiritual journey, a point of arrival, a memory.
- forms of consecration, medals and other blessed objects, scapulars as signs of belonging and of consecration

d) Most prominent Marian attitudes.

In popular piety the most prominent attitudes in relation to Mary move in these three directions:

- Mary, powerful Mother, merciful Mother, Mediatrix in the presence of her Divine Son.
- Mary, different from us who are sinners: most holy, most pure, the ideal image of the human race (the contemplation of the marvels of God manifested in Mary for us.
- Mary, close to the human race in its journey through time, shares with men and women sufferings, abandonment, comfort and hope.

e) Values and ambiguities in popular piety

Regarding this aspect, it would be useful to keep in mind a number of points that are in line with what *Evangelii nuntiandi* has to say (cf. no. 48)

- In the spiritual world every manifestation points to an interiority, an interior need to be in contact with the divine. This could be an anxiety for the Gospel not yet developed because of the lack of care or explanation, the lack of Christian formation and the neglect of attention to aspects of devotion that are deep-rooted in the hearts of the people.
- Sometimes this kind of popular piety runs the risk of being open to deformations and superstitions, without an authentic adherence to faith. In a case like this a person is more interested in satisfying an immediate need than in fundamental necessities: traditionalism becomes emphasized to the point of turning into fanaticism and individualism which has no openness to communion and finally leads to an evasion of reality where people proceed to live on the margins of the Church.
- Popular piety is not to be done away with, but *purified* (of dangers and ambiguities), *strengthened* (in what is positive) and elevated - in relation to Christ living in the Church – the Word, the liturgy, ecclesial communion.

2. The Scapular and popular piety

The Scapular in the context of popular piety points to certain perennial values of popular piety itself. They are values by which members of our Order have lived from the beginning, and shared with the whole Carmelite Family and with other people who are devoted to Mary. Carmelite Marian devotion therefore consists in the way in which people express the Carmelite Marian message. This devotion has its own sources and finds its own expressions.

a) Sources of Carmelite Marian devotion

The sources of Carmelite Marian devotion are the aspects of the mystery of Mary which we find as part of the history of Carmelite Marian piety and which are the result both of the development of the doctrinal dimension and of the way of living out certain spiritual realities.

In particular:

The PATRONESS, God's mother and our mother, mother of the Order

- in the mystery of the Mother of God, the Carmelites see the splendour of her union with God. People tried to copy this union, to the degree that was possible for them, through their prayer and their life. Thus we have a Christocentric basis for devotion to Mary (cf. the saying, "in allegiance to Christ and to Mary") The filial allegiance to Our Lady, woven from prayer and daily life (the imitation of her virtues) turns into a consecration to God and to Mary herself.
- In relation to the Patroness, the Lady of the place, the Mother of the Order, Mater Carmeli, the Carmelites themselves have a clear notion of her mediation, her powerful intercession and dispensation of graces. They see Mary taking full care of each Carmelite, body and soul, for all time and in eternity. In this setting, visions and privileges abound along with a very deep sense of belonging to Our Lady.

The VIRGIN:

- the virginity of Mary, more than in the sense of her physical integrity, is to be seen as an attitude of adherence to God, putting away everything that would separate from God, an attitude that is possible to imitate.
- the meaning of immaculate, (the most pure, the one who is totally different to sinners) led to the development of the concept of Most Pure Virgin.
- We can also talk about purity as conformity with the will of God and a participation in the divinity. It is both the condition and the effect of our union with God. It is Mary's beauty that, through her virginity, was united to the Word for eternity. Purity is related to the Carmelite characteristic of the interior life, made possible through virginity. Therefore the "Most Pure Virgin" as well as being in herself the object of contemplation in her union with God, is also the model of union with God. She is the "Flos Carmeli", the most beautiful flower of Carmel

The SISTER:

- in relation to Mary, Carmelites also talk about the similarities between her and Elijah. That gives rise to thoughts about Mary as sister. This leads to a relationship of familiarity and of presence.
- The "Most Pure Virgin" as an inspiring model becomes the one who is present in the family. The "Most Pure Virgin" from a model of inspiration becomes the one who is present in the Carmelite Family as its first member; She is the "Virgo Virginum Carmelita" (The Carmelite, Virgin of Virgins).

Therefore Patroness, Mother of Christ, Pure Virgin, Sister become the most perfect personification of the aspiration of the Order. Mary is the living ideal of Carmelite life, a life of union with God, of attention to the Word, of fraternity in the service of God. Besides being a model and a source of inspiration, Mary is at the same time a caring presence, a sister close to us, her brothers.

b) Particular expressions of Carmelite Marian devotion

With the passage of time, and with an ever deeper knowledge of these sources, Carmelites have expressed their devotion in many and var-

Particular Marian Devotions

To get a better grasp of popular Carmelite devotion it would be useful to analyse a number of expressions which we find in the Carmelite family in every age and place, in the past and in the present. The notes that follow describe briefly some of the most widely practiced devotions among Carmelites from the 16th century down to the present day.

These particular devotions may be divided into two groups :
• *those that spread within the Order*: The Seven Joys of Mary, The Seven Sorrows of Our Lady, The Most Holy Name of Mary, The Sacred Heart of Mary.
• *those that became known outside the Order*: devotion to Mary as La Bruna (which we will treat in greater detail elsewhere), devotion of the "slaves of the Mother of God"

a) The Seven Joys of Our Lady

This devotion was widely practiced in the Order in the Middle Ages. It was linked to an indulgence granted by Pope Paul V in 1606. An indulgence of 40 days was granted to those who recited every day the Our Father and the Hail Mary seven times in honour of the Seven Joys of Mary. This devotion was linked in a particular way to the prayers associated with the sabbatine privilege.

The prayer books in general say that the remembrance of these joys began with Saint Thomas of Canterbury. Joining this devotion to the veneration of Our Lady of Mount Carmel, is explained by the same prayer books, using the story which tells how Saint Berthold, in memory of the seven times that Elijah sent his servant to look out over the sea, recited the Hail Mary seven times.

The devotion of the Seven Joys had different forms, depending on the place, up until the time when everything was standardised. Every joy consists in announcing the particular joy, followed by the Our Father and the Hail Mary, both recited seven times. In Italy, for seven Wednesdays after Easter, each joy was generally accompanied by a meditation.

The most common of the seven joys were: the Annunciation, the Nativity, the Epiphany, the Resurrection, the Ascension, Pentecost and the Assumption. These are the joys that Mary enjoyed on earth in connection with the mystery of Christ. Another more modern form of the Seven Joys recalls the Seven Joys of Mary in heaven.

One author proposed, that if people did not have time for this devotion, they could follow the example of a novice who called Mary her mother and offered her each day seven flowers in honour of the Seven Joys.

b) The Seven Sorrows of Mary

Even though this practice might not have been directly related to devotion to Our Lady of Mount Carmel, it was nonetheless common among the members of the Order, both men and women, especially in Brazil and Portugal. The structure of this devotion is similar to the previous one, putting the Sorrows of Mary during Christ's passion in place of the joys.

c) The Name of Mary

There was an indulgence for everyone who, in letters, would include the words, "May Jesus and Mary be praised". The five letters of the name of Mary were used to form anagrams. In a more simple form, there was the practice of reciting the Hail Mary five times in honour of Mary's name. From Belgium and Germany came the practice of putting Mary's name on letterheads, on cards and on pictures. Sometimes an abbreviated form, MR, was used, with a crown put on top of it. There are still examples of notepaper that have the Carmelite shield at the top with this symbol.

d) Slaves of the Mother of God

This is a devotion that became widespread in the 16th and 17th centuries, especially in Spain, Portugal, Belgium, France and Poland, as well as other places. It is related to the baroque idea, by which, in order to have any dignity a Lady had to have slaves. The sign of this spiritual slavery offered to Mary was to have little marks on the hands and feet. Mathias of St. John proposed that these marks be replaced by the wearing of the Scapular, which he called, "the sign of special slavery to Mary". This devotion of slavery to Mary did not go down well with all Carmelites. Many were opposed to it because they saw themselves more as the children of Mary and not as her slaves, and Mary more as Mother and sister than as Lady and Queen.

For further study, see among others: V. Hoppenbrouwers, *Devotio Mariana in ordine fratrum B.V.M. de Monte Carmelo*, Roma 1960, pp. 278-301.

ied ways, especially in their prayer (including liturgical prayer); in acts of tender devotion towards images of Mary; fasting and abstinence from meat as expressions of devotion; and the spreading among the people of the Wednesday devotions, the Joys of Mary and the Saturday devotion to Mary.

The wearing of the Scapular underwent enormous development from the 16th century onwards, as an expression of membership of the Carmelite Family in which Mary takes total care, body and soul, in time and in eternity, of each member; and as a reminder to religious and laity alike of all the wealth of the "sources" of Marian-Carmelite devotion.

An apostolate of the Scapular, geared towards today's needs, should keep these sources of popular devotion in mind and appropriately renew the ways in which they are expressed. Therefore the first issue to be treated must be the content of this devotion, and then the forms in which it can be expressed in pastoral practice.

3. Contents

The demands of present-day Mariology assert that whatever is said about Mary must be placed within a vision of the mystery of Christ and of the Church; a demand we find expressed in the documents of the Church, as well as in theological discourse. Therefore, devotion to Mary, through the Scapular, must get to the heart of the Marian mystery without separating it from the mystery of Christ, which is its base, and without separating it from the mystery of the Church, in which it finds its meaning. Mary is everything that she is given, on account of being the Mother of the Lord, and she is also all that she is because of the Church, of which she is the figure, on account of her vocation to be Mother of God and Mother of the Church. In light of this, one must speak of Mary, Mother of Christ and our Mother, of her mediation of grace, of her intercession, of her being a disciple of the Lord. The Church "contemplates in her, as in a pure image, all that she desires and hopes to be".

In order to present the Scapular as a truly Marian devotion, in a way that is authentic, we need to look at the following points:

a) The Scapular is a means of affiliation to the Order

The first meaning of the Scapular is to be a means of association with the Order, which is clearly christocentric and Marian. This association involves a sharing in the life of the Order, its values, its ideals of union with God and of helping others.

Through the Scapular, the faithful are introduced into the entirety of the life of the Order, and not just linked to it through devotion to Mary. The Marian dimension, in itself, begins from a Carmelite Chrisotcentric stance. Therefore, being associated with the Order through the Scapular includes, along with an experience of Mary, a commitment to live according to the Christocentric nature of Carmel.

b) The Scapular is a sign of consecration to Mary

As a sign of consecration to Mary, the Scapular expresses and witnesses to our desire to climb the mountain which is Christ, along with Mary, the faithful disciple of the Lord. The concept of commitment involves the notion of a covenant pact with God, which is the highest form of fidelity to God. For the human person, such a high form of commitment bears a greater guarantee when it is supported by the mediation of Mary.

c) The Scapular is a remembrance of the mercy of God through Mary

In order to emphasise the christological value of Carmelite devotion to Mary, it is good to remember that the Scapular is a memorial of our incorporation into Christ, towards which the human person proceeds in union with Mary. The ideal of the Scapular consists in believing in the spiritual and divine Maternity of Mary and in her mediation, trusting in that, living in faithful dependence on her and witnessing, as a consequence, to her living presence in the history of salvation, cooperating so that the incarnation of Christ becomes a reality in the world of today.

d) The Scapular is a sacramental

As a sacramental the Scapular gives rise to special relationships with Mary. Here we find certain "values" from our tradition which need to be recovered and understood in the context of today, with some attention also to the interdisciplinary dimensions which includes biblical and theological data from our tradition e.g. the anthropological, symbolic and other dimensions included in these data.

Some examples and lines to follow:

• *Mary, Mother*:

- This term captures Mary's attitudes of mercy and tenderness (the Patroness), in a word, her affection. In this context we can also understand what John of Hildesheim and Michael of St. Augustine say about our participation in the affective life of Christ in relation to his Mother. The biblical images that we find in our tradition in relation to this are the Annunciation, the Mother of Sorrows at the foot of the Cross, and the Assumption.

• *Mary, Pure Virgin*:

- This expression highlights Mary's purity of heart, the transparency of her life in intimacy with God. The model of life that we contemplate in her gives evidence of the fundamental attitudes of Mary, her spiritual and mystagogical journey as a movement towards maturity. That is why Mary is a life model for Carmelites. She is a disciple on the journey. The biblical image behind this title in our tradition is the Immaculate Conception and the Annunciation.

• *Mary, Sister*

- This title represents a way of talking about Mary's presence among us: the mutual familiarity between her and the members of Carmel. This presence leads to the composition of a marian mysticism as a transformation in the Spirit and a consciousness of the mystery of God. The image behind this title in our tradition is the dedication of the Chapel on Mount Carmel to Mary, and a consonance in virginity.

• *Mary, Prophet:*

- Because Mary prays with the word (see Ribot and Bostius) she accepts and understands the mystery of Christ (see Bostius), proclaiming it (see Baconthorpe, Bostius and Soreth), witnessing to it (see Sigbert de Beka). In line with the Carmelite traditon liturgy is understood as an experience of the mystery of Christ lived with Mary.

There are also other points that should be borne in mind when considering the debate concerning the Scapular:

The vision of St. Simon Stock

• The vision is historically problematic. That it is false has not been proven and the proofs for its authenticity are neither sufficient nor satisfactory. It has to be said that this vision is handed down by a venerable tradition of the Order but it is better not to insist on the question of its historical authenticity, but rather to place the significance of the vision mostly in the context of Mary's patronage, the protection and mediation of Mary for those devoted to her.

- *The Sabbatine Bull*

  - As we have already demonstrated, this bull was not authentic. The content of the document contains contradictions that are both theological and juridical. The decree of the Holy Office of 1613, reconfirmed on various occasions afterwards, prohibits talking about this bull as a papal document which grants this privilege.

- *The Sabbatine privilege*

  - The content of this privilege was approved and confirmed by the popes from Clement VII onwards (1530). The popes allowed that people should speak about immediate liberation from purgatory especially on Saturdays, not because of an indulgence, but through the love of Mary for those who are devoted to her. Therefore, the "sabbatine privilege" has to be based on the doctrine of the spiritual motherhood of Mary for humankind and her universal mediation without any reference to the bull or to Pope John XXII.

4. Expressions

In the past, in the Order, a number of different expressions of popular devotion were cultivated in relation to the Mary in the Carmelite tradition and to the Scapular. These are:

- *Prayers* (The Joys of Mary, novenas, etc.): they gave rise to an awareness of the patronage of Mary, her protection, and mediation, with a sense of admiration and gratitude to God and to her;
- *Carmelite devotion on Wednesdays*: comes across as an experience of transcendence (devotional experiences and common prayers) as a catechesis (through the homily), as a penitential moment (abstinence from meat)
- *Saturdays*: understood as a liturgical experience (taking part in the Saturday Mass) and as a penitential moment (abstinence from meat)
- *Marian feast-days*: as occasions for festive celebration, the creating of memories and of fraternal relations within the Carmelite Family.

As can be easily seen, on the basis of a comparison with what has been said heretofore these forms of Carmelite devotion are characteristic expressions of popular devotion.

As we already recalled, in the past Confraternities were the principal and most favoured means for the practice of the Scapular devotion. From the 17th century up to the 19th, whoever wore the Scapular was of necessity a member of a recognised, local confraternity that had its own rules and regulations, commitments and activities. Calling to mind what we said about Scapular Confraternities, we can see in them very vital social and devotional elements, both as regards individuals and communities.

In particular:

- The devotional aspects were fed by the devotional practices (rosaries and novenas etc.) and the reception of indulgences both plenary and partial.
- The life of the people was marked by an intense sacramental life and the practice of penance (abstinence from meat on Wednesdays and Saturdays);
- The social aspects consisted in the members helping one another. As in a fraternal

Private Practices of Devotion to Mary

There were a number of private practices of devotion that became widespread throughout the Order. Here are some examples.

a) The Little Office of Our Lady

As well as the prescriptions of General Chapters and Constitutions relating to the community recitation of the Little Office of Our Lady, the individual private recitation was also encouraged. The Marian office spread also among Tertiaries and Scapular confraternities, after the Holy Office in 1613 decreed that it should be recited as one of the conditions for obtaining the sabbatine privilege. The individual and community recitation of the Little Office remained in the Order up to the Second Vatican Council.

We have also, in our own time, the fact that some lay Carmelites, instead of the traditional prayers which were prescribed for them, have taken to saying this Office.

b) Litanies

There was in the Order, before 1601, a great variety of litanies. In that year, Pope Clement VIII approved the final text of the Litanies of Loreto, and forbade the use of all other forms. Among Carmelites, in the aftermath of this prescription, some of their own invocations were added to the Loreto Litanies. These invocations were taken from earlier litanies. Among these the most common were, "Mother and Ornament of Carmel", "Virgin Flower of Carmel", "Patroness of Carmelites", "Hope of all Carmelites". The use of litanies became widespread in all the houses and many of the religious recited them in private. In the confraternities, the litanies were sung during processions and meetings. It was also the custom to sing litanies on feast-days, at the vigils of Marian feasts, on Wednesdays and Saturdays. Sometimes music was especially composed for the Carmelite Litanies, as for example those that are still used in Cagliari (Italy) on the first Wednesday of the year and during the Novena for the Feast of Our Lady of Mount Carmel. At the moment in Latin America the "benditos" ("blesseds") and other forms of popular litanies are still widely used in Brazil, especially in the North East, with invocations relating to the needs of the people.

For further study, see among others: V. Hoppenbrouwers, *Devotio mariana in Ordine fratrum B.V.M. de Monte Carmelo*, Roma 1960, pp. 302-319.

community, they fulfilled the works of mercy, outside and within the group, and everyone was expected to contribute in some way.

In reality, confraternities became, by reason of their structure and life, a way of fostering the Marian devotion that belonged to the Order, with particular attention to the spiritual life of the people.

From the time that large numbers of confraternities ceased to exist, due to the suppression of religious institutions in the 19th century, the pastoral dimension of the Scapular devotion began to disappear. With the passage of time, we see an attempt by the Order to look upon the wearers of the Scapular as belonging to one "general" confraternity. In this way, many of the characteristics of the former confraternities were lost. The confraternities that remained gradually began to look like sodalities in which the members could have access to great spiritual privileges with a minimum of commitment and effort. At the same time, within these groups and outside them, the Scapular was presented more in terms of devotionalism, and with an accent on indulgences and privileges, without much preparation, and without much attention to a spiritual journey. The result was that in many places the wearers of the Scapular were left entirely to their own devices. Some attempt was made, through the Third Order, offering it as a sodality that had a special devotion to the Mother of Carmel, but even this suffered from the tendency to be merely devotional.

The famous interventions of Pius XII regarding the Scapular did not produce much change, apart from a few very laudable initiatives here and there in the Order. In general, from the decade of the sixties onwards, there was little attempt to re-read our Marian heritage, and there was little effort to create new structures based on an effective pastoral approach towards the content of the devotion.

This is where the challenge for our day comes in: engage in a new reading of the heritage of the Marian tradition of the Order and look for a structure that is suitable as a pastoral approach, which will be able to help the whole Carmelite world in its growth to maturity and Christian living in the company of Mary. Of late we have seen some very valuable initiatives in this regard: studies, congresses and publications. It is the beginning of something new. There is still much to be done in terms of our pastoral approach.

5. Some pastoral suggestions

For an apostolate of the Scapular, bearing in mind our cultural situation, a first undertaking might be one of conscientisation, in order thereafter to create suitable pastoral outreaches.

We would suggest the following:

- Extend this conscientisation to all the pastoral workers: to priests, religious men and women, lay men and women tertiaries;
- Base it on the content of our rich Marian spiritual heritage and that of the nature, characteristics and demands of popular devotion;
- Through courses, meetings, sharing and live-in experiences come to a series of criteria for pastoral action.

While this work of conscientisation is going on, in its speculative and experiential dimensions, work can be done at the same time to help people in their spiritual journey with Mary the Mother of Carmel. We might, for example, suggest the following:

- Put together a suitable marian catechesis, through meetings, lectures and so on, as a preparation for the reception of the Scapular. To do this successfully a good collection of study aids will be needed;

- Place the giving of the Scapular in the context of a liturgical celebration that will better highlight its Christocentric value;
- In the churches of the Order, offer the people the possibility of having regular devotions and meetings, with celebrations of the Word, prayer groups, formation meetings, some direction and guidance in relation to the sacraments and to social commitment. This process could be helped by the traditional practices already rooted in the heart of the people, such as the Wednesday devotions, the Saturday Mass, with a proper up-dating.
- help to set up groups, even of a spontaneous nature, which will bring together the wearers of the Scapular, who would otherwise remain isolated. Failing that, at least foster the kind of interest and enthusiasm that would encourage these people to take part in the moments of celebration and prayer that are held in their "local" Carmelite churches.
- Encourage the formation of a Carmelite movement that would unite the people who wear the Scapular, the friends of Carmel and Tertiaries. Within this movement, each group should be free to follow at its own pace in order to be able to accompany the spiritual growth of its members and their movement towards an ever deeper commitment to Carmel. The dynamic of the movement should be one of helping the individual to move from a superficial relationship with Mary to one of a deeper appreciation of devotion to her in its various dimensions, contemplative, sacramental, and social, with a firm commitment to the works of justice. In this way a genuine marian spirituality will flourish.

In our fraternal dialogue, in the heart of the Carmelite Family, other possibilities will no doubt emerge as well as new forms of pastoral outreach, with abundant benefits for the life of the people of God.

ECCE SIGNVM SALVTIS SALVS IN PERICVLIS:
IN QVO QVIS MORIENS ÆTERNVM NON PATIETVR INCEN

Pages from the Anthology

1. THE SCAPULAR, SYMBOL OF THE VIRTUES OF MARY

From the letter of Pius XII, 11th of February, 1950, on the occasion of the 7th centenary of the Scapular of the Blessed Virgin Mary, Mother of God, of Mount Carmel, edit. In *Acta Apostolicae Sedis* 42(1950) pp. 390-391.

There is no one who is not aware how greatly a love for the Blessed Virgin Mother of God contributes to the enlivening of the Catholic faith and to the raising of the moral standard. These effects are especially secured by means of those devotions, which more than others are seen to enlighten the mind with celestial doctrine and to excite souls to the practice of the Christian life. In the first rank of the most favoured of these devotions that of the Holy Carmelite Scapular must be placed – a devotion which, adapted to the minds of all by its very simplicity, has become so universally widespread among the faithful and produced so many and such salutary fruits.

Therefore it has pleased us greatly to learn of the decision of our Carmelite Brethren, both Calced and Discalced, namely to take all pains to pay homage to the Blessed Virgin Mary in as solemn a manner as possible on the occasion of the Seventh Centenary of the Institution of the Scapular of Our Lady of Mount Carmel. Prompted therefore by our constant love for the tender Mother of God, and mindful also of our own enrolment from boyhood in the Confraternity of this Scapular, most willingly we commend so pious an undertaking, as we are certain that upon it will fall an abundance of divine blessings. For not with a light or passing matter are we here concerned but with the obtaining of eternal life itself, which is the substance of the Promise of the Most Blessed Virgin which has been handed down to us. We are concerned, namely, with that which is of supreme importance to all and with the manner of achieving it safely. For the Holy Scapular, which may be called the Habit or Garment of Mary, is a sign and a pledge of the protection of the Mother of God. But not for this reason, however, may they who wear the Scapular think they can gain eternal salvation while remaining slothful and negligent of spirit, for the Apostle warns us: "In fear and trembling shall you work out your salvation" Phil 2,12.

Therefore all Carmelites, whether they live in the cloisters of the First and Second Orders or are members of the Third Order Regular or Secular, or of the Confraternities, belong to the same family of our Most Blessed Mother and are attached to it by a special bond of love. May they all see in this keepsake of the Virgin herself a mirror of humility and purity; may they read in the very simplicity of the Garment a concise lesson in modesty and simplicity; above all may they behold in this same Garment, which they wear day and night, the eloquently expressive symbol of their prayers for divine assistance; finally may it be to them a Sign of their Consecration to the Most Sacred Heart of the Immaculate Virgin, which (consecration) in recent times we have so strongly urged.

And certainly this most gentle Mother will not delay to open, as soon as possible, through her intercession with God the gates of Heaven for her children who are expiating their faults in Purgatory – a trust based on that Promise known as the Sabbatine Privilege.

2. AUTHENTIC DEVOTION TO MARY AND TO THE CARMELITE SCAPULAR

From the letter of Paul VI to the Cardinal Legate for the Marian and Mariological Congress in Santo Domingo, 2nd of February, 1965. ed. *Acta Apostolicae Sedis* 57(1965) pp.377-379.

Convey our good wishes, and our words of encouragement which are inspired by the dogmatic constitution of the Second Vatican Council: May the faithful hold in high esteem the practices and exercises of devotion towards her (the Blessed Virgin) recommended by the teaching authority of the Church in the course of centuries: (LG n.67) among which we should like to mention explicitly the Rosary and the wearing of the Carmelite Scapular. This latter "adapted to the minds of all by its very simplicity, has become so universally widespread among the faithful and produced so many and such salutary fruits". (Pius XII)

When instruction is being given to the believers about Marian devotion, let it be said, with insistence and clarity, that "while the mother is honoured, the Son through whom all things have their being (cf. Col 1,15-16) and in whom it has pleased the Father that all fullness should dwell (cf. Col 1,19) is rightly known, loved and glorified and his commandments are observed" (LG n.66)

There must be an insistence that devotion to Mary, "consists neither in sterile or transitory affection, nor in a certain vain credulity, but proceeds from true faith by which we are led to recognise the excellence of the Mother of God and we are moved to a filial love towards our mother and to the imitation of her virtues" (LG n.67)

Let a devotion to the Virgin Mary that is pure and sincere be fostered in the faithful, so that they may truly be children of this Mother, imitating her virtues, giving an example of charity, harmonizing their own feelings, words and customs with the first model of Christian life, Jesus Christ, the mediator between God and humanity, the author of human salvation.

It is necessary, devoutly and faithfully, to honour the Blessed Virgin Mary, Mother of God, Mother of the Church, Mother of grace and mercy, Mother of hope and holy joy, so that, as if by a royal pathway, we may come to Jesus, and to the font of salvation.

3. THE PRESENCE OF OUR LADY OF MOUNT CARMEL IN CHRISTIAN LIFE

Address by John Paul II at the Sunday *Angelus*, in Castel Gandolfo, 24th of July 1988. *L'Osservatore Romano*, 25-26 July, 1988.

In this month of July we have celebrated the memory of the Blessed Virgin Mary of Mount Carmel, so much part of the devotion of Christians throughout the world, bound up especially with the life of the Carmelite religious family. Our thoughts are led to the holy mountain, which in the world of the Bible, has always been taken to be the symbol of grace, blessing and beauty. On this mountain the Carmelites dedicated to Mary, the Virgin Mother of God, *Flos Carmeli*, in whom the beauty of all the virtues shone, their first Church. This was an expression of their desire to entrust themselves completely to her and to unite their service of Mary enduringly to their "allegiance to Jesus Christ" (cf. the Carmelite Rule, n.1)

The great Carmelite mystics understood the experience of God in their own lives as a "way of perfection" (St. Teresa of Jesus), and as the "ascent of Mount Carmel" (St. John of the Cross). Mary is present throughout this journey. Invoked by the Carmelites as Patroness, Mother and Sister, she, as the Most Pure Virgin, is the model of contemplatives, attentive in her listening to the Word, and pondering upon it, obedient to the will of the Father, through Jesus Christ, in the Holy Spirit. Therefore in Carmel itself, and in every Carmelite heart, a life of intense communion and familiarity with the Holy Virgin is formed, as a new way of living for God and of continuing here on earth the love of Jesus, the Son of God, and of Mary his Mother.

One special grace of the Blessed Virgin towards the Carmelites, recalled by a venerable tradition linked to St. Simon Stock, has spread throughout the world, producing many spiritual fruits. It is the Carmelite scapular, a means of affiliation with the Carmelite Order, for the purpose of sharing in its spiritual benefits, a sign of tender and filial devotion to Mary (cf. Pius XII, Apostolic Letter, *Nemini profecto latet*)

By means of the Scapular people devoted to Our Lady of Mt. Carmel, express their desire to shape their lives in accordance with Mary's example, the Mother, Patroness, Sister and Most Pure Virgin, by receiving, with a purified heart, the Word of God, and devoting themselves zealously to the service of others, their brothers and sisters.

I now invite all those who are devoted to the Blessed Virgin to pray to her fervently, so that, by her intercession, she may obtain for each one the grace to walk securely along the pathway of life and to reach the "holy mountain, Christ the Lord" (cf. the collect of the Mass in honour of the Blessed Virgin Mary of Mount Carmel, July 16).

4. MARY, THE MODEL OF CHRISTIAN LIFE

Text by the Carmelite Marian Commission, *Interim Report*, Rome, 1985.

A Marian renewal is underway in the Church today. The two decades following the second Vatican Council have been a painful period with regard to the Virgin Mary, and religious families of special dedication to Our Lady have also suffered malaise with respect to her place in their lives and spirituality. The difficulties of these years have helped purge away some admitted defects of pre-conciliar piety, and in fact the Council had more to say about the Mother of the Lord than any previous ecumenical council in history. More importantly, in setting forth the Church in her true beauty, as a sacrament of Christ who is the "light of the nations" (Lumen gentium, the dogmatic constitution on the Church) the Council taught an understanding of Our Lady less in terms of privileged exceptions to general rules (e.g. all others have original sin, where she did not) than as the archetype of the divine design for all human beings. She is the perfect exemplar, the ideal model of the plan of the Father of mercies to bring all his human children to grace and glory through his Son made man ("for us and for our salvation") in the power of the Holy Spirit.

The Council presented a portrait of Mary as the great Gospel woman of Faith, from her consent at the Annunciation to Calvary and Pentecost, where the Acts of the Apostles describe her as joined to the disciples in common prayer for the outpouring of the Spirit, obedient to the command of the risen and ascended Christ her Son (Acts 1,13-14). The Council extended its considerations of Mary by salient reflections from the Fathers, particularly Irenaeus, Ambrose and Augustine. Mary's obedience untied the knot of Eve's disobedience (Irenaeus). She is the faithful disciple, conceiving Christ in her heart even before she conceived him in her womb (Augustine). The Mother of Jesus is the "figure of the Church" (Ambrose). Special veneration and love are due the Blessed Virgin because God made her the holy Mother of the Saviour. She is joined to him now in glory in the communion of saints and is a "sign of sure hope and comfort for the pilgrim people of God" (Lumen gentium, n.68). In the careful thought of St. Anselm (+1109) the patristic insights are carried into medieval monastic theology about the Blessed Virgin.

The Council sought to present a pastoral portrait of Mary, in intimate association with Christ, as the freely consenting and faithful Mother of the Saviour, completely given over to her Son's saving work (ch. 8 of Lumen gentium). In their first constitution, on the liturgy, at the second session, 1963, the conciliar Fathers put it succinctly: "In celebrating the annual cycle of Christ's mysteries, holy Church honours with special love the Blessed Mary, Mother of God, who is joined by an inseparable bond to the saving work of her Son. In Mary the Church holds up and admires the most excellent fruit of the redemption, and joyfully contemplates, as in a faultless model, that which the Church herself wholly desires and aspires to be" (*Sacrosanctum Concilium*, n.103, on the liturgical year)

Here we have the key elements of Marian devotion: it is as we honour Christ that we show also special love for Mary; she is intimately associated with his salvific work, even though through the Immaculate Conception she herself was redeemed; she is the flawless model (technically, archetype, first achievement) of the Church in all its hopes.

The revised western liturgy was a result of the Council, and the changes effected in the Marian sections reflect well the imperatives and intuitions of the Council.

On Feb. 2, 1974, *Marialis cultus* (On devotion to Mary in the Church and its promotion) of Pope Paul VI was published, as an answer to fears that the Church was forgetting the Mother of the Lord. It is a warm presentation of Our Lady's role, especially in the liturgy, with attention also to the rosary and the Angelus, and a rich selection of texts from the current liturgical books. Like the Council, *Marialis cultus* addressed modern needs, such as woman's dignity and ecumenism. Pope John Paul II has continued to relate the Blessed Virgin to contemporary problems, not least in his many addresses to young people in every land he visits. As well as many individual bishops, a number of national Episcopal conferences have issued Pastorals on Our Lady, e.g. in Switzerland, Germany, Italy, the Philippines and the United States of America (this last Pastoral, *Behold Your Mother, Woman of Faith*, Nov. 21, 1973 may be regarded as a Carmelite contribution, for the principal author was Eamon R. Carroll, O.Carm.).

Even a cursory survey of current writing would show the serious attention being given to Our Lady in many sectors: Scripture, the Fathers, ecumenism, etc. In the decades after the Council, the work of Scriptural exegetes has shown the enormously rich portrait of Mary the woman and of her role that is to be found in what we might easily have regarded as only brief references to her in the Bible.

The Council called for the renewal of religious life, recommending loyalty to the charisms proper to individual orders and congregations. We have experienced in Carmel efforts at renewal of our heritage of prayer. A similar task awaits us with respect to our Marian inheritance, not as an historical heirloom but as a vibrant way of living and praying our Carmelite vocation, which is not simply for ourselves as a family matter but in service to the Church at large. Some significant steps have already been taken by the Order to promote a recaptured appreciation of Mary as the Mother and Ornament of Carmel (*Mater et decor Carmeli*). She is our sister as well as our mother, for she is the model disciple, our guide along the way of faith, to Calvary as well as to Bethlehem and Nazareth, but also to Easter and Pentecost (recall Carmelite devotion to the seven joys of Mary).

These interim puncta aim to draw attention to the central areas of Carmelite "Mariology", using the word "Mariology" here not simply for formal study (as in a seminary course) but for the whole reality of the mystery of Mary in Carmelite register – doctrines, devotion (liturgy and other forms), pastoral, the historical and present role of the Scapular etc. These areas of Carmelite concentration (e.g. patroness, mother, sister ....) will be related to present-day theology and spirituality.

To appreciate our Marian charism we must know its origins, but for that charism to be living and productive we must integrate our history with what is best in contemporary biblical, liturgical, ecumenical and anthropological perspectives. We will focus on Our Lady of Mt. Carmel as our Mother and sister, as the sinless one, the pure Virgin who draws us from the fears that haunt humanity to the experience of God's love and merciful care. (...)

A great encouragement in our task is the shift that has taken place in recent decades. (....) Even though this shift may seem new, even novel, it has roots in Christian antiquity, back in the New Testament itself, and in early Christian authors (new Eve, holy ever-Virgin etc.) for Mary is model for all, for men and for women, with different nuances. She shows the way to full discipleship of Christ, who also is the perfect model for men and women. Mary as model of Christian life has great appeal for our contemporaries: both as recipient of God's gifts and as the one who responded so generously to God's invitation. She thus was at the beginning of a new stage in God's plan for the liberation of his people. Without ignoring the danger of condensing a rich development into short phrases, we might say that current Mariology has moved from a "privilege" vertical mentality to a "communion of saints" horizontal outlook, which is enriching also for the renewal of our Carmelite Marian charism.

For further study and reflection

I. Bibliography

- E. Esteve, *Lo Scapolare della Madonna del Carmine* (note di pastorale) in *Studi Francescani*, 65(1968) pp.386-391.
- E. Boaga, *Reflexions pera una pastora de l'escapulari del Carme*, in *Butlleti informatiu de la provincia Carmelitana de Catalunya* 19(1988)152, pp. 127-133.
- L. Saggi, *Espressioni principali di pietà popolare mariana carmelitana*, in *La dimensione mariana del Carmelo*, I, pp.79-86.
- E. Monari, *Contenuti mariani dai testi devozionali*, in *La dimensione mariana del Carmelo*, I, pp. 87-92
- Carmelite Marian Commission, *Interim Report*, Rome, 1985
- C. Cicconetti, *La pietà mariana carmelitana: prospettive* in AA.VV., *Maria icona della tenerezza del Padre*, Palermo, 1992, pp.192-210
- L. Nasta, *La diaconia dei santuari mariani nella chiesa locale*, in AA.VV. *Maria icona della tenerezza del Padre*, Palermo, 1992, pp.223-230.

II. For individual or group study

1. Read the basic text, recording the ideas that seem most significant.

2. From the text and the inserts, list the expressions of popular piety that you find. What values do they express?

3. What Marian characteristics can be found in your community? In your apostolate? How are they expressed?

III. Prayer and Life

1. Pray with the Word of God

   Lk 11,27-28
   Lk 2,1-14
   Zech 1,14-17
   Is 61,1-9

2. With regard to "Some suggestions for the apostolate", look into the question of what can be done to renew Marian devotion among the people.

3. Check the Marian values you find in the songs and hymns you sing in your own community.

4. What suggestion would you make regarding a revitalization of Marian devotion among the people, with elements that come from our spirituality, with due consideration for the nature, demands and expressions of this devotion?

9

ICONS OF TENDERNESS

Sing with a heart on fire,

The woman whom I always desire to love,
    And without whom I have no desire to live,
    Queen of heaven and earth,
The woman whom I always desire to love.

    All those who have no thought for her
Cultivate meaningless loves
    Corrupt and corrupting
All those who have no thought for her

Because she is the only one of her kind
    There is no other like her
    And there never will be
Because she is the only one of her kind.

                        (Arnold Bostius,
                         De Patronatu et patrocinio, n. 1534)

9 ICONS OF TENDERNESS

An iconographical study of Saint Mary of the Carmelites

1. Introduction

Religious art was not invented by artists. It is rather a representation, in visual form, of what people believed and how they lived at the time that the work of art was produced. The artist, in order to produce the desired image, has to go deeply into the emotion and the culture, the spirituality and the vision of his world and the world of the person who commissions the work. In accordance with the ability of the artist, "his" image will move the heart of the person who looks at the work of art, which becomes a message that is visible and alive. This is where the importance of iconographical study comes in, which as well as pointing to the work of the artist, also discovers the message that helps us to understand the vitality and wealth of the various eras.

We offer here some details on the topic, "Saint Mary of the Carmelites". They will help us to understand what has been said about Mary through art within Carmel, that is, how Mary was presented in the art that was commissioned for the Churches of the Order. As a result, some light will be shed on how Mary was presented in the world of the Carmelite confraternities, and in churches not run by the Carmelite Order.

2. Themes in Marian iconography

A. The most common Marian iconography between the 13th and 15th centuries

At the time of the origins of the Carmelite Order, and the first stage of its development in Europe, (the second half of the 12th and first half of the following century) there is a common thread in the artistic conception of Mary that is connected with the most dominant forms in the Christian world of the east. The norms of this style were set down in a well-known manual, called the Mount Athos Manual.

These norms, which determined the whole of Byzantine Marian iconography, can be divided in two groups:
- The *icon-portrait* of Mary
- The *festive-icon* with representations of the episodes of the life of Christ, of Mary and of the saints

a) The icon-portrait of Mary

We have a number of different types and models on this theme available to us, most of which come from the 12th and 13th centuries:

The *Odighitria,* the one who points the way
In this image Jesus Christ, the Child, has an expression on his face of one who is "Eternal Wisdom"; with his right hand he blesses and with the left he holds the scroll of the Sacred Scriptures. Mary, the Mother of God, facing forward, turns her eyes towards us; with one arm she supports her child while with the other, she points to him, "He is the way".
This iconographical motif, which exalts the divinity, began to spread from the 6th century onwards. During the Crusades, up to the year 1261 a picture of this kind was always carried in processions.
- *The Eleusa,* or Our Lady of Tenderness (in Greek also called *Glicofilussa* - the one with the sweet kiss).

This iconographical motif sets out to exalt the human aspects: the faces of the mother and the Child rest on one another in an expression of gentle intimacy. In this Marian icon the position of the hands is typical: all four are very visible and the affectionate embrace between Mother and Child is very expressive. This motif gave inspiration to a number of different Marian icons, the most notable of which is the one by Vladimir, painted in the first half of the 12th century, in Constantinople.

- *The Kyriotissa*, the Queen

  This icon exalts the royalty of the subject. Mary appears seated on the throne with the Child in her arms. In general, icons of this type are adorned with angels and saints.

- The *Platytera*, "the One who is greater than the heavens"

  In this image Mary appears standing, like "the One who contains the uncontainable, the God-Child, represented inside the circle".

In all of these images we find common elements in the composition:

- Three stars visible on the head and on the shoulder of Mary (sometimes one of them is covered by the Child) are the traditional sign of the virginity of Mary, before, during and after the birth of her child. The star with a tail, on the right shoulder means the same thing.
- The blue colour of the mantle indicating the Maternity of Mary.
- The red colour of the clothing over the mantle, partially covering the Child is a sign of the love the Mother has for her Child.

b) *The festive, or composite, icon.*

This type of icon presents Mary within the mystery of Christ, highlighting a particular feast, or a particular gospel passage. This type became much more common from the 14th century onwards. The icons themselves can be adorned with a series of pictures juxtaposed on them, which at their centre, portray the mystery that is being contemplated.

B. - *Later developments*

In Europe, the laws of the Mount Athos Manual exercised an influence throughout the Middle Ages. With the coming of Cimabue (+ 1302) a movement away from Byzantine models began to be seen. He in fact was responsible for spreading the title of the Queenship of Mary (Our Lady in Majesty) that sees Mary seated on the throne surrounded by angels.

Giotto (+ 1337) finally cuts with the past and begins a new cycle in the chapel of Scrovegni in Padua depicting Mary as a very real woman. Mary appears as a woman who is conscious of the importance of the mission announced to her by the angel: she is very motherly, engrossed in her child. She is depicted in deep sorrow when she holds in her arms the body of her dead Son.

The new development then gave rise to new themes in the composition of the paintings. The figure of the Lady takes on new dimensions: she is the heavenly lady, the woman with a heart that rejoices and weeps with humanity, one who is felt to be close, one who shares in the joys and sorrows that people bear in their hearts.

The figure that exalts the divine maternity of Mary is complemented by the image of Our Lady of Mercy who, in statues and pictures, is seen to gather the city and the people under her mantle.

We find the following in a guide for the artists of the 15th century written by Giovanni Dominici (+ 1419): "It is beautiful to see the Virgin and the Child in her arms, along with the little bird, or a pomegranate in her hand. The image of Jesus sucking at the breast is very appealing, Jesus who sleeps in his Mother's arms, Jesus being tender with his mother; Jesus is seen in profile, and Mary, caressing Jesus, also in profile. The

Baptist is also there: he is dressed in camel skin, a child who goes into the desert, plays with the little birds, tasting the sweet leaves, sleeping on the ground ….."

In the iconographical development in the 15th and 16th centuries there is a movement away from the image of Mary as Queen to Mary as the Immaculate Conception and the Assumption of Mary.

From the Renaissance onwards, new problems arise in relation to content and form. Alongside what emerges from the theological area, we may add the concepts of pure fantasy, and Marian themes, as a consequence, come to be interpreted through a vast array of images and figures.

In the subsequent evolution, the norms issued by the Council of Trent are very important. This succeeded in avoiding an irreverent art, at variance with the communication of Christian spiritual truth. Also in relation to these Tridentine norms we find the intervention by the ecclesiastical authorities in favour of the art and decoration of Churches. For example we could recall the interventions of Cardinal Charles Borromeo at the diocesan synods of Milan. These became guidelines for subsequent synods. Likewise Cardinal Paleotti, in his Discourse on sacred and profane images, conducted a dialogue with artists on the value of sacred images in the diffusion of religious ideas and messages.

3. Carmelite images

a) the Mother of God (13th-14th cent.)

The most frequently used iconographical themes that we find in the first Carmelite churches are the Mother of God in the form of:
- *Eleusa*, the most widely used (and the only one in the 13th century)
- *Odighitria*, (which appears in the 14th century).

All the images of the Eleusa kind which could be found in Carmelite churches in the 13th and 14th centuries are connected with the legend which claims that its origin was on Mount Carmel. The symbolic language in these legends is very clear:
- In the iconographical production of that time there existed in the East the legend that images of Mary came from St. Luke, while in the West, it was said that they came from the hand of an angel.
- In this context, to claim Mount Carmel as the origin means finding in the Eleusa iconographical theme, a reason for belonging (i.e. affection for Mary) and perhaps it also suggests that this picture stood in a niche in the Prior's cell in the Wadi ain Es-Siah on Mount Carmel.

There would appear to be some confirmation of this symbolic interpretation in the Marian literature of the Order. " To love Mary as Jesus loved her is the mission of the Order", which was proposed by John of Hildesheim, is seen when the tenderness motif is transformed into other forms (Idighitria, Kyriotissa etc.)

The following are very ancient examples of the Eleusa type of picture:
- "La Bruna" from the 13th century in the Church of the Carmine Maggiore in Naples. It has been the most widely known icon in the Order especially in the 16th century, in Italy and beyond, especially in Holland and Belgium. This is due to the numerous miracles attributed to it in the triumphal pilgrimage of the Holy Year of 1500 when it was exposed in the Vatican Basilica. Devotion to "La Bruna" is connected to the emergence and development of the Carmelite devotion that dedicates Wednesdays to Mary.
- Our Lady of Mount Carmel, from the end of the 13th century, in the Church and afterwards in the house of S. Martino ai Monti in Rome.
- Saint Mary of the Wearers of the Mantle from the end of the 13th century or the beginning of the 14th in the Carmelite Church in Siena. It appears that before being moved to its present position inside

La Bruna

The origins of this devotion are linked to the picture that is venerated in the Carmelite Church in Naples, Carmine Maggiore. It spread outside Naples after the miracles that occurred when the picture was taken to Rome on pilgrimage in the holy year of 1500. In 1524 the General Chapter of the Order placed the Carmine Maggiore under the special care of the Prior General in order to help to spread the devotion. Many of the Carmelite churches in Europe came to have a copy of this picture: the secretary of the Prior General Henrique Silvio, at the beginning of the 17th century, counted 55 examples in the Order. Under the express instructions of the superiors of the Order, copies were made, for example in Belgium, where in 1657 it was decreed that this picture should be used in all the churches, and if possible, also in the houses. Michael of St. Augustine was a great propagator of this devotion in Belgium. Today, with the reproductions of the icon by Riccardo Pallazzi (+ 1999) once again the picture of "La Bruna" is becoming known far and wide and can be found in many of the houses of the friars and of the sisters, helping in the rediscovery of those values that were found in the original iconography of the Order.

The day that is dedicated to this particular devotion continues to be Wednesday, for which there are special prayers and exercises. In the past the picture was covered. In order to expose it to the public, on Wednesdays, more solemn celebrations were organised, with Confession and Communion in the morning and the singing of Litanies in the evening.

Cf. E. Boaga, *La Vergine Bruna e il Carmine Maggiore di Napoli: fede, storia, arte*. Napoli [Basilica del Carmine Maggiore], 1988. Id. *Como Piedras Vivas...* p. 103.

the Church, it was part of the façade of the Church.
- Our Lady of Mount Carmel from the 13th century in the Church of Santa Maria in Traspontina in Rome. It had previously been in the first Carmelite church in Rome, called S. Giuliano ai Trofei di Mario, and was moved to the old Traspontina at the end of the 15th century and to the new Traspontina in 1587.
- Another work of the 14th century is the icon of Our Lady of Mount Carmel called Our Lady of the People. It now stands in the Carmelite Church in Florence. It was placed in the Brancacci Chapel in 1422.

Further images of the Odighitria kind from the 15th century may be found in the frescoes by unknown artists in the church of S. Pietro in Tivoli, near Rome, representing Our Lady of Mount Carmel, and in Poland in various Carmelite houses, there are other paintings on cloth from the year 1500 taking their inspiration from the picture in the Order's church in Wola Gulowska.

b) The Mother of God – The Patroness (14th and 15th centuries)

At the beginning of the 14th century, and even more, in the 15th century, the representation of the Mother of God tended to underline her patronage regarding Carmelites. This was expressed in two forms:
- With the spread of the Kyriotissa type in which the reference to the divine maternity appears in the form of Mary's majesty as she sits on the throne with the saints of Carmel flanking her on either side.
- With the introduction of a new iconographical element, related to the previous tradition, or of the Mother of Mercy, no longer holding the Child Jesus, but standing. Under the mantle of the Mother that covers the Carmelite Family as a sign of protection, the images of the "fathers" of the Order appear, Saints Angelus and Albert of Sicily. This iconographical motif which spread in the 15th century and the beginning of the 16th, continued to be commonly used after that.

The Patroness motif that was characteristic of the 14th and 15th centuries also continued after that and became quite common.

Some examples of the representation of the Mother of God, and Patroness of Carmelites, corresponding to the Kyriotissa type are:
- Our Lady of Mount Carmel by Pietro Lorenzetti from 1329. The panel painted for the Carmelite Church in Siena (Italy) is now broken into sections and is in the local art gallery.
- Our Lady of Mount Carmel, a fresco from 1487 in the Carmelite Church in San Felice del Benaco (Italy)
- Mother of God, Protector of Carmelites, in the church of St. Cassian in Nicosia on the island of Cyprus. The painting by an oriental artist is from the 14th century (perhaps from the beginning of the century). On either side there are small pictures that seem to be a series of commentaries on the antiphon "Sub tuum praesidium" related to local historical events.
- A processional banner painted by B. Bonfigli (14th century) in the Carmelite Church in Perugia (Italy).
- An example of continuity also in later periods of the iconographical type known as the Patronage is the canvass of Pastura (1501) in the Carmelite Church in Catania in Sicily. Mary the Patroness is presented wearing the habit of the Order and in the company of Elijah and Elisha above and the "fathers" of the Order, Saint Angelus and Saint Albert, down lower. This canvass contains, alongside the picture of Mary, some small pictures referring to the history of the privileges of the Order to justify the affiliation of lay people to it.

We have the following examples of the type known as Mother of Mercy:

- Our Lady who protects the Carmelite Family, a miniature from the 15th century in the Carmelite Missal which today is kept in the Vatican Library.
- Mother and Ornament of Carmel, a banner from the early part of the 16th century used for processions. It is kept by the Carmelite nuns in Sutri (Italy).
- Our Lady, Mother of Carmelites, a famous work by Filippo Lippi, Carmelite. This work is in the Berlin Museum.
- Our Lady of Mount Carmel, from the beginning of the 16th century, painted by John Antonio Licinio, "Pordenone" so named because of his place of origin. The work today is housed in the Fine Arts Museum in Venice.
- Our Lady of Mount Carmel of the museum of the Discalced Carmelites in the Theresianum in Rome. This is an image made of birds feathers, constructed at the end of the 18th century in Mexico.

c) Most Pure Virgin (15th and 16th centuries)

In the 15th and 16th centuries we find a very interesting development in Carmelite iconography alongside a development in Marian thought and reflection in the Order that sees Mary as the life model of the Carmelites.

In this period, in fact, something very important was happening. The historical and concrete representation of the conception by Saint Ann is being replaced sometimes by the ideal image of a young woman, surrounded by celestial brightness. Within the globe of the earth, we find the moon, standing like a curved object ready to strike the serpent.

This development is made up of the following stages:

- *The representation of the event of Mary's conception*
   Up to the 15th century we have a form of iconography which came from the east, based on the apocryphal text of the Proto Gospel of James. The reference is to the sacrifice of Joachim and Ann because of her sterility: the message of the angel to Joachim (in an isolated place outside the city, weeping) and to Anne (who looked at the birds in the garden, thought about their fecundity and lamented her own sterility); the meeting of the two at the Golden Gate. We find an example of this in various Carmelite books and in the London Missal from the end of the 14th century as an illustration for the feast of the Immaculate Conception of Mary. More than the fact of the conception from Ann, consideration is given to the conceiving of Mary which is celebrated as we learn from the title of the feast, *conceptio vel pocius veneratio sanctificationis B. Mariae Virginis*. It was clearly the conception of the one who will be the mother of the Redeemer. It is interesting to note that the relationship between the conception of Mary and the Carmelites is to be found in *"Universis christifidelibus"* (1300-1320), where it is stated that the first Carmelite house in the Holy Land was in Jerusalem, close to the Golden Gate, afterwards called after Saint Ann. The statement was repeated often after that.
   The picture of the encounter, close to the Golden Gate, continues to be used still as a way of talking about the conception of Mary.
- *Representation of the sinless origin of Mary, daughter of Eve*
   Alongside the traditional representation of the actual moment of her conception a new kind of iconography came to the fore in the 15th and 16th centuries with the intention of giving form to what was essential. The image of the Golden Gate and of Saint Joachim is left behind in favour of the image of the Virgin. The iconography of the family tree of Mary and Saint Ann form the essential part of the representa-

tion, together with the idea of messianic salvation in the image of the Mother of the Saviour, preserved free from sin and made holy by God.

From the trunk of Jesse a pure shoot springs forth which in turn produces the flower which frees us all from original sin: a grace which she enjoyed already from the time of her conception. The plant sown in the contaminated earth of humanity remains uncontaminated.

We find similar ideas in the Carmelite literature of the time: the sermon by the Bishop of Armagh on the Immaculate Conception in 1342; The Book of the First Monks by Felip Ribot which, for the first time among Carmelites, applies to Mary the little cloud that Elijah saw; commentaries on the Song of Songs by Michael Aiguani of Bologna; and finally the *De Patronatu et patricinio* by Arnold Bostius.

In this context we have a passing phase of iconography, which was influenced by this interpretation of the little cloud of Elijah. Elijah prays to Saint Anne in the same way that Saint Anne prays to Mary at the centre of the cloud. This scene is represented for example in a miniature of the Antiphonale of the 15th century.

- *Representation of the Immaculate Conception, a characteristic trait of the Mother of the Saviour*

  Subsequently the representation of the Immaculate Conception becomes separated more and more from Saint Ann (Jesse etc.) and artists sought a more plastic image in which Mary occupies the dominant position. That brings us to the 15th and 16th centuries, in which Mary is viewed exclusively from the point of view of the divine predilection, the unique place she holds in the plan of God, and her intimacy with God. This is a new humanity, a creature who comes directly from the hands of God, just like Eve, but without the stain of original sin. She is young, clothed in all the beauty of the new creation. She is not touched by the corruption of the earth. She is not so much sanctified as preserved; she is the friend of the Father, following an interpretation of the Song of Songs, found in a miniature of the Office of the Hours of the Blessed Virgin Mary from 1516.

This highlighting of the mystery of Mary does not ignore however the profound idea that Mary is beautiful because she is the Mother of the Son of God.

That gave rise to a type of pictorial representation that surrounds Mary with the light of the Sun, including the symbols of the quarter moon (in the form of a pruning hook) with Mary standing on the globe, crushing the serpent. This means that she is preserved from sin through the merits of the Redeemer who clothes her in light. This picture is clearly inspired by the passage in the Book of Revelation: A woman clothed with the sun, with the moon under her feet … (Ap 12:1) This woman is present always in the company of Christ: She is the Mother of God, the Immaculate Conception, following the Platytera model.

The Virgin, presented as the woman of the Apocalypse so impressed the Carmelites of the 14th and 15th centuries that they chose this image as the best representation of Our Lady of Mount Carmel.

At the end of the 15th century a series of images appeared which were very significant as a synthesis of Marian devotion in Carmel. These were the images of Mary, Carmelite, Virgin of Virgins. The most well known of these pictures is to be found in the Carmelite Church in Corleone (Sicily). It was painted by Tommaso de Vigilia in 1492. The composition is a synthesis of the devotion to Mary in the Order in relation to the Mother of Christ, the Immaculate Conception, Most Pure Virgin, Queen of Heaven. It reveals at the same time the justification for granting the habit of the Order to lay people affiliated to the Carmelite Family. In this picture in Corleone, perhaps the most ancient representation, there is a remembrance of the vision of Simon Stock as an isolated detail. This detail is missing from the picture in Palermo, which is a copy of the picture in Corleone, with some small differences.

In relation to this kind of iconography there was an evolution of the elements of the *Vexillum Ordinis*, the Order's coat of arms, the representation of the seal that we find in official publications from the end of the 15th century onwards. This evolution contains a confluence of elements (the woman of the Apocalypse, Elijah, Elisha, Purity, the divine Maternity of Mary) in the symbolism of the Carmelite shield.

d) Our Lady of the Scapular (16-20th centuries)

Mary, Our Lady of Mount Carmel, as a subject underwent major changes in terms of iconography from the post-Tridentine period and the baroque period up to the present day. Our Lady of the Scapular appeared as a type, in two ways:
- The re-emergence of the model of Mary the Mother of God, the primitive type, represented by La Bruna to which a reference to the Scapular was added;
- The development of the vision of Simon Stock.

As a basis for the first of these, we have the picture painted by Geronimo Massei in 1595 for the church of San Martino ai Monti in Rome. This was spread most of all to the Scapular Confraternities and thereby became the most widely preferred image for holy cards. The composition recaptures the characteristic of tenderness from the La Bruna icon of Naples and became very popular because of its relationship to purgatory.

At the beginning of the 16th century, pictures of Our Lady of Mount Carmel show her coming out of the flames of purgatory. In 1613 the Holy Office issued a decree prohibiting the use of this type of image. It would no longer be possible to paint Our Lady as coming out of or going into purgatory. This task was limited to the angels who went there to bring souls out of the flames and into heaven. After this decree, Our Lady of the Scapular is placed at the top of the picture, in the midst of clouds, with the souls in purgatory below.

It is also interesting to note the evolution in popular representations, from Mary who protects to Mary who sets souls free from purgatory and finally the protection of souls from purgatory through devotion to Our Lady of Mount Carmel.

The increasing attention to the Scapular and its ever wider diffusion as a form of pastoral mediation among the faithful lead to a presentation of Mary no more as the sublime ideal of Carmelite life but rather as the Mother of God who brings help and favour to the world. The attention moves from Ornament and Splendour to Mother, from the *Flos Carmeli* to *Da privilegia*. The artistic composition, still artistically valid, greatly reduces the very fruitful element of the preceding period, that of Our Lady of Mount Carmel as the ideal of the most perfect personification of the aspirations of the Order, which is to possess a pure heart, prepared for union with God.

The second direction that characterises the iconography of the modern era is the representation of Our Lady with the Scapular in her hand, very often giving it to Simon Stock.

There is a great variety in the way artists depict the giving of the Scapular to Simon Stock. Without going into the variety of details, the location of the vision, or the place where Simon was standing etc. we can note the following variations: sometimes Mary appears wearing the habit of the Order, with the child Jesus and without him; she gives the whole habit to the Order, the white cloak, the large Scapular or the small one. These variations represent various ways of highlighting particular details.

Of the giving of the Scapular to Saint Simon Stock we have a number of paintings by famous artists as well as lesser artists: Palma, the younger († 1628), Francisco Barbieri, called the Guercino (†1666), Murillo (†1682), Mattia Preti († 1699), Carlo Maratti († 1713) Ludovico Carracci, Giovanni Battista Tiepolo (1721) Sebastiano Conca (†1764) Sebastiano Ceccarini († 1773), Antonio Cavallucci († 1795), Dominguez, Keating, Mignard, Roncali, Jose Zannoni († 1903) Alexander Franchi (†1914) João Soler Blasco (†1970) etc.

Very often, in the pictures of this period, we find inscriptions, mostly using the terms Mother and Ornament of Carmel. The use of the inscription Queen of Carmel is more restricted even though it appears quite often in the Portuguese and Spanish cultures.

The practice of the Middle Ages of painting Our Lady with the habit of the Order influenced, from the 17th century onwards, the way of sculpting stone images of Our Lady. In the acts of provincial chapters of the Belgian province in 1664, and of the Portuguese province in 1669, norms were issued for the painting of wooden and stone statues.

4. Today's orientation

In recent years we have seen a widespread tendency to go back to the image of tenderness, in the Eleusa, under the influence especially of La Bruna and the art of the end of the last century, like that of Franz van Oert, which people came to know through the 1938 Carmelite breviary.

Among recent images of Our Lady, in this renewed approach, the most relevant are:

- The canvass by R. Bittelinch Brink, a German artist, painted in 1954 for St. Albert's College in Rome. The symbolism is very striking. It contains elements from the Apocalypse, the picture conveys the tenderness of Our Lady of Mount Carmel, for a world crying out for peace.
- The picture painted in 1986 by the artist Sr. Claire S.M.M.I. from India. Its symbolism, typically oriental, shows us the contemplative attitude of Mary allied to the characteristics of the Mother of God.

Pages from the Anthology

1. A FAMOUS PICTURE

Text Emanuele Boaga, O.Carm. *S. Maria dei Carmelitani. Note d'iconografia*, pp. 668-670.

The most well known of the pictures of Mary, Virgin of Virgins, Carmelite, is without doubt the painting that is in the Carmelite Church in Corleone, painted by Tommaso de Vigilia in 1492. The work met with great success, if we take it that there are at least four copies of it that come from the 16th century. The whole pictorial composition is a summary of the Marian spirituality of the Order in the 15th and 16th centuries, with its references to the Mother of Christ, the Immaculate Conception, the Virgin Most Pure and Queen of Heaven. It also affords a justification for the giving of the habit to lay people, thus allowing them to become part of the Carmelite Family. The picture also shows the time and the setting of the development among Carmelites in Sicily of devotion to Our Lady of Mount Carmel.

Taking an overall look at the picture, it is made up of four parts in the centre and a series of smaller pictures on both sides. The image of the Mother with the child in her arms right in the centre of the picture, is pointed to by the scroll held by the Prophet on the right above the picture itself, as Mary, Virgin of virgins, Carmelite, i.e. as an image of Our Lady of the Carmelites. This is confirmed by the presence at the top of the central section of St. Elijah and St. Elisha, believed to be the founders of the Order.

The way in which Our Lady is depicted is full of meaning. Her image is placed at the centre, surrounded by a luminous almond; from her head over which two angels hold a crown, a gracious flowery mantle descends while at the two feet we find a globe and a half moon, a reference to the woman described in Chapter 12 of the Apocalypse. The Virgin Mother holds the child Jesus on her left arm and with the right shows her breast, as if to say, that from her virginal milk, as from a fountain of innocence, all of us are to be nourished. This depiction then reveals profound theological meaning; the divine motherhood of Mary, her virginity, her being the new Eve, the woman of the Apocalypse, are the ways through which Jesus the Saviour comes to us, in the same way that through the hands of Mary all the graces necessary for an intense living out of each one's Christian and religious ideals come to those that are devoted to her.

Still looking at the central section, lower down on the right there is a detail that shows the vision of Our Lady by Simon Stock in which he receives the Scapular. This detail – perhaps the oldest depiction of it – added to by details showing people being saved from hell and being freed from purgatory, will appear again in pictures after a lapse of a century until the point where it becomes a characteristic depiction of Our Lady of Mount Carmel.

Still in the lower part, on the right, we find St. Brocard with the Book of the Rule in his hand and behind him we can pick out the first oratory on Mount Carmel, while on the left hand side we find the Fathers of the Order, Angelus of Sicily and Albert of Trapani.

In the eight small pictures on either side, following in clockwise direction, we see through the presence of two figures – Pope John XXII on earth, and Mary in heaven – the benefits that come to the men and women who are members of the Confraternity of the habit of the Order. The painter does not limit himself simply to painting the picture: to each subject he also adds written phrases to every scene in the popular Sicilian language, a fact which points to the purpose of this work in relation to the people.

The collection of scenes introduces the following subjects:

- A general chapter of the friars sends two of its members to Pope John XXII to obtain a new confirmation of the Order.

- The two friars set out and get to the Pope but they run into difficulties as can be seen in their gesture of perplexity

- At night while the Pope was asleep Our Lady appears to him, dressed in the white mantle of the Order, holding a long parchment in her hand (a reference to the so-called "Sabbatine privilege") and commands him to confirm the Carmelite Order. Strangely, the two friars are there while the vision is taking place.

- The Pope shows the two friars the parchment (the "Sabbatine bull") received from Our Lady. The Pope, it must be noted, except in the nighttime vision, is always surrounded by cardinals; meaning that the Church and its hierarchy are present.

- The friars clothe lay people with the sign of the "habit of the Virgin Mary" i.e. with the white mantle. In a niche down at the bottom Our Lady is depicted along with the "Fathers" of the Order.

- The souls in purgatory are set free on the Saturday after their death, by Our Lady. The souls, separated from the body, are painted naked, wearing the "night" scapular of the religious. It might be possible to explain this by saying at that time lay people affiliated to the Order were not allowed to wear as their distinguishing mark the habit of the Order (the Scapular) because Canon Law at the time prescribed that anyone who wore the habit of a religious order for an entire year became automatically a professed religious, with all the effects and consequences of that. That is why in the previous scene that illustrates the affiliation of lay people, they are given the white mantle, which is a sign of this habit. But because heaven is not bound to observe Canon Law, valid only on the earth, we see how souls wear the same habit as that of the Order although in a reduced form, the "night" habit. We can also see in the following picture a religious with a tonsure, who is wearing the small scapular.

- The souls are pictured under the mantle of Mary to signify her protection in the hereafter. One of them is a religious, as we said before. What is not easy to understand is the presence of the two angels who sound the trumpet. The painter perhaps wanted to say that those souls will remain under the mantle of Mary until the final resurrection.

- Finally, the souls are presented to St. Peter by the angel; Mary receives them and presents them to the Most Holy Trinity (the three Persons are depicted in the oval setting).

2. THE CARMELITE KYRIOTISSA

Text by Riccardo Palazzi, *Sotto il manto della Madre*, in *La Madonna del Carmine*, 43(1989) n. 7-8, pp. 24-29.

In Nicosia there was an ancient Carmelite house. Some maps, that try to reconstruct the city as it was in the middle ages, place the house in the area now occupied by the Turks. In this section of Nicosia there is the magnificent basilica of St. Sophia with its three naves, today a Salenic Mosque. The church of the Carmelites could not have been very far away. Towards the end of the 13th century the Carmelites in that house painted an icon of the Virgin Mary, Carmelite, and they donated it to the basilica. This is one of the most ancient depictions of Our Lady as she was seen and venerated by the Carmelites. Despite the disastrous events of 1571, the icon was not lost. It turned up again in the church of St. Cassian that was built close to the Famagosta gate in Nicosia.

As soon as I arrived in Nicosia, Fr. Xavier, the superior of the Franciscans, who live in that house and Fr. Massimino, brought me straightaway to the Church (…). Inside the small church, somewhat unused and neglected (the Mass is celebrated there only on Sundays) there is a great wealth of icons, but when I got to the Carmelite image of Our Lady that I was looking for I felt an enormous disappointment. What was there was a very poor photograph and nothing of the original. It didn't matter. A Hail Mary would be fine. There was no point in asking the caretaker, an elderly lady, where the original might be. She spoke Greek and I would not be able to understand anything beyond, *Karitos* and *Parakalo*. A little more disappointed I went in the direction of the house, going by the ancient venetian walls that surround the old city. At a certain point I found myself standing in front of the Archepiscopal Palace, with its giant statue of Makarios I. I got closer, going into the courtyard where I began looking for the museum that I knew had many icons. It was there between the ancient residence of Makarios and the modern Episcopal palace. In the great hall I found the icon I was looking for. My earlier disappointment turned into joy and enthusiasm.

The icon measures 206 cm by 160 cm, painted on skin attached to a board. The Virgin Mary is depicted seated on a throne in the centre of the plate. She is the Kyriotissa, the Lady and the woman who points the way – Jesus. She holds the Divine Son in her left arm: with her right she spreads her mantle wide to protect the group of religious kneeling beside her.

It is precisely this group of religious that shows that the picture is Carmelite. There are sixteen in the group, each wearing a brown habit and white mantle: the Carmelite habit. Each one's hands are joined, turned upwards towards Mary, they are praying and at the same time they are pointing to Mary and to her Son Jesus. The group of religious is the best-preserved part of the painting that despite recent restoration work still shows the signs of a long life.

Two angels turned towards Mary dominate the upper section of the painting. Right and left of the central section there are sixteen small scenes: eight on each side. Each one is described by a short phrase in Latin written at the top. The majority of these small pictures is in bad condition: the lower ones almost unrecognizable. A mark of each of these scenes is that they depict the same person towards whom all the others are turned. More than likely the person who recurs is the Virgin Mary who miraculously intervenes in the lives of different people. The sixteen scenes refer to things that happened in peoples' lives.

The Carmelite who donated the picture to the Basilica of St. Sophia wanted to narrate, like in a film, the miraculous actions of Mary. They themselves are the witnesses. They pray and look not only to Jesus but also to his Mother, worker of wonders in whom Jesus finds support and to whom Jesus belongs. Their attitude leads us to understand that not only does Jesus belong to Mary, but also all those who place themselves under her mantle.

The lateral scenes are a concrete proof, the proof of faith, we might say: in those events, known to the people of that time, we can see and recognise the protection of Mary. They are a memorial to all she did: episodes that have the ability to sustain the faith of the believer. Many of the descriptive phrases begin with the words, "Here, in this picture" and above all, "Here, in this situation …. Mary stepped in".

Standing before this icon, rich in history and faith, I repeated over and over again the "Sub tuum praesidium" and it seemed to me more and more the material depicting of this ancient Marian antiphon.

3. MARY, AN ICON OF OUR LIVES

Text from the introductory address by Fr. Titus Brandsma at the Mariological Congress celebrated at Zenderen from the 15th to the 18th of August, 1931.

Mary, a sublime woman is, like us, what she became through the grace and goodness of God. It is true that by the will of God she was chosen by a special grace, but she responded to it without the slightest hint of hesitation and allowed herself to be taken over. She opened her heart to God and God gave himself completely to her.

We want to be one with Christ. We want to receive Christ in our hearts, despite the fact that these same hearts oftentimes are not open to his visit. Mary, however was given totally to God from the earliest years of her life. From the time she went up to the Temple, where she committed herself to the service of God, her whole life was a continual service and constant offering to God. Her heart remained always open to Him. From Mary we have to learn how to put away everything that does not belong to God, and open our hearts entirely to our God, in order to be filled with grace. Jesus will then come down to us, be born anew in us, grow in us and be seen in our actions as one who is alive in our life. The less we are filled with God the poorer will be the way we live. Along with Mary, filled as she was with the grace of God, we are called to live the life of God, and in our union with God, seek our glory and our good.

Mary is the model of all the virtues and for that reason is twice a Mother for us. Her life is a mirror for us to see how we are to be united with God (….) That is why we have to be mirrored in her, and live in her presence. We would like to see, as in an image placed before our eyes, every stage of her life, to the point where these scenes become familiar to us, speak to us, and shape our lives. After all, we are all of us flesh and blood and we cannot nourish our souls without the help of our senses and the work of our imagination. Therefore there should be place for a picture of Mary in the room where we live just as the picture of our Mother should always be there in our minds. Finally, we should have a great interest in what we find about her life in pictures, music, songs and every other form of art, that keeps her image before us.

In this way, not only is Mary brought closer to us, but also the glory of Mary becomes part of us, as it were. We have to react, i.e. we have to show forth what is happening inside us, something that should not remain hidden. All that is taking life inside should be manifest outside. We have to give expression to this beauty and goodness that cannot remain hidden and stifled in our hearts. The more we are filled with love and affection for Mary the more we will be filled with the glory and beauty of her life and our tongues will proclaim her praises and our mouths will speak of her glory. Our love and devotion cannot remain lifeless or static inside us. They should shine through our lives, they should burn and burst into flame for others. In every dimension of our lives that bright flame should appear in the same way that our devotion to Mary shines forth.

We have to be human even in our devotion to Mary, Holding on to our human nature as individuals and as members of community, we offer our homage and praise to Mary and recognise that we are her children. We should see it as a great honour that we are so devoted to her. We should be very happy to wear her habit as a sign that we honour her and place ourselves under her protection. We should be very happy to pray to her, not only on our own but also with others, to place ourselves under her protection and intercession and give voice to our praise of her great dignity.

We should have a great regard for both the Scapular and the Rosary. We should see them also as schools of prayer that teach us how to speak to our Mother. In a word, we should welcome anything that unites us closely to our Mother and helps us to express our love and devotion for her. Through the external expression we become more aware of what is inside us, all that lies within, grows, flowers and gives good fruit.

For further study and reflection

I. Bibliography

- G. Saggi, *Appunti d'Iconografia Carmelitana*, in *Lo Scapolare*, 1(1950), pp. 16-32; 2(1950), pp.90-91
- B.Borchet, *L'Immaculée dans l'iconographie de Carmel*, in *Carmelus*, 2(1955) pp. 85-131
- C. Gonzalez Coloma, *Iconografia carmelitana*, Madrid, 1060.
- C. Edmond, *L'Iconographie carmélitaine dans le anciens Pays-Bas méridonaux.* Brussels, 1961
- E. Boaga, *S. Maria dei Carmelitani, Note di iconografia* in *Confraternite, Chiesa e Società* a cura di L. Bertoldi Lenoci, Fasano: Schena Editore, 1994, pp. 655-716.

For further information on paintings and Marian art in the churches and shrines of the Carmelite order, see J. Smet, *The Carmelites* (4 Volumes, Darien, Ill.: Carmelite Spiritual Center, 1976-1988)

II. For individual and group study

1. Examine the principal types of pictorial representations of Mary of the Carmelites and note the message they contain in relation to Marian spirituality.

2. Carry out research into other kinds of Marian iconography that can be found in your part of the world. Get to know the most well known representations and note the message they transmit.

III. Prayer and Life

1. Pray with the Word of God

    - Ap 11,19-20;12,1.
    - Eccl 24,23-25

2. Of the images of Mary that you know which one impresses you most? Why? What do you learn from it?

3. Which of these images would you chose to help people remember the most essential values of our Carmelite identity? Why?

10

HER PRESENCE TODAY

Virgin Daughter of Sion,
the ardent desire in your heart,
is that there will be peace and unity
among all who believe.
Help us, from your splendour,
so that we too may be a prophetic sign
of God's kindness.
Help us, out of your goodness,
to be in communion with those around us
and those we meet along the way.
Just as it was once
for the group gathered in the Upper Room
so let the radiance of your presence
make the community of believers today
one in heart and spirit.
Help us, to make the love of God known
to the ends of the earth.
Along with you, Daughter of Sion,
we lift up to God, the God of mercy,
a festive hymn
of praise and thanksgiving
of joy and jubilation
a hymn of love
because the Lord has done great things in us.

10 HER PRESENCE TODAY

Mary in Carmel today

It is natural that every era should have its own way of approaching Mary. In every age, a particular image of Mary emerges (i.e. Mary as the figure, the icon, the model, the type of the Church and of every Christian). These ideas correspond to the content of faith and the spiritual characteristics of the particular time in history.

In today's world, changes in society and religious culture are leading to the formation of a new image of Mary, which can be seen both in theological reflection and in the *sensus fidelium*. The profile that is emerging has the following characteristics:
- Mary who is close to us
- Mary, a responsible woman, servant of the Lord, faithfully listening to the Word
- Mary, a woman of faith, attentive disciple, one of the little ones of the Kingdom
- Mary, image of freedom and liberation of humanity and of the cosmos
- Mary, guided by the Spirit

In this post-Conciliar age, the reflection on Mary taking place in our Order, in comparison to what was said in the past, prefers to look towards the dynamism of Mary's inspiration. Without denying the wealth of Marian devotion in the past, there is a need to look for a more solid theological foundation, as indicated by the Second Vatican Council.

In popular literature, or in specialised studies, rather than look for a new interpretation of the Scapular devotion for today (a devotion which is going through a time of crisis among Carmelites), many people meditate on the exemplary role of the Virgin Mary and on Mary as one of the poor of Yahweh, highlighting her prayer, her listening to the Word of God, her example of willingness, the simplicity of her life, her being there for others in an attitude of self-giving and service.

The figure of Mary thus becomes an inspiration especially with reference to what happened in her life. The contents and events of her life are referred to often and given much attention in the official documents of the Order. In particular we might mention:
- Her faithful listening to the Word of God
- Her willingness to serve
- Her commitment to the needs of each day
- Her continual conversion of heart
- Her influence on the early community of Jerusalem
- Her belonging to the poor of Yahweh.
- The linking of people's relationship with Mary to the preferential option for the poor.

In all of this we have a rediscovery of the deepest values of our tradition, linked to Mary as the Patroness, the Most Pure Virgin, the sister.

There is an attempt also to integrate the elements of a typically Carmelite language in a cultural setting that is totally transformed. We find an example of this in the document titled "Return to the Sources": Mary is presented there as the model for almost everything that is considered essential to the Order. She is a model for fraternity, for prayer and contemplation and as a simple woman in the midst of the people.

As the document "*Return to the Sources*" (1979) showed, a consideration of the biblical image of Mary leads Carmelites, in a changing cultural environment, to be more and more open to the Word of God in all that is happening in the world at the present time, through discernment of the will of God for the world, and for their own lives in community and in apostolic service.

In that same document, Mary is presented as the model for all that is essential for the life and

"Mary, Mother of Christ and Most Pure Virgin, the Carmelite ideal"

25. All that we desire and all that we wish to be today was fulfilled in the lives of the Prophet Elijah and of the Blessed Virgin Mary. In their own way, both had "the same spirit, the same formation, and the same teacher - the Holy Spirit." By looking to Mary and to Elijah, we can more easily understand and internalise, live out and proclaim the truth that makes us free.

27. Mary, overshadowed by the Spirit of God, is the Virgin of a new heart, who gave a human face to the Word made flesh. She is the Virgin of wise and contemplative listening who kept and pondered in her heart the events and the words of the Lord. She is the faithful disciple of wisdom, who sought Jesus - God's Wisdom - and allowed herself to be formed and moulded by his Spirit, so that in faith she might be conformed to his ways and choices. Thus enlightened, Mary is presented to us as one able to read "the great wonders" which God accomplished in her for the salvation of the humble and of the poor.

Mary was not only the Mother of Our Lord; she also became his perfect disciple, the woman of faith. She followed Jesus, walking with the disciples, sharing their demanding and wearisome journey - a journey which required, above all, fraternal love and mutual service. At the marriage feast in Cana, Mary taught us to believe in her Son; at the foot of the Cross, she became Mother to all who believe; with them she experiences the joy of the Resurrection. United with the other disciples "in constant prayer," she received the first gifts of the Spirit, who filled the earliest Christian community with apostolic zeal.

Mary brings the good news of salvation to all men and women. She is the woman who built relationships, not only within the inner circle of Jesus' disciples, but beyond that, with the people: with Elizabeth, with the bride and bridegroom in Cana, with the other women, and with Jesus' "brothers".

Carmelites see in the Virgin Mary, Mother of God and archetype of the Church, the perfect image of all that they want and hope to be. For this reason, Carmelites have always thought of Mary as the Patron of the Order, its Mother and Splendour; she is constantly before their eyes and in their hearts as "the Virgin Most Pure." Looking to her, and living in spiritual intimacy with her, we learn to stand before God, and with one another, as the Lord's brothers. Mary lives among us, as mother and sister, attentive to our needs; along with us, she waits and hopes, suffers and rejoices.

Text from *Carmelite Constitutions*, Rome, 1996.

action of the Order: contemplation, prayer and fraternity in the midst of the people. "We, as Carmelites, look to Mary to understand and live in depth Her attitude of listening and answering to the Word of God, thus avoiding identifying religiosity with alienating pietism or with secularism which closes the way to transcendency. Like her we would like to tend towards an ever more intimate habit of life with God and to build, through this, profound and vivifying relations with others. When we consider Mary as an inspiring model of life for us we ultimately mean to approach Christ and to conform ourselves to him in a triple openness: to God, through listening and through prayer; to ourselves, through the incarnation of our own identity; to others, through generous service, especially towards the humble and abandoned". (Return to the Sources, n.7. 1979). This approach is deepened as time goes on, especially in the Constitutions of the Order, approved by the General Chapter in 1995.

In the biblical figure of Mary, the most perfect and faithful of all Christ's disciples, Carmelites pick out three principles for their particular way of life: continuous prayer (contemplation), fraternity and *diakonia* understood as service, ministry, mission among the people of God.

- Carmelites today, contemplating Mary in the mystery of Christ and of the Church, find in her all they desire and hope to be in the present situation of their lives in the world and in the Church. She is the guide and the example in terms of the incarnation of the three principal characteristics of their way of life.
- Contemplation: like the Pure Virgin, who listens to, accepts, ponders and contemplates the Lord in her heart, Carmelites listen to the voice of the Spirit and allow themselves to be shaped and formed by what they hear. Like Mary, they are capable of discerning God's plan of salvation, and of being at one with her "Fiat" and with her hymn of praise for all the Lord has done in her.
- Fraternity: like the Mother of the Lord and our Mother, the perfect disciple of the Lord, present in the Upper Room, united with the Apostles and with the women, the "household of the Lord", Carmelites, seeing in Mary their sister, commit themselves to a journey of fraternity, sharing with others in their work and commitment, in their joys and sorrows, in their hopes and expectations, and in their love and service.
- Diakonia: like Mary who hastened to help her cousin (Lk 1:39-56) and the young couple at Cana (Jn 2:1-12), Carmelites are attentive to the needs of others, being present, helping, loving. They are also willing to welcome all those who are little and do not count, into their own community, into their own lives.

Thus, Carmelites are led by Mary, and journey with her, to the fulfillment of their own lives, based on the absolute foundation of existence: Jesus Christ. Just like living stones in the building of the Church, they are called to give a prophetic witness based on the Word of God and the Eucharist, in fraternity and in growth in a spirit of openness towards everyone who is a neighbour, especially the least, the *minores* of history.

Oh Virgin Mary
Cover us with the mantle of your love
And we will be happy as we journey through life.

Pages from the Anthology

PRAYER WITH MARY, OUR MOTHER AND SISTER,

Text by the Carmelite Fraternity in Pozzo di Gotto, Sicily.

>God, Our Father,
>On the solemn day
>When we celebrate the Blessed Virgin Mary
>Mother and sister of Carmel
>We come into your presence
>And ask for the gift of your Spirit.
>May your Spirit who is light and wisdom
>Come and dwell in our hearts
>So that we may follow Jesus, with a pure heart and total commitment
>And that we may receive Mary, his most pure mother,
>Along with her virtues and her criteria
>In the house of our lives.
>
>>Rejoice, Mary, full of grace.
>>Exult, Virgin of the pure heart,
>>because the Lord is with you.
>>You are blessed among women,
>>You are our mother,
>>and our sister.
>>Come and live with us,
>>And pray for us to your Son Jesus
>
>BLESSED are you, Mary, the model of perfect charity.
>Even though you were the Mother of the Lord,
>You wanted to live as one of his disciples;
>Like them, you came to know the Lord,
>The Teacher who taught everyone what love and fraternity are.
>Like them you walked along the painful way
>Following the way of the Cross,
>Going up to Calvary.
>At the moment that Christ was reconciling the world with the Father
>You and the disciple that Jesus loved

Come to form one family,
Becoming Church, united in faith and in love.
Along with you, Mary, mother and sister,
We offer our prayer of supplication to the Most Holy Trinity,
the source and the model of fraternity,
thus shall we become one heart and one soul,
in solidarity one with the other;
and there will no longer be among us,
rich and poor,
powerful and vulnerable
wise and ignorant,
because each of us will grow
as a true brother or a true sister of the Lord.

> Rejoice, Mary, full of grace.
> Exult, Virgin of the pure heart,
> because the Lord is with you.
> You are blessed among women,
> You are our mother,
> and our sister.
> Come and live with us,
> And pray for us to your Son Jesus

You are blessed, Mary, Virgin of the new heart,
listening always to the Word of the Lord,
receiving in faith the word of the Gospel,
You gave a human face to the eternal Son of the Father.
In recognising the Lord,
You, the perfect disciple,
learned to ponder in your heart,
His words and actions,
Signs to the world
of a new era of justice and peace.
Along with Joseph, your husband,
for three days, you looked for your son Jesus,
and when finally you found him in the Temple,
He is seated in the middle of the doctors,
Listening to them and asking questions.
He, Jesus, is the true wisdom of the Father,
Light and guide on the uncertain pathways of our life;
And you, Mary, found that,
By going through the dark night of faith, like we do.
Therefore, together with you, Virgin Mother,
We pray to your Son, Jesus,
Eternal Word of the Father

So that he will make our hearts open
In constantly listening to his Gospel
And may he grant, through the Spirit, an understanding of his Word;
Now become a light for our steps
Wisdom for what we do,
Until we see, in the face of every human being
The loving face of the living God.

> Rejoice, Mary, full of grace.
> Exult, Virgin of the pure heart,
> because the Lord is with you.
> You are blessed among women,
> You are our mother,
> and our sister.
> Come and live with us,
> And pray for us to your Son Jesus

Blessed are you, Mary, the Virgin who prays,
The dwelling place of the Holy Spirit,
When you went to visit Elisabeth,
The mother of John, the precursor,
You were filled with joy as you listened and recalled
The great things that the Almighty had done in you
For the good of his people!
And your song of praise,
Daughter of the prophets,
From the home of Elizabeth
Reached the whole world,
And gave hope to the lowly,
Strength to the disheartened,
Consolation to the afflicted.
In Cana of Galilee
Your attention to the worrying situation of the spouses
Made you, without hesitation, Mother,
Ask your divine Son
For wine, new and abundant
The Gospel of salvation and love
That makes the heart happy,
And makes our faith stronger.
In your company, Mary, the Apostles
Were assiduous in prayer and united in heart.
You, true temple of God,
prayed with the young Church
and you were a support for it
through your silent attention to the Spirit

so that, with power from God,
it might become free and fruitful.
We too, today, Mother,
Like the first Christians
Want to pray with you
And speak to your Son Jesus.
He renews our prayer:
With an outpouring of the Spirit
He makes it more true and authentic
More in obedience to his will,
Open to the marvels of the Reign of God
And close to what is happening in daily life.

> Rejoice, Mary, full of grace.
> Exult, Virgin of the pure heart,
> because the Lord is with you.
> You are blessed among women,
> You are our mother,
> and our sister.
> Come and live with us,
> And pray for us to your Son Jesus

BLESSED are you, Mary,
Virgin daughter of humanity
And Lady of our people.
You shared our life
In the midst of the lowly and the poor.
When you gave birth to Jesus,
You found no place for yourself and Joseph,
Apart from a cave,
And when you brought the child to the Temple of Jerusalem
To offer him to the Lord,
You offered a pair of turtle doves or two young pigeons
As it is written in the law of the Lord
For the families of Israel that are poor.
You, Mary,
Who listened every day to the Word of the Lord,
And who belonged totally to God
How well you understood the needs of the people
And how you shared their problems!
You know the faith and the joy,
The pain and the hopes of the poor.
That is why, Mary,
You chose to be the servant of the Lord
And to serve the lowly and the poor

And showing yourself to be an attentive and concerned woman,
With Elisabeth, and with the poor spouses at Cana.
That is why, Mother,
You chose to be close to the first Christians
Praying with them,
Breaking with them the bread of the Eucharist,
Sharing with them property and life.
With the passage of time, Mother,
You desired to continually show
The signs of your presence among us;
The holy Scapular that we devoutly accept
Is a reminder to us of the tenderness you have for the lowly
And the love you have for every creature.
In contemplating you, Mother of humanity
We turn to God, our Father
Through Jesus Christ, our brother.
May He, that lived among us,
Taking on our weariness and pain,
Guide our Church
Through love for the poor,
And the liberation of the marginalized;
Enlighten, with the light of the Spirit,
The city where we live,
So that peace may radiate from it,
That it may live in justice,
That it may grow in honesty
And work for the good of all.

> Rejoice, Mary, full of grace.
> Exult, Virgin of the pure heart,
> because the Lord is with you.
> You are blessed among women,
> You are our mother,
> and our sister.
> Come and live with us,
> And pray for us to your Son Jesus

BLESSED are you, Mary, the temple of God,
Beauty and splendour of Carmel.
In you we contemplate our destiny and the way ahead,
The way which leads us to Christ,
Our one and only hope.
You, Virgin of Carmel,
Most tender mother,
Be merciful to Carmelites.

By your example,
And in the spirit of the prophet Elijah,
Help us to live as brothers of the Lord,
Guide us to the constant contemplation of the face of your Son
And teach us to zealously serve our people.
To you, Mother and sister,
We want to entrust, on this festive day,
Our whole life:
Our commitment to follow the Gospel,
The harmony of our communities and of our family,
The education and the future of our young
The work of each day
The joy and the pain of the elderly.
Take us lovingly by the hand,
O Lady of Carmel,
and guide our steps
to Christ Jesus,
Our brother, and Lord of history.
To him be honour and power and glory,
With the Father and the Holy Spirit
now and forever. AMEN.

For further study and reflection

I. Bibliography

I. Calabuig, *La imagen de la Virgen en la perspectiva del tercer milenio de la era cristiana*, in *Congreso Mariano internacional*, pp.9-36.

L.M. De Candido, *Orientamenti di vita e di pietà Mariana nei testi legislativi degli Ordini Mendicanti: rassegna documentaria* (1967-1977), in *Marianum*, 39(1977), pp. 469-473 (Carmelitani), pp. 473-479 (Carmelitani Scalzi)

G, Vallejo Tobon, *Lo mariano del carisma carmelitano en América Latina*, in *Vida Espiritual*, 54(1977), pp. 49-59.

J. Castellano Cervera, *El impacto de la doctrina mariana del Concilio Vaticano II en la familia del Carmelo Teresiano*, in *Marianum*, 45(1983), pp.479-504.

Carmelite Marian Commission, *Interim Report*, Rome, 1985.

Pellegrini verso l'autenticità, Documenti dell'Ordine Carmelitano, 1971-1992, ed. by E. Boaga, Roma: Casa Editrice Institutum Carmelitanum, 1993.

Towards a Prophetic Brotherhood, Documents of the Carmelite Order, 1972-1982, Melbourne: The Carmelite Centre, 1984.

II. For individual and group study

1. Based on this study of the Marian character of the Carmelite Order, identify the Marian values that have inspired the Carmelite vocation from the beginning.

2. Has your province, congregation and/or community come to a new understanding of these values in working out its own way of life and its work? How have these values shaped the process? How do they appear in the Constitutions you follow?

3. What are the expressions of the exemplary nature of Mary and of our familiarity with her? How do these appear in the modern documents of the Order?

4. What in our Marian spirituality can be of use in our daily lives and in our formation?

5. A new image of Mary is emerging in the Church. How should the Carmelite Family relate to this new situation? What specific contribution could it make to it?

> If Carmel lives the fidelity of the loving Mother,
> why should I fear?
> Where Mary's gaze falls,
> there the gifts of God are abundant

CONCLUSION

At the end of this work, we would like to say that it has been good to have followed this course. By following the thread of the history of the experience of Mary in the Carmelite Order, we have together contemplated the "beauty of Carmel" and savoured the familiarity Carmelite men and women in the past have had with their Patroness and sister, and our familiarity too.

Together, we can appreciate what Michael of St. Augustine wrote a long time ago, as a way of kindling our desires and purposes in life, with Mary and for her, until "we reach the summit of the mountain that is Jesus Christ". May his words find an echo in the way we live:

> "… all those who profess to be your servants,
> children, brothers and sisters,
> have to make their lives conform
> to the demands of that profession,
> in the effort in some way to be similar
>   to a PATRONESS who is so holy,
>   a MOTHER who is so lovable,
>   a SISTER who is so gentle and kind,
> imitating her virtue
> and savouring her goodness.
>
> Therefore, if you love her as a Mother,
> imitate her humility, poverty and obedience;
> imitate her in her love for God and her neighbour
> and in all her other virtues".

INDEX OF NAMES AND SUBJECTS

Aaron 38 59 104

Ahab 26

Aiguani, Michael: *Mary strong and unasailable fortress* 27, *Arise like the dawn in order to enlighten* 28, Mary Mediatrix 48, Immaculate 63 77, the little cloud 27 77, Mary's virginity 185

Albert of Trapani, saint 184 190

Albert the Great, saint 115

Albert, Patriarch of Jerusalem, saint 13 24

Alberto di San Caetano, OCD, Manual for Confraternities 131

Alexander IV 102

Alexander of St. Teresa 78

Alexander V: sabbatine bull 102 106

Alexander VII 67

Alexius, Saint 146

Alfonsus of Liguori, saint 182

Ambrose, saint 19

Angelus of Sicily, saint y martyr 183, 189

Anne, saint, Mary's conception 38 62 145 184, feast 15 38 104 185

Annunciation, patronal feast 143-145

Anselm, saint 27, 63, 115, 173

Antonio of Piacenza, Marian legend 22

Antonio of Viterbo, see Pastura

Aragon and Valencia, the defence of the Immaculate Conception 63 64

Arenas, Jacinto de, Marian preacher 78

Argentina, the spreading of the scapular confraternity 129

Arrais, Amador, Marian Doctrine 77

Artists who portrayed the Blessed Virgin of the Scapular 187

Assumption, patronal feast 145

Audet, Nicholas, prior general: the sabbatine bull 103, 109, 124

Audience, devotional exercise 144

Augustíne, saint 27, 63, 173

Aylesford: the place of the vision of St. Simon Stock 101

Baconthorpe, John: white cloak, 41 61 65, miracle of Chester "You are my brothers" 67, Marian commentary on the Rule 45, imitation of Mary 85, Immaculate Conception 63 77, Mary announces the mystery of Christ 165, Mary, sister, in the juridical sense 60, the little cloud 19 77, *Mary and Carmel* 22 26, Mary, the Lady of the Place 34, Marian title 37, the virginity of Mary 16 114.

Baetica: vow relating to the Immaculate Conception 64 65

Bagnari, Pedro Luis: Manual for Confraternities 131

Baptist Spagnoli, blessed 12, Loreto 42

Barbieri, Francisco, see Guercino

Baronio, Cesar: against the sabbatine privilege 107

Basso de la Rovere, Jerome 42

Battuti: type of confraternity 121, in Carmelite churches 122

Beauty of Carmel 45

Beauty of Mary: purity and union with God 62

Beauty of the purity of Mary 73

Beka, Sibert of: Mary, witness to Christ, 165

Bellarmine, Robert, Card: sabbatine privilege 107

Benedict XIII 126, 148

Benedict XIV: sabbatine privilege 108

Benedict, saint 38

Bernard of Clairvaux, saint: elements of Marian devotion 14, 23, 26,

Bernardine of Buste 46

Bertold, saint 132, 150, joys 163

Best way to honour the Virgin 136

Bitterlink Brink, R: the Virgin of St. Albert 187

Blessed Virgin, prioress of the Carmelite community 46

Boaga, E.: *A famous image* 8, 10, 30, 50, 61, 105, 127, 139, 176, 182, 188, 194, 206

Bolivia: spread of the scapular confraternity 129

Bonaventure, saint 112

Bonfigli, Benedict 183

Boniface VIII: the Bull annulling the *nota vacillationis*

Borchert, Bruno. 194

Bordeaux 1294, GC: the Marian title 37

Borghese, Camillo: against the sabbatine privilege 106, vedi Paul V

Bostius, Arnold: Marian doctrine 80, *Exhortation to love and to intimacy with Mary-Sister* 52, *Speaking to you Mary my sister* 68, imitation of Mary 85, Mary, Sister 60, Mary, prioress 46, Mother of the Order 48, Mary, praying the word 165, Marian legends 104 16, *O Holy Mother* 32, *O my sweet love!* 178, the "prior Simon" 96, *Virgo Carmelita* 62, the Patronage of Mary 80 105, Mary's Virginity 114 185.

Bradley, Thomas: *Mater Carmeli* 48, Marian title 40, the miracle of Chester, 67

Brandsma, Titus: Like Mary, generating Christ 90, Mary, icon of our life 192, Marian mysticism 82 84.

Brazil: the spread of the scapular confraternity 129

Brocard, saint: testament 38, 45, in Corleone 189

Bruna, the Blessed Virgin, in the 16th and 17th centuries, A famous picture 188, *La Bruna* 182

Bruyne, Peter: Mary, mother and sister 48

Bulhões, Manuel de Dios, Marian preacher 78

Busserio, Felipe 20

Calabuig I. 206
Calciuri, Nicholas 62, 100
Cambridge: the place of the vision of St. Simon Stock 101
Camprodón: Marian confraternity 124
Canticle, *Salve Regina* 109
Caprioli M. 10
Carmel and Mary 13, biblical questions 19, Marian legends 20, Marian Oratory 22-23, the title of the oratory: Marian mystery 22, Mary and Carmel 26
Carmel, Mount: Byzantine laurel 22
Carmelite authors: Mariology 77-78
Carmelite confraternities 120-135, administration of property 134, of *signo Ordinis* 121, participating in the meritorious actions of the laity 122, Carmelite confraternities in the world 123, demands and conditions 125, the Roman arch-confraternity 125, oratory 134, dependence upon the bishops 128, 17th-18th centuries 128, 19th-20th centuries 134, spread throughout Latin America 129, spiritual union with the Order 129, statutes 129-130, daily practices 130-131, manuals 131, demands and conditions in 19th-20th 134, members, social classes 131, faculties for giving the scapular 135
Carmelite Confraternities in the world 123
Carmelite devotion: familiarity and presence of Mary 164, expressions: prayer, scapular, relation with the Order 164, experience 168, knowledge of it 168, life commitment 169, present tendencies 197, elements: contemplation, fraternity and service 199
Carmelite devotions: historical summary 22, devotional exercises in Carmel, 132 144: Seven Joys 162, Seven Sorrows 163, in the name of Mary 163, Slaves of the Mother of God 163, little Office 167, Litanies 167

Carmelite images: *La Bruna* 181, history 182, Rosian Codex 183, Filippo Lippi 184, Mother of God 181, Blessed Virgin of the Mantellini (wearers of the cloak) 183, S. Martino ai Monti: picture 181, Elements of representation in the 14th cent. 183, Blessed Virgin of Valdes Real 183, S. Felice del Benaco 183, Nicosia 183, Carmelite Kyriotissa 191, Perusa 183, Pastura (Catania) 183, Sutri 184, Venice 184, Teresianum of Rome 184, Most Pure Virgin 184, Most Pure Virgin in Traspontina 183, Blessed Virgin of Lorenzetti 183, Blessed Virgin of the People 183

Carmelite Marian Commission: Mary model of Christian life, 173

Carmelite Order and Mary: the Marian character of the Order 13, the election of the Patroness 33, founded in honour and in praise of Mary 34-35, Imitation of Mary 33, Oratory dedicated to Mary 18-23, the presence of Mary 33, reciprocal relationship 78, takes the place of the Jesus' love for his mother 84

Carmelite Third Order 135
Carmelite Virgin 62
Carmelite Wednesdays 126 128
Carmelites and the Mediatrix 153
Carmelites, Brothers of the Blessed Virgin 37
Carracci, Ludovico 187
Carroll, Eamon 74, 105, 174
Caruana E. 10 156
Castellano Cervera, Jesús 156 206
Castilho, Pedro de Portuguese inquisitor: denounces the sabbatine privilege 106-107
Castilho, Pedro de 106
Castro Cotta, C. Augusta de 10
Catalogue of saints 96
Catena C.: studies of the Immaculate Conception 66 74 126 127
Catez Elizabeth, see Elizabeth of the Trinity
Cavallucci, Antonio 187
Ceccarini, Sebastiano 187
Cesar de Heirsterbach 105
Charlemagne 15
Charles Borromeo, saint 181
Cheminot, John de: the origin of the Marian title 36 37, our Mother 48, Virgin 59, sister in the juridical sense 60, the little cloud 62, *scientes virginitatem*" 65, Marian legends 104,

Cheron, John, Fragments 101
Chile: spread of the scapular confraternity 129
Chivalry: influence on spirituality 15
Christocentricism 33
Church of Carmel 20
Churches dedicated to Mary 38-40, title mysteries 40
Churches in the Holy Land 17
Cicconetti, Carlo 176
Cimabue 180
Clement V: in honour of Mary 34, decreeing indulgences 103
Clement VI: Marian title 36
Clement VII: *Dilect filii,* sabbatine bull 103, *Ex clementi* confraternities 106, 124, approves the sabbatine privilege 166
Clement VIII: confraternities 126, litanies of Loreto 167
Clement XIII: indulgences 126
Conca, Sebastiano 187
Confidence in Mary 152
Confraternities, formation of groups 169, membership of 166, social and devotional 167, suppression of the Order, consequences for the confraternities 168
Confraternities, types of 121, of *signo ordinis* 122, for Marian devotion 122-123
Constitutions 1281: the clothing formula 34 40; 1294: our Patroness 34; dedication to Mary 34
Constitutions 1996: Mary, Mother of Christ and Virgin Most Pure: ideal of Carmel 198
Content of Carmelite *devotio mariana:* the mystery of Christ 164
Copsey, Richard. 118
Coredemption in Mary 77
Costa Ribeiro, F. C. 47
Costantino, Antonio 74
Council of Trent: iconography 181, indulgences 106
Couronne, Matthias de la: mariological tract 78
Crisippo of Jerusalem: the little cloud 19
Crusade legends 15-18
Cum nobis: sabbatine privilege 10
Cum sacra Pentecostes 147 148
Cyril of Alexandria, saint: belonging to the Order 37 38 104, the little cloud 19 14 63 132

Daniel of the Virgin Mary: Mary, cause of the Order 49, sister 9 50 52 60 68
De Candido, L. M. 206
De Elias a Maria 50
De Inceptione Ordinis: title of the Order 37

Decree for the spread of devotion to the Immaculate Conception in Spain 67
Dedicated to Mary: Constitutions 1281: clothing formula 34; 1294: our Patroness 34; 1324 dedication to Mary 34, Malinas, John de: devoted to Mary 34, Urbani IV: founded in honour of Mary 34, Tolosa: dedication to Mary 34, Millau, Pedro, Prior General: dedication to Mary 34, Edward II of England: dedication to Mary 34, Fredol, Berengario, Cardinal protector: devoted to Mary 36, John XXII, : Marian title 36, Clement VI: Marian 36, Innocent VI: his Patroness 36, Gregory XI his Patroness 36, B. Oller: explain patronatus 38, liturgical instructions 41, profession 40, dedication of Churches 38-41, conformity of life 45
Deogratias 27
Deus qui excellentissimae 148
Dilecti filii: Sabbatine bull 103, *Ex clementi*: Sabbatine bull 106
Discalced Carmelites, celebrations of their own 146
Diziani, Gaspar 187
Dominic of St. Albert 59
Dominic Guzmán, saint 38 96 150
Dominici John, blessed: sacred representations 180
Edam, Gerard de: cause of the vision 102
Edith Stein, *At the foot of the Cross of Jesus* 90, Marian mysticism 82
Edmond C. 194
Edward II king of England: dedicated to Mary 34
Eleusa 179
Elijah prophet, saint 19 22 26 27 38 48 50 53 59 60 61 63 65 77 78 104 161 163 183 185 186 188 198
Elisabeth of the Trinity: *Janua coeli* 72, *Faithful Virgin* 71, Marian mystcism 82 16 82
Escobar, María: conversations with Mary 137
Esteban de San Pablo: Mariological tract 78-9
Esther 60
Esteve, Enrique M: *The rhythmic praying* of the *Flos Carmeli* 114 118 139 176
Eve 185
Ex clementi: confraternities 124, sabbatine bull 106
Exercises in honour of the Child Jesus, a Carmelite devotion 132
Exercises of Marian devotion: the Twelve Star Rosary Exercise in honour of the Child Jesus, Novena in honour of Mary's expectation, Three Hail Marys 132, the Audience 144
Exhortation to celebrate the feasts of the Virgin 147
Exhortation to love and intimacy with Mother and Sister 52

Faci, Alberto Roque 137
Fadda, Carlo 67
Falcone, Joseph: number of Carmelite confraternities 128
Federico di S. Antonio: We are children of the Mother of Jesus 151, Manual for confraternities 131
Feijoo de Villalobos, John, Prior General: Mary, cause of our Order 49, Patronal feast 141
Feudalism: influence on Marian devotion 13
Fitzralph Richard: Immaculate Conception and the Order 61 62 65 185
Flos Carmeli, sequence for the Solemn Commemoration 148 100
Foppa, Vincent 183
Forcadell, Agustín M. 152, 156
Foscarini, Paolo Antonio: Mariology within Christology 77-78
Frachet, Gerard de, O.P.: witness on the Prior Simon 96 97 98
Franchi Alessandro 187
Francis of Assisi, saint 15, 102
Francisco de la Madre de Dios: Marian filiation 137
Francisco da Natividade 78
Francesco Saverio Maria Bianchi, saint 182
Fraternity of Pozzo di Gotto: *At prayer with Mary, our Mother and Sister*, 200
Frederick II, King of Naples 126
Fredol, Berengarius 36
Friedman, Elias: Bizantine laurel 22
Gabriele di S. Maria Maddalena: *Marian devotion is a call to the interior life* 91
García Eliseo: Mariological Doctrine 78
Garrido P. 9, 92
Geagea N. 8 10 13 30 56 92
General bibliography 8
General Conclusion 207
Gerard de Frachet 96 97 98
Gerard da Maiella, saint 182
Gerard of Bologna: title of the Order 34 44, Immaculate Conception 63
Gerard of Edam 102
German of Costantinople, saint: little cloud 19 117
Giacomo di Verona 21
Giotto 180
God and the Virgin Mary 86
God in Mary and Mary in God 89
Godfrey, prior general 98, 101
González-Coloma C. 194
Gostaldus of Chester 67
Götz, Tobias 116

Gracián, Jerónimo 132
Grammatico, Albert: Studies on the Immaculate Conception 66
Grassi, Simon, O.Carm. Manual for Confraternities 131
Grayer Gaspare de 187
Gregory IX 97 98
Gregory XI 36 38
Gregory XIII 106
Grimaldi, F. 42
Grossi, John, prior general: Mother of the Order 44, 48, 61, 65, 96, 98
Grosso, G. 118
Guatemala: spread of the scapular confraternity 129
Guercino 188
Guerricus d'Igny: Mary as model 15, Marian doctrine 84

Habit: Marian symbolism 40-41
Henry of Lagenstein 43
Hildesheim, John of: dedication of churches 40, Mary, founder 48, Sister in the juridical sense 60, little cloud 62, relationship with Mary, our Mother 165, the patroness is not Mary the Egyptian 37, title of the Order 38, Mary, successor of Elijah 59, symbol of the cloak 61, love of Carmel for Mary 84, 181, not talking about the vision 99
Hisdin, John of 37
Holy Places in the Holy Land 17
Honorius of Autun 19
Honorius III 97 98 104 147 148
Honorius IV: favours for the Order 147
Hoppenbrouwers, V. studies on the Immaculate Conception 8 9 47 54 56 64 66 74 79 92 109 127 133 137 139 144 150 156 164 167
Hornby, John, O.Carm. controversy 1374: Marian title 38, dedication of churches 40, consonance with the race 59, does not talk about the vision 99
Hugh of Saint Cher: little cloud 19
Hyperdulia, veneration of 77

Iconography: the artist and the viewer 179, in the 12th-13th centuries 179, in the 14th-15th centuries 179, the Renaissance 181, in the 16th-17th 186,
Icons: common elements 180, festive icon of Mary 179 180, icon portrait of Mary 179
If I were a priest 154
Ignatius of the Child Jesus 10
Ildefonso of the Immaculate Conception 9 92

Imitation of Mary 14, conformity of life 45, in the ways of God 78, Bostius 80

Immaculate Conception 62 77, patronal feast 62 145, interior life 63, representations of the Order 63, woman of the Apocalypse 63, Carmelite doctors 63, special vows in Spain and Portugal 63-64, Rome 1609, GC: Immaculate Conception, solemn and principal feast 62,

In defence of the Immaculate Conception 64

Incarnation: merits of Mary 77

Innocent IV 24 34 97

Innocent VI 36

Innocent XI 108

Inviolabilis antiquitatis 148

Inviolata: Marian antiphon 41

Irenaeus of St. James 116

Irenaeus, saint 173

Isidore, saint 117

Itinera ad loca sancta 15 17

Jansen Thomas 113

Janua coeli 72

Jerome, saint: little cloud 19, 59, name of Mary 116, 117

Jesi 185

Jesse 185

Joachim, saint 38, 184

João de S. Tomé: sabbatine privilege 107, 108

John Damascene: Mary dispenses graces 14, little cloud 19, burning bush, a sign of Mary 117

John of St. Samson 59 82 86

John of the Cross, saint 16 172

John Paul II: Our *Lady of Mt. Carmel in the life of Christian* 172, Mary and modern issues 174, *La Bruna* 182

John XXII 36 102 103 104 106 108 124 166 189

Jordan, blessed 96

Joseph, saint 43, 77

Juan de Jesús María: *Best way of honouring Mary* 136, 147

Kallenberg, Arie patronal feast 143-144 156

King Arthur 15

Kyriotissa 180

Lantana Bartolomeo 79

Laudesi, type of confraternity 121, in Carmelite churches 122

Lay people, clothing with the Scapular 121

Leers Baldwin, Marian mysticism 82, Marian legends 104, 105

Leo VI the Wise 19

Leo XIII 43

Leondelicato, Egidio: Mary and the Rule 45

Lezana, John Baptist de: Mary cause of the Order 49, Mary-Elijah: dependence 59, moderation Mary Sister 60, 150

Licino G.A., see Pordenone

Life of intimacy with Mary 88

Like Mary, generating Christ 90

Lippi, Filippo 184

Litterae affiliationis 121 124

Litterae fraternitatis 121 124

Little cloud, little cloud and the Immacolate Conception 62

Liturgical texts, Confidence in Mary 152, Carmelites and the Mediatrix 153

Liturgy: Mary in the liturgy 41, Marian liturgical themes 43

Lombardy CP 1333: Mary, Mother of the Order 48

López-Melús, Rafael. M. 9, 44

Lorenzetti, Pietro 183

Ludovico of the Presentation 80

Louis IX saint 97

Lynn, Nicholas of : Solemn commemoration 146

Lyon II 1274, Ecumenical Council, suppression of religious orders 37, *nota vacillationis* 34, motive of the Commemoration 101

Malines, John of, O.Carm.: Carmelites devoted to Mary 34 59

Mallorca: sabbatine bull, document 102, Marian confraternity 124

Mantegna, Andrea 183

Mantellati wearers of the white cloak 122

Mantuan Congregation: Immaculate federation of nuns 65

Manuel de Sá 64

Maratta, Carlo 187

María Perpétua da Luz: *Prayer to the Blessed Virgin* 54

Marian devotion, a call to the inner life 91, total dedication to God 78

Marian devotions, updating, prayers 166, Carmelite Wednesdays 166, Saturdays 166, Marian feast-days

Marian feasts of the Order 41 143, liturgy of the Resurrection 143-145

Marian filiation 136

Marian legends of Carmel 22, Marian legends 104

Marian mysticism: 80-84, forms or degrees 82, Michael of St. Augustine, Marieform life 80-81, Serafina de Dios 82, Leers, Baldwin 82, Teresa of Jesus 82, Therese of the Child Jesus 82, Elisabeth of the Trinity OCD, Blessed 82, Edith Stein 82, Titus Brandsma, O.Carm. Blessed 84
Marian salutations 44
Marian spirituality in Europe in the 17th-18th centuries 14
Marian themes in the 13th century: Theotokos, All Holy, Intercession 15
Marian title of the Order 36, controversies 37, adding "Virgin" 38, Marian title of the Order 24, historical summary 24-25
Marie of St. Teresa Petyt: mystical Marian doctrine 81-82
Marieform life: Michael of St. Augustine 80, Marie Petyt 81
Marielology 78
Marti, Francisco: Immaculate Conception 63
Martin V 102
Martino, Albert 42 74
Mary of James 41
Mary Magdalen de' Pazzi, saint: *Ascend with Mary* 69, Beauty and purity of Mary 73, Purity 66, Marian mysticism 16 58 66 76
Mary Salome 41
Mary the Egyptian, saint 37 38
Mary of S.Peter 82
Mary, our Sister: Elias-Mary, line and virginity 59, equivalent of Mary the Most Pure Virgin 60, sister 33
Mary's day 83
Mary's marriage 77
Mary's protection 45
Massei, Jerome 186
Mastelloni, Andrea: *This is how we honour Mary* 54, preacher and Marian expert 78, life in and for Mary 80 60
Matthias of St. John: *How to preach about the Scapular* 111, Mary cause of our Order 49, Mariological tract 78 59 164
Medieval devotion, contact with the holy person 17, geographical contact, prayer, imitation 18
Meucci Vincent 187
Michael of St. Augustine: *To Jesus through Mary* 87, *La Bruna* 182, relationship with Mary Mother 165, Mariaform life 80-81, Mystical life with Mary 16, 80, 82, Jesus' love for Mary 84, final exhortation 207

Millau, Peter de, Prior General: dedication to Mary 34
Millini, Garzia card.: sabbatine privilege 107
Miracle of Toulouse 39
Miracula et exempla 15
Monari E. 176
Mondini Francesco: Confraternities in Venice 129
Monsignani Eliseo. 9
Montpellier 1287, GC: Dedication to Mary 34
Most Pure Virgin, 59-66, the beauty of Mary 185, iconography, conception of St. Anne 184, little cloud 184, Mary preserved from sin 185, Woman of the Apocalypse 185, representations of the Conception of Mary 184, Corleone 185, Virginity of Mary, central Carmelite theme 59 33
Mother of the Scapular 93-110
Murillo Bartolomé Esteban 188
Mysteries of Mary: Crusades 18
Mystical life of Mary 88

Names of Mary in Carmel 109
Nasta L. 176
Nestorius 37
Nicholas IV 102
Nicholas of Lynn: Calendar and Solemn Commemoration 145 146
Nicholas the Frenchman 65
Novena of Expectation; Carmelite devotion 132
Nunzio Sulpizio, blessed 182

O'Donnell, C. 9
Odighitria 179
Oliviero 15
Oller, Bernard, Prior General: Marian title 38, explanation of the Patronage 38, Rule and Mary 45
Orlando 15
Oudewater John, O.Carm., see Paleonidorus
Our Lady of Mount Carmel: in Christian life 172, Mary, strong and unassailable fortress 27, Mother 185, Mother of the Order, 48, Lady of the Place 13, forms of presence in Carmel 33, Sister 161, updating 165, in the history of salvation 33, imitation 33, Icon of our life 192, Model of Christian life 173, Patroness 33-49 161, Most Pure Virgin 33 161, Virgin of the Scapular 33, Mother and sister 33, prophet, updating 165

Padilla Pedro: Marian doctrine 77
Palazzi Riccardo: *Carmelite "Kyriotissa"* 190, 192
Paleonidorus John: Mary Mother of the Order 49, Mary sister 60 46 48

Paleotti, Gabriel Card.: Images
Palma the Young 187
Palumbo E. 105
Paris: antiphon *Inviolata* 41
Pastura 183
Patronato: Bostius, ascendent-descendent 80
Patroness, Mary: expressions 36-43, based on divine maternity 48
Paul III, *Provisionis noatrae*: sabbatine privilege 106
Paul V: sabbatine privilege 107, Carmelite fraternities 128
Paul VI: *Authentic devotion to Mary and to the Carmelite Scapular* 3 171
Pereira, José 79
Perpetual virginity of Mary 77
Peter the Hermit 132, 150
Peter Thomas, saint 104
Petijt, Mary de S. Teresa: *Intimate life with Mary* 89, *god in Mary and Mary in God* 89, Marian mysticism 81-82 16, Immaculate vow 64
Phillip III king of Spain: in favour of the sabbatine privilege 107, 129
Phillip IV king 67
Phillip of Harveng 19
Pironio, E. 159
Pius IV, : *Cum nobis:* sabbatine privilege 106
Pius V, saint *Suprema dispositione*: sabbatine privilege 106 126
Pius X, saint : Summary of indulgences 108
Pius XII: *Scapular symbol of the virtues of Mary* 170, interventions in favour of the scapular 168, *Neminem profecto latet* 108 172
Platytera 180
Pordenone 184
Portugal: vow related to the Immaculate Conception 64 65
Possanzini, S. 74 92
Prayer, expression of Carmelite devotion 164 40 63
Prayers: *Conversations with Mary* 137-138, *Speaking to you, my Sister* (A.Bostius) 68, *My Mother* (M. Perpetua da Luz) 54, *My sweet love Mary* (A.Bostius) 178, *Mary, Faithful Virgin* (CDP) 158, *O Blessed Mother* (A.Bostius) 32, *Mary, Mother and Queen of Carmel* 120, *O God, Our Father* 200, *Salve, Flower of Carmel* (canticle) 94, *Virgin, daughter of Sion* 196
Praying to Mary 14
Praying with the Flos Carmeli 100
Preaching about Mary 79
Preaching about the Scapular 111

Presence of Mary in the spiritual life 80
Preti Mattia 187
Private devotions, Little Office of the Blessed Virgin, Litanies 167
Procopius 19
Provisionis nostrae: sabbatine privilegi 106
Pseudo-Anthony of Piacenza 22
Pseudo-Epiphanius 19
Pseudo-Methodius: little cloud 19
Purity of Mary 62-66, Carmelite characteristic of prayer 65, Habit 65, Mary Magdalen de' Pazzi 66, relationship with the Annunciation 65, devotional practices of the Third Order 66, interior life 65

Quaecumque a Sede Apostolica: confraternities 125

Raised up with Mary 69
Reformatio Ecclesiae and Marian devotion 15
Religious profession: reference to Mary 40
Return to the Sources 197
Reuver M. 118
Rhythmic prayer of the *Flos Carmeli* 114
Ribot Phillip: Mary prophet 165, *From Elijah to Mary* 50, little cloud 62 77 185. Marian interpretation of the Bible 22, Marian title 38, Marian legends 104, Elias and Mary, virgins 59, white cloak 65
Richard of St. Victor 115
Richard of the Heart of Mary 44
Rite for the giving of the Scapular, updating 169
Robert Bellarmine, saint 107, 148
Robert d'Arbrissel 46
Robert de Turlande 46
Roberto di S. Severino 21
Rome 1609, GC: Immaculate Conception, Principal and Solemn commemoration 62
Rosary, 150
Rossi John Baptist, Prior General: Scapular and its spreading 124-125, Preaching about Mary 79, Indulgences 106, singing of the Salve Regina 109
Rouen: Priests against the sabbatine privilege 108
Rubrica prima of the Constitutions 1281, 1294: Marian title 37
Rule and Mary 13, consonance 45, John Baconthorpe 45

Sabac see Sobac
Sabbatine Bull 102, content 103, places where there are copies 102, present position 166
Sabbatine privilege 102-108, present attitude 166, Benedict XIV 108, Sabbatine bulle 102, content

103, contradictions 103, decree 1613 107-108 186, contrary dispute 106-108, *Ex clementi*: Sabbatine bull 106, history 103-108, Mallorca: document 102, Pius X: summary of indulgences 108, Pius XII: *Neminem profecto latet* 108, *Provisiones nostra* 106, theological sense 108, Sicily: origin of the sabbatine bull 102, University of Bologna: in favour of the sabbatine privilege 107
Saggi L.: Studies of the Immaculate Conception 66, 8 42 56 74 101 102 118 176 194
Salve Regina: sung in the Order 109, St. Martin of Bologna 109
San Giuliano ai Trofei, church of, 184
Saul 26
Scapular: clothing of lay people 121, popular piety 160, Marian dimension 161, affiliation to the Order 164, sign of consecration to Mary 164, memory of the mercy of God 165, sacramental 165, symbol of the virtues of Mary 170, symbol of authentic devotion to Mary 171, preaching the scapular 111, dignified life 112, devotion and life 113
Scellato C. 52
Scrope, see Thomas Bradley
Serafina di Dio: Marian mysticism 82
Sfondrati card.: sabbatine privilege 107
Shrine of Loreto and the Carmelites 42
Sibert of Beka 165
Sicily: origin of the sabbatine bull 102
Signum Ordinis 121, clothing of lay people 121, see White Cloak
Silvestrani Brenzone Cristophorus: Marian doctrine 77, life in and for Mary 80
Silvio Enrico Prior General: organization of confraternities 125, statutes of the confraternities 129, sabbatine privilege 107, 192
Simon Stock, saint: 95-102, life 95-96, witness of de Frachet 96, lists of Priors General 96, Catalogue of saints 96, entry to Carmel 97, Term as General 98, death 98, veneration 99, interpretation of the vision 100, a promise for the friars alone 122, extension to lay people 124, scapular and vision 130 172, vision and solemn commemoration 152, updating 166, vision in Corleone 186 189 115
Sixtus IV, 48 103
Smet J. 139 194
Sobac 104
Solemn Commemoration, patronal feast: history 143-148, Time and place 145, title of the feast 145, Discalced Carmelites 146, rite and rank of the celebration 146, content and objective 147, liturgical texts 148, present texts 149
Soler Blasco Juan, painter 187
Solomon king 26, 29
Soreth, John, blessed Prior General 46, 132, 165, 182
South America: the spread of scapular confraternities, 129
Spiritual union with Mary 80
Sr. Claire, SMM, artist of modern icon 187
Staring A. 9 26 67 105
Steggink Otger 92
Stein Edith, see Teresa Benedicta de la Cruz
Stephan of St. Paul 78
Stokes, John 38
Straccio, Teodoro 128, 129
Sylveira João: *The Palmtree and the Queen of Carmel* 60 117
Teresa of Jesus, saint 16 46 82 172
Teresa Benedicta of the Cross (Edith Stein), saint and martyr 16, Marian mysticism 82, At the foot of the cross of Jesus 90
Terrena Guido, O.Carm.: against the Immaculate Conception 63
That my brothers might carry my Son's cross! 35
The Carmelite Fifteen days 144
Theodorus the Studite: little cloud 19
Therese of the Child Jesus, saint: Marian mysticism 82, *Why I love you Mary* 155, *If I were a priest* 154 16, visit to Loreto 43
This is the way they named Mary 110
This is the way we honour Mary 54
Thomas Aquinas, saint 2
Three Hail Marys, Marian devotion 133
Tiepolo, Giovanni Battista 187
Titus Brandsma, saint and martyr, see Brandsma 82, 84, 90, 192
To Jesus through Mary 87
Toulouse, dedication to Mary 34

Universis Christifidelibus 184
Urban IV: founded for the honour of Mary 34
Urban V: indulgence for the antiphon *Inviolata*
Urban VI: approval for the Marian title 38
Uruguay: spread of the Scapular confraternity 129

Valentine of St. Amandus: Mariological tract 78
Valls: Marian confraternity 122
Van den Bergh, Alexander: Marian devotion 80
Veneta, John of,: Marian title 37
Vexillium Ordinis 1499 186

Virgin of the Scapular 33 186, devotional aspect and intercession 186, the Carmelite habit 187, vision of St. Simon Stock, general introduction 95
Virgin: title applied to Mary 62
Virgo Fidelis 71
Vischi Camillo: first mariological tract 78
Vision of St. Simon Stock: present position 165, in Corleone 186, sources 95, historical data 99, historical nature 101, meaning 101

Voersio, Francesco, O.Carm.: confraternities in Naples 129
We are children of the Mother of Jesus 151
White Cloak, symbol of the Immaculate Virgin 61
Why do I love you Mary 155
Witness of pilgrims in relation to the Church on Mount Carmel 20
Woman in majesty 180
You will be my brothers 67

INDEX

Preface .... p. 3

Hymn to Mary .... p. 5

Bibliography .... p. 8

1. A Loving Presence
The Presence of Mary at the origins of the Order p. 11

1. The Marian characteristic of the Order, p. 13 - 2. Marian Spirituality in the 9th-13th centuries, p. 14 - 3. Marian spirituality during the Crusades, p. 15 - 4. The Dedication of the Oratory on Mount Carmel, p. 18 - 5. Is the Marian title generic or specific?, p. 22 - 6. Conclusion on the Marian Origins, p. 23.
Inserts Life in allegiance to Mary, p. 16 - Witness of pilgrims to the church on Mount Carmel, p. 20 - The Marian title of the Order, p. 24.
Páges from the Anthology: Mary and Carmel (J. Baconthorpe), *p.* 26 - Mary: the Strong and Unassailable Castle (M. Aiguani), p. 27 -"Arises" like the dawn to illuminate the faithful (M. Aiguani), p. 28.
For further study, p. 30.

2. The Heavenly Lady
Mary as Patroness .... p. 31

1. Different forms of the presence of Mary in the history and life of Carmel, p. 33 - 2. The Presence of Mary as Patroness, p. 33, a) To the honour and praise of Mary, p. 34; b) Various ways of expressing Mary's patronage: The Marian title of the Order, p. 36; The dedication of churches of the Order to Mary, p. 38; The formula and rite of religious profession, p. 40; The symbolism of the habit, p. 40; Liturgical regulations 41; c) Further reflection : Conformity of life, p. 45; The Mother of the Order, p.48
Inserts: My Brothers carry the Cross of my Son, p. 35 - The Miracle of Toulouse, p. 39 - The Shrine of Loreto and the Carmelites, p. 42 - The Visit of St. Therese, p.43 - Marian greetings, p. 44 - Our Lady as Prioress of the Carmelite Community, p. 46.

Pages from the Anthology: From Elijah to Mary (Ph. Ribot), p. 50 - Intimacy with Mary, Mother and Sister (A. Bostius), p. 52 - Prayer to Our Lady (Sr. María Perpétua da Luz), p. 54 - This is how we honour Mary (A. Mastelloni), p. 54.
For further study, p. 56.

3. Most Beautiful Sisters
Most Pure Virgin, ... p. 57

1. Sister, p. 59; a) Harmony in virginity, p. 59; b) The theme of sister, p. 60; c) The Carmelite Virgin, p. 62, - 2. Purity, p. 62; a) The Beauty of the Virgin, p. 62; b) The Immaculate Conception, p. 62; c) Purity and the interior life, p. 65.
Inserts: The white cloak as a sign of the Immaculate Virgin, p. 61 - In defense of the Immaculate Conception, p. 64 - "You are my brothers", p. 67 - A Royal Decree to spread devotion to the Immaculate Conception in Spain, p. .67.
Pages from the Anthology. Speaking to you, my Sister (A. Bostius), p. 68 - Raised up with Mary, (S. Mary Magdalen de Pazis), p. 69 - Virgo fidelis (Faithful Virgin) (B. Elizabeth of the Trinity), p. 71 - "Janua coeli" (Gate of Heaven) (Elizabeth of the Trinity), p. 72 - The beauty of Mary's purity (St. Mary Magdalen de Pazzis), p. 73.
For further study, p. 74.

4. Life hidden with you
Mystical Presence of Mary .... p. 75

1. Contemplating the mystery of Mary, p. 77 - 2. With Mary on the pathways of God, p. 78 - 3. At the summit of love, p. 80 - 4. Reproduce and continue the love of Jesus for Mary, p. 84.
Inserts: Preaching about Mary, p. 79 - Day by day with Mary, p. 83 - Model of Carmelite life, p. 85.
Pages from the Anthology: God and the Virgin Mary (John of St. Samson), p. 86 - To Jesus through Mary (Michael of St. Augustine), p. 87 - The mystical life with Mary (Michael of St. Augustine), p. 88 - Intimacy with Mary (María Petijt), p. 89 - God in Mary and Mary in God (María Petijt), p. 89 - Like Mary, we bring forth

Christ (T. Brandsma), p. 90 - At the foot of the Cross of Jesus (Edith Stein), p. 90 - Marian devotion, a call to an interior life (Gabriele di S. María Maddalena), p. 91.
For further study, p. 92.

5. Mother of the Scapular
Our Lady of the Scapular . . . . p. 93

A. The life and vision of Simon Stock, p. 95, a) The life of St. Simon Stock, p. 95; b) The vision of Simon Stock, p. 99, - B. The sabbatine privilege, p. 102, a) the "Sabbatine Bull", p. 102; b) The content of the "Sabbatine Bull", p. 102.
Inserts: The "Flos Carmeli", p. 100 - Marian legends, p. 104 - Names given to Mary, p.109 - The "Salve Regina", p. 110.
Pages from the Anthology: How to preach about the Scapular (Matias de St. Jean), *p.* 111 - Exhortations in favour of a worthy life, at the reception of the Scapular (Giovanni di S. Giov. Battista), p. 112 - A devotional view of the Scapular (T. Jansen), p. 113 - The rhythmic praying of the "Flos Carmeli" (E. Esteve), p. 114 - The Palmtree and the Queen of Carmel (J. Sylveira), p. 117.
For further study, p. 118.

6. In Fraternity
The Carmelite Confraternities . . . . , p. 119

1. Preface, p. 121 - 2. Medieval confraternities in Carmelite Churches, p. 122 - 3. The confraternities "de signo Ordinis", p. 122 - 4. Confraternities for devotion to Mary, p. 122 - 5. The Scapular Confraternities, p. 124 - 6. Characteristics of the Scapular Confraternities of the 17th-18th centuries: spreading, concept of spiritual union with Order, regulations, members, the oratory, Care for the patrimony, pp. 128-134 - 7. The Carmelite Confraternities from the 19th to the present day, p. 134.
Inserts: Carmelite Confraternities around the world, p. 123 - Carmelite Wednesdays, p. 126 - Marian devotional exercises: The Crown of 12 Stars, Devotion in honour of the Child Jesus, Novena in expectation of the delivery. The Three Hail Marys, p. 132
Pages from the Anthology: The best kind of devotion to the Blessed Virgin (Juan de Jesús María), *p.* 136 - Children of Mary (Francisco de la Madre de Dios), p. 137 - Conversations with Mary(Sr. María Escobar), p. 137.
For further study, p. 139.

7. The Feast of Love
The Solemn Commemoration of Our Lady of Mount Carmel. . . . . p. 141

1. Marian celebrations in the Order, p. 143. - 2. The Solemn Commemoration, A. Date and place of origin; B. The name of the feast; C. The day of the celebration; D. The Rite for the celebration; E. the object of the feast, p. 143-148 - 3. The Liturgical Texts A. The Divine Office; B. The Mass, p. 148.
Inserts: Devotional exercises in Carmel: The Novena, The Carmelite Fortnight, The Audience, p. 144 - An exhortation for the devout celebration of the feasts of the Blessed Virgin, p. 147 - The Rosary, p. 150.
Pages from the Anthology: We are children of the Mother of Jesus (Federico de S. Antonio), p. 151 - Trust in Mary (Text from the liturgy), p. 152 - The Carmelites and the Mediatrix (Text from the Liturgy), p. 153 - If I were a priest, (St. Therese of the Child Jesus), p. 154 - Why I love you, Mary (St. Therese of the Child Jesus), p. 155.
For further study, p. 156.

8. In the Life of the Church
The Scapular from the pastoral point of view , p. 157

1. Popular piety: a) An explanation of concepts, b(Characteristics of popular piety, c) Expressions of popular piety d) Most prominent Marian attitudes, e) Values and ambiguities in popular piety, 160-161 - 2. The Scapular and popular piety, a) Sources of Carmelite Marian devotion b) Particular expressions of Carmelite Marian devotion, p. 161-162 - 3. Contents, a) The Scapular is a means of affiliation to the Order, b) The Scapular is a sign of consecration to Mary, c) The Scapular is a remembrance of the mercy of God through Mary d) The Scapular is a sacramental, p. 165-167 - 4. Expressions: prayers, Carmelite Wednesdays, Saturdays, Marian feast-days, p. 166 - 5. Some pastoral suggestions, p. 168.
Inserts: Particular Marian Devotions: The Seven Joys of Our Lady, The Seven Sorrow of Mary, The Name of Mary, Slaves of the Mother of God, p. 163 - Private practices of Devotion to Mary: The Little Office of Our Lady, Litanies, p. 167.
Pages from the Anthology: The Scapular, Symbol of the Virtues of Mary (Pius XII), p. 170 - Authentic Devotion to Mary and to the Carmelite Scapular (Pablo VI), p. 171 - The Presence of Our Lady of Mount Carmel in Christian Life (John Paul II), p. 172 - Mary, the Model of

Christian Life, (Carmelite Marian Commission), p. 173
For further study, p. 176.

9. Icons of Tenderness
An Iconographical Study of Saint Mary of the Carmelites .... p. 177

1. Introduction, p. 180 - 2. Themes in Marian Iconography, A. The most common Marian iconography between the 13th and 15th centuries, B. Later developments, p. 180-181 - 3. Carmelite images: a) The Mother of God, p. 182; b) The Patroness, p. 183; c) The Most Pure, p.185; d) Our Lady of the Scapular, p. 187 - 4. Today's orientation, p. 188.
Insert. "La Bruna", p.182.
Pages from the Anthology: A Famous Picture (E. Boaga), *p.* 189 - The Carmelite "Kyriotissa" (R. Palazzi), p. 191 - Mary, an icon of our lives (Bl. Titus Brandsma), p. 193.
For further study, p. 194.

10. Her Presence Today
Mary in Carmel today, ... p. 195

Mary in the present-day reflection of the Order, p. 197.
Insert: Mary, Mother of Christ and Most Pure Virgin, ideals of Carmel, *p.* 198.
Pages from the Anthology: At prayer with Mary our Mother and Sister (Carmelite Community of Pozzo di Gotto), p. 200.
For further study, p. 206.

Conclusion .... p. 207

Index of subjects and names .... p. 208

General Index .... p. 208

NOTES

NOTES

NOTES

NOTES

Finito di stampare nel ottobre 2015
dalla Tipografia Città Nuova della P.A.M.O.M.
Via Pieve Torina, 55
00156 Roma - tel. 06/6530467